A Guide to CIVIL WAR WASHINGTON

To Pat.
Enjoy the book!!!
Steve [illegible]

To Fran, Gertrude, Cory, Jamie, and Randi—
A loving and supportive family.

All information is accurate as of press time. However, all information herein should be regarded as a guidemark and is not guaranteed by the author or publisher. In the interests of keeping this book accurate, we would appreciate hearing from you regarding any errors.

Edited by Mary Ann Harrell and Lise Sajewski
Designed by Gibson Parsons Design
Map research by Glen B. Ruh
Printed and bound in the United States of America

Any inquiries should be directed to
Elliott & Clark Publishing
P.O. Box 21038, Washington, DC 20009-0538.
(202) 387-9805

Library of Congress Cataloging-in-Publication Data

Forman, Stephen M. (Stephen Michael), 1943–
A guide to Civil War Washington / by Stephen M. Forman.
p. cm.
Includes bibliographical references and index.
ISBN 1-880216-29-9
1. Historic sites—Washington (D.C.)—Guidebooks.
2. Washington (D.C.)—Guidebooks. 3. Washington (D.C.)—History—Civil War, 1861–1865. I. Title.
F195.F64 1995
917.5304'4—dc20 95-1673
CIP

8 7 6 5 4 3 2 1 1995 1996 1997 1998 1999 2000 2001 2002

A Guide to Civil War Washington

Stephen M. Forman

Elliott & Clark Publishing
Washington, D.C.

Table of Contents

Foreword *8*
Introduction *9*

Part I—Washington During Wartime
An Abode of Bats and Owls 17
We Are Coming Father Abraham 31
Contrabands 42
Washington's Wounded 49

Part II—Tour of Washington
West Georgetown 62
East Georgetown 68
Foggy Bottom 77
White House Area 81
Downtown/Commercial District 93
The Mall 102
Capitol Hill 104
Anacostia 109
Surrounding Neighborhoods 113

Part III—Cemeteries

Arlington National Cemetery 122
Battleground National Cemetery 143
Congressional Cemetery 144
Glenwood Cemetery 163
Mount Olivet Cemetery 166
Oak Hill Cemetery 170
Rock Creek Cemetery 180
Scottish Rite Temple 185
Soldiers' Home National Cemetery 186

Appendices

Appendix I—Civil War Sculpture in Washington, D.C. 190
Appendix II—Washington Street Directory 191
Appendix III—Civil War Forts in Washington, D.C. 201

Bibliography *202*
Index *205*
Acknowledgments *208*

Left: General Custer presenting captured battle flags at the War Department, Washington, D.C., October 23, 1865.

Washington, D.C.

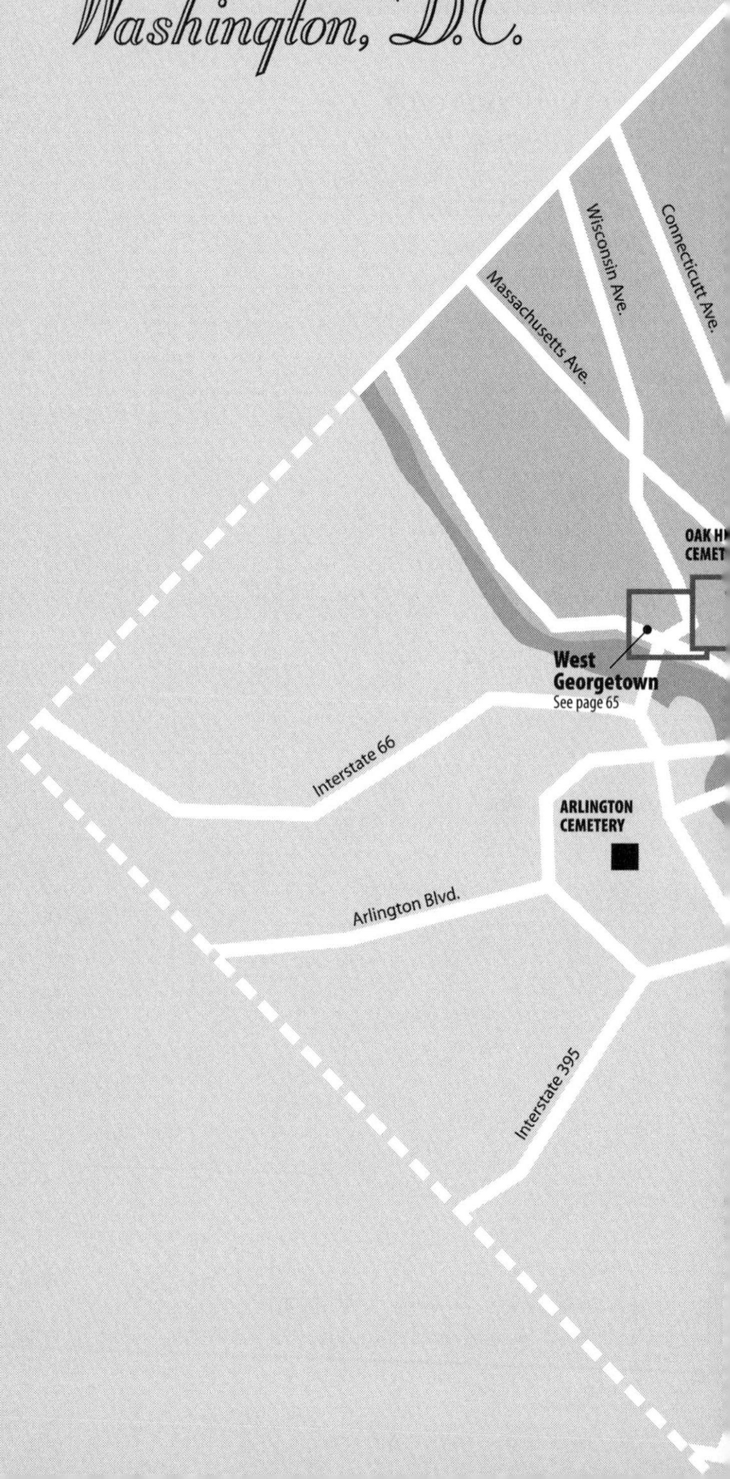

Massachusetts Ave.
Wisconsin Ave.
Connecticutt Ave.
OAK HI
CEMET
West Georgetown
See page 65
Interstate 66
ARLINGTON CEMETERY
Arlington Blvd.
Interstate 395

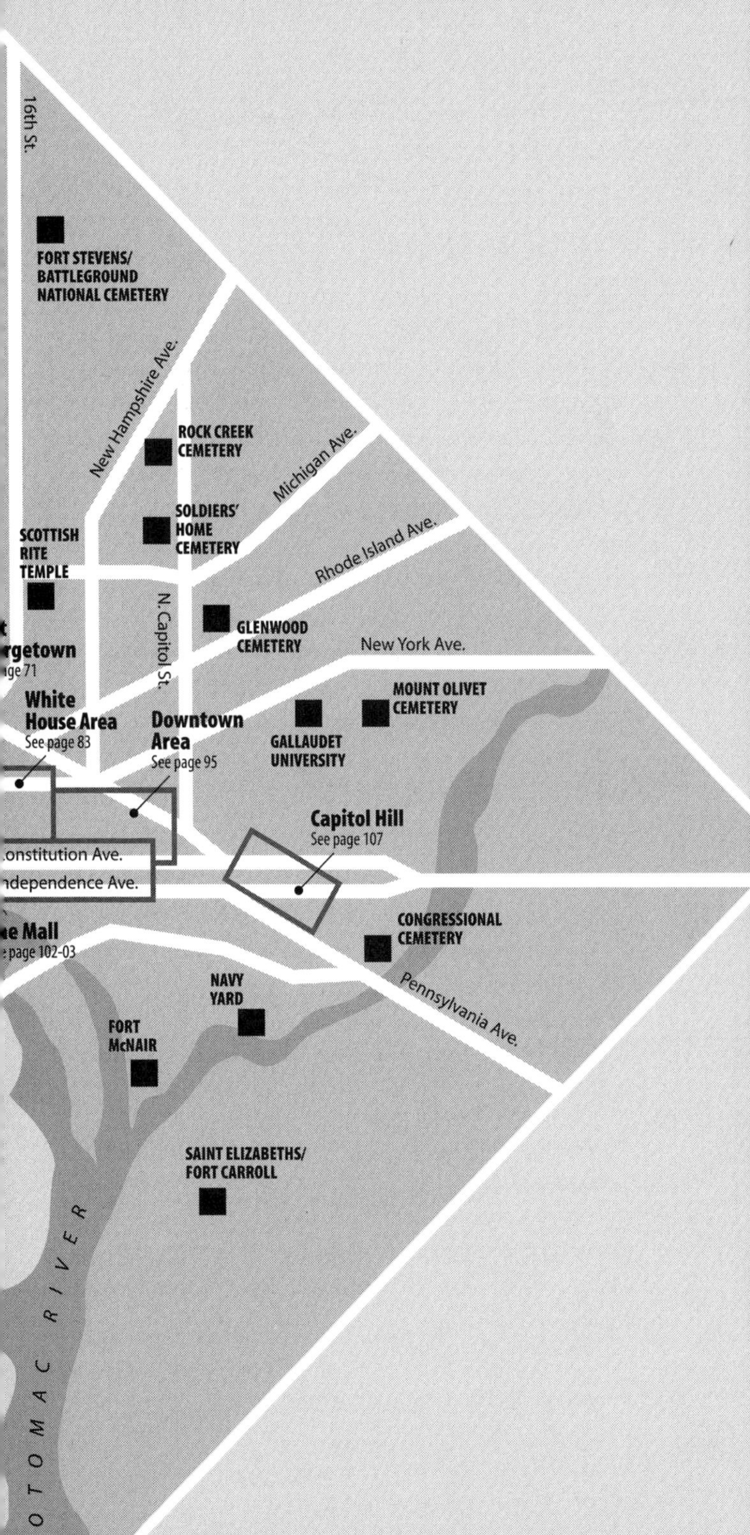

16th St.
FORT STEVENS/
BATTLEGROUND
NATIONAL CEMETERY
New Hampshire Ave.
ROCK CREEK
CEMETERY
Michigan Ave.
SOLDIERS'
HOME
CEMETERY
SCOTTISH
RITE
TEMPLE
Rhode Island Ave.
N. Capitol St.
GLENWOOD
CEMETERY
New York Ave.
White
House Area
See page 83
Downtown
Area
See page 95
MOUNT OLIVET
CEMETERY
GALLAUDET
UNIVERSITY
Capitol Hill
See page 107
onstitution Ave.
ndependence Ave.
CONGRESSIONAL
CEMETERY
Pennsylvania Ave.
NAVY
YARD
FORT
McNAIR
SAINT ELIZABETHS/
FORT CARROLL
POTOMAC RIVER

Foreword

During my perambulations around Washington as an educator, tour guide, and historian, I am often frustrated by seeing a massive government building built upon acres of land as I read a description of an event that took place on that spot. The description, of course, bears little resemblance to what I am looking at.

Tour guidebooks usually show a "then and now" photograph that usually satisfies the most casual tourist. I have to "picture" what happened there. Likewise, as I stand above the final resting place of a Civil War-era personality, a sense of history and personal attachment flows through me.

Edwin C. Bearss, former chief historian of the National Park Service, once wrote:

> *Many people like nothing better than visiting out-of-the-way historic sites and places, especially when they are associated with our Civil War battlefields and military past. A major manifestation of this phenomenon is a desire to visit sites associated with the Civil War, to walk in the footsteps of the soldiers and civilians of the 1860s, see and touch the landscapes, structures, and objects in a conscious effort to recapture the past.*

In this spirit, I have attempted to locate and identify buildings, sites, and graves of the people involved in events in Washington City during the Civil War.

May the fire and passion of the Civil War flow through you as it does through me when you stand in the shadows of greatness and history.

—S. M. F.

Introduction

Prior to the Civil War, Washington was a far different place than the magnificent international city it is today. George Washington and other early promoters of the city envisioned the nation's capital as an international seaport. By 1850, the Chesapeake & Ohio (C & O) Canal was completed, linking Cumberland, Maryland, with Washington in an attempt to attract the Ohio farm-produce trade. Unfortunately, the Baltimore & Ohio Railroad reached beyond Cumberland and captured the farm trade for the port city of Baltimore.

The venture bankrupted Washington and set the tone for serious financial problems up to the Civil War. Congress was reluctant to support local development, and continual silting of the Potomac River near the ports of Georgetown and Washington reduced the number of deep-water ships that could make their way up the river.

Thomas Moore, an early visitor to the city, wrote about it:

> *This famed metropolis, where fancy sees,*
> *Squares in morasses, obelisks in trees;*
> *Which traveling fools and gazetteers adorn*
> *With shrines unbuilt and heroes yet unborn.*

Little changed in Washington the first half-century of its existence. In 1842, Charles Dickens wrote in his *American Notes:*

> *Spacious avenues, that begin in nothing, and lead nowhere; streets, miles long, that only want houses and inhabitants; public buildings that need but a public, to be complete; ornaments of great thoroughfares, which only lack great thoroughfares to be ornament—are its leading features. One*

might fancy the season over, and most of the houses gone out of town forever with their masters. To the admirers of cities it is a Barmecide Feast: a pleasant field for the imagination to rove in; a monument raised to a deceased project, with not even a legible inscription to record its departed greatness. Such as it is, it is likely to remain.

And remain it did until the Civil War. Washington was a small Southern city, not in the same league with Charleston or Savannah, let alone New Orleans. Designer Pierre L'Enfant's grand avenues were superb in their length and width, a painful contrast to the low sheds and shanties scattered along them. Most of the public buildings worth looking at were unfinished, and the finished shacks and shanties looked as if they should have been torn down generations before.

Even though industrial development was hampered by lack of investors, a number of businesses were established. Georgetown boasted several flour mills; and because of its proximity to the C & O Canal, the Washington Canal, and the Potomac River, the area called Foggy Bottom became an important industrial center. Several lime kilns (the remains of one can be seen from Rock Creek Parkway, near Virginia Avenue) and a brewery were opened.

These industries employed several hundred unskilled and semiskilled workers. The average daily wage of an unskilled worker was $1.03 and that of a skilled worker was $1.62. Skilled workers in Washington included blacksmiths, carpenters, engineers, machinists, painters, and printers.

Antebellum businesses were small and their activities centered around the immediate community. Seventh Street near the Center Market was commercialized with dry goods and clothing stores. Service businesses located near the Patent Office on 7th and F Streets included patent agents and lawyers. Advertisements in the *1860 Boyd's Washington and Georgetown Directory* included improved billiard tables; cabinet making; undertakers; photography studios; plumbers and gas fitters; carpeting and oilcloths; groceries; wallpapers, wines, liquors, and havana segars [*sic*]; livery stables; and many restaurants, hotels, and boardinghouses.

Even with the development of small businesses, Washington was still a government town. By 1861, there were 2,199 federal employees living and working in the city.

The major mode of transportation was walking. An irregular system of hacks and carriages ran between distant neighborhoods and the Capitol. Omnibuses, as they were called, transported members of Congress almost one mile from their accommodations at the Willard Hotel, Kirkwood House, and other lodging establishments on lower Pennsylvania Avenue to the Capitol. Other hacks ran between faraway Georgetown and the Navy Yard, almost three miles distant. In the spring and autumn, the entire west end of the city was a vast slough of impassable mud. Residents often had to walk many blocks before they found it possible to cross a street.

In 1848, the Washington Gas Light Company was chartered by Congress and by 1860, there were gas street lamps on Pennsylvania Avenue and gas lamps in the White House. More than 30 miles of gas mains crisscrossed the city and 500 street lamps illuminated the dangerous streets.

One of the most serious problems confronting Washington related to sanitation and disease. The streets were strewn with garbage and filth, and the stagnant water of the Washington Canal was, as one citizen described it, "the receptacle of all abominations." Sewage ran into open creeks that polluted the Potomac and Anacostia (Eastern Branch) Rivers. As a result of the unsanitary conditions, the city's death rate was very high. The number of children's graves in the cemeteries mentioned in the text attests to the fact that living in antebellum Washington was indeed precarious.

Free black people, "free persons of color" in the legal term, were part of Washington's business class. They owned and operated carts and hacks, and black women earned their wages as seamstresses and laundresses. Several men owned restaurants and other retail businesses. By

1860, there were 9,209 free black people and 1,774 slaves out of a total population of 61,122. The free blacks lived throughout the city, in the Southern fashion. Black churches and private black schools provided educational opportunities for many of the city's black children. The most respected of the private black schools was operated by Myrtilla Miner, a white woman from New York State.

Even though the Compromise of 1850 abolished the trading of slaves in Washington, slaveholding remained legal. A strong national fugitive slave law was passed, which discouraged runaways from coming into the city. Free blacks had to register with the mayor's office and they could hold no public meetings without the mayor's consent.

The Civil War changed Washington faster than any other event in its history. By 1864, the population of the city increased to almost 140,000. At the beginning of the conflict, the population had a Southern flavor, but as the war expanded so did the government. Southerners and their sympathizers left the city, to be replaced by government employees who filled the many new bureaus created by the war. Doctors and nurses arrived daily to care for the thousands of sick and wounded soldiers. Businessmen came to sell their wares to the government, while others sought government contracts for feeding and supplying the army.

With the shortage of men for the work force, women took jobs as clerks at the Government Printing Office, Treasury Department, Navy Yard, and U.S. Arsenal. (At the end of the war, these women generally lost their jobs to former soldiers.)

With thousands of soldiers, businessmen, contractors, and the ever-present con men arriving, daily life changed drastically. Saloons, gambling salons, brothels, and myriad other businesses came into existence to cater to every imaginable whim. Theaters and playhouses offered inexpensive entertainment. Shoeshine boys were constantly polishing muddy boots, and innocent soldiers were divorced from their money at shady gambling halls. One of the most notorious areas was called Hell's Bottom, an area bordered by Q, T, 9th, and 10th Streets. National Race Course was opened near the insane asylum across the Anacostia River. Often horses raced for purses larger than $1,000!

Sanitary conditions remained primitive. Washington had some storm drains, but no sewer system. Houses or hotels that installed water closets simply ran their sewers to a creek, if one flowed nearby, or to a vacant lot. Residents still threw their garbage in the same vacant lots or on the streets. The army tried to haul away garbage on a daily basis, but poor sanitation existed throughout the war.

Private investors improved public transportation with regularly scheduled omnibuses traveling between Georgetown, the Navy Yard, and various business districts. The improvement of the transportation system was a double-edged sword. With the thousands of army carts, wagons, gun carriages, and daily omnibuses, the unpaved roads became rutted dust holes or muddy quagmires, depending on the season. As before, Congress refused to pay for paving the roads, and the city had no money to pay the costs.

Even with the wartime influx of people and the resulting hustle and bustle, the city still gave some the impression of only a fancy facade. In 1865, an English visitor wrote of Washington:

> *The whole place looks run up in a night, like the cardboard cities Potemkin erected to gratify the eyes of his imperial mistress on her tour through Russia; and it is impossible to remove the impression that, when Congress is over, the place is taken down and packed until wanted again.*

This was the world of Civil War Washington. This book will take you to buildings and locations where significant events took place. Part I gives more background information on Washington City during this period. Part II is divided by geographic areas. While it doesn't include every surviving building, it does mention and describe most of the buildings that were standing during the Civil War. Part III locates cemeteries and identifies gravesites where civilian and military personalities are buried. A biographical sketch puts each life into the context of the Civil War. The Appendices include a directory of Civil War sculpture; addresses of forts around Washington; and a street directory that converts period addresses to the current Washington Street Grid.

Unless you concentrate on one area, you will need your car or a taxi, bus, or Metro to visit the sites. All of the buildings, cemeteries, and statuary are easily accessible. But most of the buildings are private property; please respect the owners' privacy. Several of the cemeteries are located in outlying areas and some are in transitional areas, which may not be considered particularly safe. As on any other touring, you'll want a game plan and common sense.

Perhaps the best encouragement to the casual tourist or historian is the biblical adage, "Seek and ye shall find."

PART ONE

Washington During Wartime

An Abode of Bats and Owls

Perhaps, suggested a New York newspaper in December 1860, the nation's capital would become a mere abode of bats and owls. More practically, a Richmond editor suggested that Washington be occupied as the capital of a new Southern federation. The District of Columbia was, after all, surrounded by slave states, with Delaware, Maryland, and Virginia as barriers to the North, and many of its residents would count themselves as Southerners in sentiment.

All of the District's residents—like citizens elsewhere—were under strain that Christmas season. For the first time a president had been chosen by a purely sectional vote: Abraham Lincoln, the Republican, had carried all the free states and none of the slave states. The tea had been thrown into the harbor, said the Charleston *Mercury*: "The revolution of 1860 has been initiated." South Carolina proclaimed her secession from the Union on December 20. "Thank God! Oh, thank God!" shouted a South Carolina congressman when a telegram gave him the news at a wedding reception. His fellow guest President James Buchanan weakly asked his hostess, "Madam, might I beg of you to have my carriage called?" His subsequent political actions were equally polite and less effective.

Other deep South states renounced the Union: Mississippi, Florida, Alabama, Georgia, Louisiana, and Texas. In his farewell speech as senator from Mississippi, Jefferson Davis stated the constitutional case for secession and deplored the necessity for ending a cherished confederation. On a conciliatory note he explained:

> *That flag shall not set between contending brothers and that when it shall no longer be the common flag of the country,*

it shall be folded up and laid away, like a vesture no longer used; that it shall be kept as a sacred memento of the past, to which each of us can make a pilgrimage and remember the glorious days in which we were born.

Davis concluded his speech by adding: "If there cannot be peace, Mississippi's gallant sons will stand like a wall of fire around their State, and I go hence, not in hostility to you, but in love and allegiance to her, to take my place among her sons, be it for good or for evil."

Senators and representatives of the seceded Southern states resigned and left for home; other civil officials followed suit; officers of the army and navy resigned their commissions and, as the current term had it, "went with their state." Lesser officials followed the famous.

Some of those civilians might have left in any case. Only a few experts and specialists could escape the normal turnover of the spoils system. Every new administration would hand out federal jobs to its friends and supporters, and there were always far more claimants than places. In 1860 the District of Columbia had about 2,200 federal workers, with some 1,200 more employed at the Navy Yard. These small numbers are deceiving because government was the major element in the District's economy, albeit a fairly sluggish industry in peacetime.

In December 1860, rumors of a plot to kidnap or assassinate President-elect Lincoln had drifted through the city, repeated in private parlors and crowded hotel lobbies. Creaky but clear-headed, the aged Lt. Gen. Winfield Scott chose a reliable colonel to investigate the loyalty of four local militia units—the best-equipped and most fashionable proved most secession-minded—and to raise new volunteer companies. Scott collected eight companies of Regulars from hither and yon and found quarters for them with some difficulty.

Political tensions were felt in society circles, too. Normally, winter was the high social season, even in an election year. "The young ladies are … trying to be gay—but as yet politics has entire sway & there is nothing else

****

****

Parks & History Association Oct 08/96
Lincoln Memorial
23rd & Lincoln Memorial Circle

Qty	Price ISBN/PKU		Total
1	3.95 6-00-002453-3 ENPMA		
	NATL PARKS STAMP SHE		3.95
		Subtotal	3.95
D. C. Tax: 5.75%			0.23
		Total	4.18

1 Units Sold
Sales No.73373 Dr.ID 4 CASH $20.18
RK @22:38 Chg.: $16.00

thought or talked of," wrote Elizabeth Blair Lee. Daughter of the powerful Blair family and wife of a Lee of Virginia (a naval officer named Samuel Phillips, cousin of an army officer named Robert), Mrs. Lee watched the scene from her home on Pennsylvania Avenue near the White House.

Hostesses had long since become wary of inviting political foes to the same dinner. Now ladies and gentlemen were literally showing their colors, wearing cockades of colored ribbon: red, white, and blue for the Union; blue for secession. At the president's reception on New Year's Day, "secesh" ladies snubbed their host. But those Southerners were to leave his administration, and Union men took their places. It seemed that the government would last until Inauguration Day, March 4. The city waited, shivering in a nasty winter, its streets white with snow or yellow with frozen or thawing mud.

Tagged as a city "of magnificent distances" early in the century, it had struck visitor English author Charles Dickens in 1842 as a city "of magnificent intentions." The major government buildings were worthy of manifest destiny. Dominating the landscape on its noble hill rose the white mass of the Capitol, its dome still unfinished. Wide avenues radiated from it, crossing the gridiron of streets that measured their distance from it by rising numbers or letters. To the northwest ran Pennsylvania Avenue, the only thoroughfare in town paved at federal expense. (Wrangles over federal help for the city were an old story already.) The cobbled surface had reached Rock Creek by 1861; but mud often washed down to it from higher ground to the north, where only a few blocks had been paved at the expense of property owners in the Northwest quadrant.

Two imposing structures of white marble rose on the west side of 7th Street: the Post Office with its overhead telegraph wires and the Patent Office with its Greek Revival portico. The latter housed the Department of the Interior, with 702 clerks and bureaucrats of the Pension Office, Census Bureau, Bureau of Indian Affairs, and Bureau of Public Lands. After 1862, when a Congress without Southerners created the Department of Agriculture, the new agency shared the Patent Office space.

A third cluster of buildings stood about a mile and a half from the Capitol. At 15th Street, the massive Treasury Building blocked the vista to the White House, or Executive Mansion. Between the Treasury Building and the White House, on the corner of 15th and Pennsylvania, the modest two-story brick State Department housed its 35 paid employees. The grounds of the White House, with its glass conservatory and other outbuildings, were enclosed by decorative iron fencing. West of the mansion was the headquarters of the fighting services—two buildings, both adequate for peacetime. A foreign correspondent, William Howard Russell of the London *Times,* described the two-story red-brick Navy Department as "very plain and even humble." Its staff had charge of a total of 90 vessels, of which only 40 were in commission and no more than 2 were available to defend the Atlantic Coast (the steamer *Brooklyn,* with 25 guns, and the storeship *Relief,* with 2). The War Department, in a similar building, administered an array of 18,006 Regulars, mostly scattered west of the Mississippi to confront the Indians. Congress did not provide a retirement pension for officers, and some of them soldiered on into their 70s, 80s, even 90s. (A pension law was belatedly passed in August 1861, but the commanding general, Lt. Gen. Winfield Scott, continued to serve at age 75.)

Highrise structures of the time were the five-story Winder Building, at 17th and F, and the Corcoran, at 15th and F, put up by entrepreneurs hoping to lease space to the government. These buildings would come in handy before long.

Federal funds had provided some amenities for the public. Across from the Executive Mansion, on the north side of Pennsylvania Avenue, Clark Mills's equestrian statue of Andrew Jackson reared boldly over Lafayette Park. (Jackson's defiance of South Carolina was remembered wistfully by Union loyalists exasperated by Buchanan's timidity.) Farther west on the avenue stood another bronze by Mills, a statue of George Washington in solitary splendor on the circle at 23rd Street. Its dedication on February 22, 1860, was remembered as the last great public gathering not marred by partisan sectional rancor.

In conspicuous contrast, the unfinished stump of the Washington Monument, begun in 1848, rose 154 feet into the air from a knoll south and a little east of the Executive Mansion. Quarreling in the society that sponsored it and lack of money in a year of depression had stopped the project in 1855. Inscribed stones lay strewn about or stored in nondescript sheds. Some of the city's notorious free-roaming livestock—cows, sheep, goats, pigs, and poultry—routinely grazed and wandered about this cluttered, malodorous area.

Cutting off the Mall expanse from the rest of town ran—or oozed—the old city canal, the Washington Canal (now covered by Constitution Avenue). Opened with pride in 1815, it supposedly linked the Chesapeake & Ohio (C & O) Canal terminus in Georgetown with the wharfs on the Anacostia (Eastern Branch) River, but repeated efforts at dredging had failed to keep it from silting up. Its feeble currents carried the remains of dead livestock as well as poultry innards and other offal, rotting produce, and spoiled fish from the popular Center Market. While market vendors tossed their garbage into the canal out back, farm carts, wagons, and city vehicles jammed the venue in front at 7th Street and Pennsylvania Avenue. Washingtonians bought their fresh meats, birds, fish, fruits, and vegetables here; such delicacies as spring shad, terrapin, duck, wild turkey, and venison attracted the prosperous.

A gentlewoman, however, would let her husband or servants do the shopping at the Center Market, for the south side was definitely the "wrong" side of the avenue. Seedy shops, saloons, gambling houses, cheap theaters, so-called "rooming houses," and other dingy buildings south of the avenue catered to the underpaid. In striking contrast, the street boasted plantings of ailanthus trees, each sheltered from livestock by a little whitewashed wooden palisade.

Property values were high on the north side of Penn-

Balloon view of Washington, D.C., in the spring of 1861.

sylvania Avenue, where owners had paid taxes for a brick sidewalk 30 feet wide. Fashionable shops, restaurants, and imposing new hotels flourished here. Small boardinghouses still served the public—a widow named Mary Surratt would soon acquire one at 604 H Street—but hotels appealed to legislators, justices of the Supreme Court, Cabinet members, and other men of affairs who swelled the city during sessions of Congress, as well as visiting politicos, businessmen, inventors, office seekers, journalists, and sight-seeing travelers.

During the fateful winter before the Civil War, delegates hoping "to avert so dire a calamity" as "a permanent dissolution of the Union" converged on Washington. The Virginia legislature had called for a special national convention "to adjust the present unhappy controversies." None of the seceded states took part, but in February of 1861, 131 delegates gathered in the capital city, choosing former President John Tyler to preside over the Peace Convention. Yet again the familiar issues were debated: slavery and its status in the territories, constitutional amendments to placate the slave states, and other measures for compromise.

At least the delegates had a convenient meeting place:

Willard Hall, formerly the First Presbyterian Church, at 14th and F Streets. The owner of the Willard Hotel had bought the structure in 1859 and turned it into a setting fit for meetings and cultural events, useful for city residents and hotel guests alike. The hotel proper was immense, reported William Howard Russell: "a quadrangular mass of rooms, five stories high, and some hundred yards square," with a writing room, a smoking room, a bar, a barbershop with deft black barbers, and a ladies' drawing room with a piano. In a vast uncarpeted dining room, "not less than 2,500 people" a day chose favorites from an endless menu, and servants shoved chairs "to and from with a harsh screeching noise." Tobacco-stained carpets ("despite a most liberal provision of spittoons"), bustle and turmoil, and central heating annoyed Russell, but the place—a favorite of Northern visitors—was a kind of national nerve center. The Willard housed the main office of the American Telegraph company, and the wires carried reports from the Peace Convention and brought in dispatches from afar.

On Monday, February 11, President-elect Jefferson Davis left his Mississippi plantation for his inauguration in Montgomery, Alabama, capital of the Confederacy; President-elect Lincoln left Springfield, Illinois, on his roundabout way to Washington. In Columbus, Ohio, he said, "There is nothing going wrong....nothing that really hurts anybody," and in Cleveland he called the crisis "artificial."

Perhaps these remarks reassured the merchants of Washington's principal business section along 7th Street (which boasted cobblestones all the way from H Street to Virginia Avenue, near the river). This area north of Pennsylvania Avenue most resembled a city; it included substantial residences, shops, and a dozen of the city's newer churches. Local government—suddenly significant in days of uncertain loyalty—was administered from City Hall on Judiciary Square, which held the office of the mayor and the rooms used by the Board of Aldermen and the Common Council. The city police force, with 27 uniformed officers for daytime duty and a night watch of 40, delivered suspects to the nearby county jail. Circuit and criminal courts sat in City Hall, which also held the office of the U.S. marshal for the District. In the block behind it, facing E Street between 4th and 5th, was the city's only general hospital, the E Street Infirmary.

Any of several slums contributed to hospital and jail rosters. Just southwest of the White House, between 13th and 15th Streets, was the canalside spot notorious as Murder Bay. Gangs roamed the Island—the portion of Southwest penned between the canal and the marshy banks of the Potomac. Just north of the Capitol, beside fetid Tiber Creek, poor immigrants—workers, ne'er-do-wells, drunks and toughs—made the shantytown called Swampoodle a byword for trouble.

A source of more worry than of crime, the black population was scattered throughout the District. Slaves lived in or behind their owners' homes as a rule. For decades, slaves hired out as workers had been earning enough money to buy their freedom; they formed a close-knit, self-respecting community, supporting their own churches, schools, and friendly societies. The law might forbid a person of color to run a shop or restaurant, but the mayor would give him a license anyway. Still, whites worried that the District might shelter fugitive slaves, and events like John Brown's raid at Harpers Ferry stirred waves of apprehension.

Although the founders had expected Washington to expand eastward, things hadn't worked out that way. One significant community in Southeast centered on the Navy Yard. It was the home of office workers, carpenters, mechanics, and day laborers employed there. Early in 1861, only a disabled steam sloop was moored on the Anacostia River. Russell of the London *Times* noted the Navy Yard's high brick walls, white-gloved sentries, agreeable plots of grass and trees, "some few trophies of guns taken from us at Yorktown," and bustling foundries. But, he remarked, the latter only cast brass fieldpieces and boatguns. Compared to British establishments, this dockyard was "a mere toy." Three blocks north on 8th Street SE stood the Marine Barracks, which had sent 90 combat-ready men to quell John Brown's insurrection.

From the foot of 11th Street, the Navy Yard Bridge crossed the Anacostia en route to the government insane asylum (now St. Elizabeths Hospital). The distinguished reformer Dorothea Lynde Dix had persuaded Thomas Blagden to sell his farm on the hills overlooking the river, and in 1855 the asylum had received its first inmates. Troubled residents of the District—regardless of sex or color—and men of the armed services received enlightened treatment under the supervision of Dr. Charles Nichols, with farm or household chores as a kind of therapy in this tranquil, beautiful setting.

Also remote, enlightened, and peaceful was the Soldiers' Home (formerly called the Military Asylum), authorized by Congress in 1851 to shelter enlisted men too old or infirm for active service. From his base pay—as low as $132 a year for a private—a soldier gave up 12 ½ cents a month as a deduction for the home's support. The complex stood on high ground out the 7th Street Pike, three miles from Boundary Street (now Florida Avenue). President Buchanan used a stone cottage there to escape the muggy summer heat, especially oppressive on the riverside flats at the White House.

Countryside dotted with large estates and occasional farms still covered much of the District in 1860. Neither Washington nor Georgetown had spread up the escarpment to the north. Carts took "night soil" from town privies to a dumping ground about ten blocks north of the White House. Weedy fields and unimproved lots abounded. Charles Dickens had compared such wasteland to "a small piece of country that has taken to drinking, and has quite lost itself."

Had the nation lost itself? On February 18, a mild sunny day in Montgomery, a happy crowd gathered outside the Alabama capitol to see Jefferson Davis take his oath as provisional president. Secession, he said, "illustrates the American idea that governments rest on the consent of the governed," and he warned that the Confederacy might need to secure its place among nations by war. On Washington's Birthday in Philadelphia, Lincoln also invoked the

Declaration of Independence, stressing its promise "that *all* men should have an equal chance."

By now, more rumors of danger to Lincoln—perhaps to derail his train, perhaps to kill him in a riot when he had to change trains in Baltimore—had convinced level-headed advisers that no chances could be taken. With his burly friend Ward Hill Lamon and detective Allan Pinkerton, Lincoln quietly boarded a special train at Harrisburg, passed safely through Baltimore in the small hours of the night, and arrived unnoticed in Washington at 8 a.m. on Saturday, February 23. Lamon never had to use his two pistols, two derringers, and two large knives. When crowds gathered at the Baltimore & Ohio Railroad station at New Jersey Avenue and C Street hoping to see Lincoln arrive as announced, he was already installed in the best suite at the Willard, parlor number 6 on the second floor.

Newspapers hostile to Lincoln had a field day with stories about the midnight journey. Few editors of that era hesitated to slant their coverage, even at the cost of accuracy. In this case, they didn't bother to find out that Lincoln had worn an old overcoat and a soft hat. The Cincinnati *Commercial* and the *Crisis* of Columbus, Ohio, copied the Louisville *Courier*'s "Yankee Doodle" verses such as:

They went and got a special train
At midnight's solemn hour,
And in a cloak and Scotch Plaid shawl,
He dodged from the slave-Power
Lanky Lincoln came to town
In night and wind and rain, sir
Wrapped in a military cloak
Upon a special train, sir.

The *Courier* added insult in prose, while the "Scotch Plaid" story spread around the country:

The men who made the Declaration of Independence did not make it good in that way. They fought for rights; Lincoln runs for his … and leaves his wife. They ought to swap clothes. She is a true Kentuckian. Lincoln began the exchange by assuming her striped petticoat, called by his friends a "Scotch Plaid." ... No Kentucky-born man would have run all the way from Harrisburg to Washington, with but the ghost of an enemy in sight.

Washington's own newspapers reflected the splintered opinions of the times. Oldest of the lot was the *National Intelligencer,* founded in the fall of 1800, with offices at the corner of D and 7th Streets. Its venerable editors were Joseph Gales and his brother-in-law William Winston Seaton. Both trained in shorthand, they had reported the debates and orations of Daniel Webster, Henry Clay, and John C. Calhoun until 1850. The paper's motto was "The Union and the Constitution." In the four-candidate presidential campaign of 1860, it supported the hastily formed Constitutional Union Party and its nominee John Bell, a Tennessee slaveholder but a staunch nationalist.

The *Evening Star,* founded in 1852, had its office at 11th Street and Pennsylvania. Selling for a penny a copy and focusing on local news, it had the largest circulation in the city. Its publisher, W. D. Wallach, had Southern connections and sympathies, and in 1860 the *Star* backed the

"Flight of Abraham, 1861" ridiculing Lincoln's secret arrival in Washington before his inauguration.

nominee of the Southern Democratic faction, John C. Breckinridge of Kentucky.

Deep South extremists had walked out of the Democratic convention in Charleston after bitter wrangling, and the Northern wing of the party had nominated the "Little Giant," Senator Stephen A. Douglas of Illinois. Douglas had built a splendid house on I Street and had married one of the belles of the city, the beautiful Adele Cutts, a grand-niece of Dolley Madison. There was no more distinguished social connection in the capital, and the Douglases' hospitality was most fashionable, but these factors did not earn him a local endorsement.

Founded in 1860, the *Daily National Republican* was located on 9th Street between C and D. It was basically a house organ or party newspaper and, predictably, supported Lincoln. Lewis Clephane, the principal member of the ownership group, would soon become postmaster of Washington.

While Lincoln was forming his administration, John W. Forney was founding the city's first Sunday paper, the *Sunday Morning Chronicle,* with offices on the northwest corner of Pennsylvania Avenue and 7th Street. Forney, a Democrat and a strong supporter of the Union, advertised his paper as entirely independent of party.

Lincoln's first day in the city would have taxed the most dogged reporter. He had breakfast with Senator William H. Seward of New York, who had hurt his own chance for the Republican presidential nomination by a speech about "irrepressible conflict" between free and slave states. With Seward, Lincoln had paid a ceremonial call on President Buchanan at the White House. He conferred privately with General Scott and other key figures; he met Douglas and the rest of the Illinois delegation in the afternoon. He dined at 7:00 p.m. at Seward's house, which faced Lafayette Park on the street numbered 15 ½ (now Madison Place), and then received Peace Convention delegates in his private parlor at the Willard. He was cordial with men from the upper South, but unyielding. After 10:00 p.m. he received other callers and finally discussed Cabinet choices with Senator James Harlan of Iowa. His days soon became even more demanding.

Meeting the mayor and city officials in 1861 was something more than a formality; well-founded suspicion of a disloyal mayor and police chief in Baltimore had been an important reason for Lincoln's midnight journey. Lincoln assured the civic leaders, "When we shall become better acquainted—and I say it with great confidence—we shall like each other better."

On February 26, the Peace Convention forwarded six proposed constitutional amendments to Congress, measures that would entrench the status of slavery. It adopted a resolution urging the federal government to abstain from "all counsels or measures of compulsion" toward the seceded states, and adjourned forever.

On the same day President Davis named three special commissioners to Washington to establish friendly relations and settle such questions as sharing the public debt and disposing of U.S. arsenals, dockyards, and forts—many already taken over by Southerners. One, Martin J. Crawford, arrived before Inauguration Day and found President Buchanan too "fearfully panic-stricken" to receive him, with signs "of anxious care and gloomy forebodings" among men of all sections alike.

On Monday, March 4, the city of Washington saw an inauguration unlike anything it had ever seen before. General Scott and members of a Republican association feared an attempt on Lincoln's life. They had a scant protective force to work with, but they managed to set up a strong guard around the president and along the parade route. Scott ordered an engineer company of Regulars to march in front of the open barouche carrying the president and president-elect. A squadron of District cavalry rode close-packed around it; militia infantry marched behind. Although there was a float with 34 pretty girls—one for each state, seceded or not—the military presence set the tone. Riflemen stood guard on the roofs of buildings on either side of Pennsylvania Avenue from the Willard to the Capitol, and others were posted there in the windows. Armed guards were concealed under the ceremonial platform at the East Front, U.S. Marines guarded key entrances, and two light artillery batteries waited nearby to fire in salute—or defense.

Lincoln had drafted his speech in Springfield and revised it carefully, and he read it in his clear, high-pitched tenor. He repeated a point he had often made: he would not interfere with slavery in the states where it existed. He acknowledged his "great and peculiar difficulty. A disruption of the Federal Union, heretofore only menace, is now formidably attempted." Nevertheless, he argued, the Union was perpetual and secession "legally void." He appealed for calm and patience. At the end he spoke specifically to the South as well as the crowd: "I am loath to close. We are not enemies but friends. We must not be enemies. Though passion may have strained, it must not break our bonds of affection."

Reporters rushing to the telegraph office had no violent incidents to describe. The police had easily coped with a few rowdies and drunks, and there was no truth to the rumor that Virginians would gallop across the Long Bridge from Alexandria and kidnap the new president at his inaugural ball that night.

This grand Union Ball was held in a specially constructed plank structure fancifully called the "White Muslin Palace of Aladdin." Five big gas chandeliers supplied light for the white and blue decorations and for the finery of the ladies who crowded the dance floor in their huge hoopskirts. The "Palace stood just behind City Hall, and gentlemen left their coats in a courtroom while ladies left their shawls and cloaks in the Common Council chamber. Many of the guests had come from northern and western states and were painfully surprised to learn that their wraps were missing—taken by mistake or stolen—when it was time to go home." But overall the day was a success as these things go.

We Are Coming Father Abraham

"From California, Texas, from the Indian Reserves, and the Mormon Territory, from Nebraska, as from the remotest borders of Minnesota, from every portion of the vast territories of the Union, except from the seceded States, the triumphant Republicans had winged their way to the prey." So William Howard Russell of the London *Times* noted in early March 1861.

The prey, of course, was President Lincoln. Or, failing him, one of his Cabinet, a senator, a representative, or anybody who might have the ear of somebody powerful.

Office seekers crowded into the city, their pockets bulging with testimonial letters. One, failing an appointment as a judge or a postmaster, offered to manage a lighthouse—any lighthouse would do. A drunken prizefighter declared that he was going "to get a foreign mission from Bill Seward."

Secretary of State William H. Seward was not only dealing with European diplomats but also sparring with American envoys. Refusing to meet the three Confederate commissioners, he used Supreme Court Justice John A. Campbell as a go-between. Each side grew more suspicious of the other.

Meanwhile, local institutions were doing their best to carry on as usual. At 2nd and D Streets SE, the Sisters of Charity tended the patients of Providence Hospital. Benevolent ladies of the city continued their supervision of the Washington City Orphan Asylum founded in 1815. The original executive, or "first directress," had been Dolley Madison, followed by Marcia Burnes Van Ness, wife of a prominent banker. The orphanage stood on H Street NW

General Thomas swearing in volunteers at Washington, D.C.

between 9th and 10th, on what was known as Mausoleum Square. (The name reflected an undertaker's premises there.)

Local indigent children and disabled offspring of servicemen were studying at the Columbia Institution for the Deaf, Dumb, and Blind. Chartered by Congress in 1857, it stood at the edge of town at 7th and Boundary Streets NW. Its house and two-acre grounds had been given by Amos Kendall, a Jacksonian Democrat who was postmaster general from 1835 to 1840. The Department of the Interior paid $150 per year to support the school. (In 1864, Congress would authorize a collegiate department, and the "National Deaf-Mute College" would become famous as Gallaudet University.)

Columbian College, opened in 1822 under Baptist auspices, stood on what was known as Meridian Hill—the high ground north of Boundary Street west of 14th Street NW. Its finances had long been a problem, but it owned 46 ½ acres of land (originally bought for $7,000) and its medical department was a community asset. It worked from the old city infirmary on Judiciary Square.

At Gonzaga College on F Street NW between 9th and 10th, young men were studying for liberal arts and science degrees. At its founding in 1826, it had been Washington Seminary, where Jesuit priests prepared their pupils for admission to Georgetown College.

Farther west in the legally distinct city of Georgetown, the oldest Roman Catholic College in the United States enjoyed its special distinction. This Jesuit school had opened its doors in 1791. In March 1861 the faculty of 18 Jesuit priests were teaching 350 students, but more than a hundred withdrew in just two days as tensions heightened. Some went north, some south, for parents in both sections were disturbed by the course of events.

Opinions were divided about whether there would be a war. Senator William Yancy, one of the most extreme of states' righters, said in a speech in Montgomery, Alabama, "I have a good reason to believe that the action of any State will be peaceable and will not be resisted under the present of any probable prospective condition of Federal affairs." His optimism was ill-placed.

"I am tired and weary of this perpetual jabber about Fort Sumter," noted William Russell on April 7. At that island fort in Charleston Harbor, Maj. Robert Anderson and his 84 Federals were coming to the end of their food supply. South Carolina was refusing to sell them provisions, and 5,000 armed Confederates were at hand. The Southerners ran out of patience first. They demanded Anderson's surrender. He refused. Confederate batteries began their bombardment at daybreak on April 12. Anderson surrendered the next day. The war that no one wanted and no one had been able to prevent had begun.

President Lincoln issued a proclamation declaring a state of insurrection and calling for 75,000 militiamen (the militia act of 1795 that he relied on was originally passed to suppress the Pennsylvania whiskey insurrection) and a special session of Congress to convene on July 4. While Northern states responded eagerly, the governors of North Carolina and Kentucky refused. So, ominously, did the governor of Virginia. In Richmond, a state convention endorsed secession and called for volunteers to defend the state.

Washingtonians wondered whether their city could be

defended or not. Refugees left in haste from the capital and from Georgetown. Shops were closed, houses boarded up. Hotel owners found themselves with vacant rooms. Emergency plans were made to house the president and his Cabinet in the massive Treasury Building: its entrances were barricaded, sandbags were piled around it, and flour was stored in the basement, which contained a deep well. Senator Jim Lane of Kansas brought an improvised company of toughs to camp in the East Room of the White House. Loyal militia took up night guard duty. U.S. cavalry guarded the bridges over the Potomac, the Anacostia, and Rock Creek.

The first victim of the loyal Union response was its own War Department. Secretary Simon Cameron, a powerful boss in Pennsylvania, was swamped by telegrams offering men and pleading for weapons. Col. Robert E. Lee, invited to take command of the new army, declared that he could take no part in an invasion of the South. "Lee," said Lt. Gen. Winfield Scott sadly, "you have made the greatest mistake of your life." Lee rode back across the Long Bridge to Arlington and resigned his commission in the U.S. service. Quartermaster General Joseph E. Johnston and others resigned.

At the Navy Yard, Cdre. Franklin Buchanan and subordinate officers also resigned. Across town at the Naval Observatory, located on a hilltop between 23rd Street and the Potomac, the noted superintendent Matthew Fontaine Maury resigned his rank of commander; he received the same rank in Confederate service.

First of the units to reach the jittery capital were five companies from Pennsylvania—"unlicked patriotism ... ragged and unarmed," said Lincoln's secretary John Hay. The Washington Artillery Company of Pottsville had brought along an old black man known as Nick Biddle. As the Pennsylvanians crossed Baltimore, a mob had stoned them, hitting Nick Biddle in the head. Blood was still oozing from his bandages when the train pulled in on the evening of April 18; he was the first casualty among the city's defenders.

When the 6th Massachusetts Regiment reached Baltimore, they, too, met mob resistance. These troops, however, fired back when fired upon. Three of them were killed; eight of the wounded were left in Baltimore; 31 were brought on to Washington and taken to the E Street Infirmary. The rest were housed in the Senate Chamber, where Senator Galusha Grow franked their letters home.

On Saturday, April 20, Washington's rail links with the North were broken. Riots raged in Baltimore. On Sunday the telegraph wires were cut. The city was isolated. On Wednesday, President Lincoln received the walking wounded of the 6th Massachusetts, commenting: "I don't believe there is any North. The New York 7th Regiment is a myth. Rhode Island is not known in our geography any longer. *You* are the only Northern realities." They left, said John Hay, "easy, proud and happy."

Finally on April 27, relief arrived. The 7th New York and the 8th Massachusetts had come safely by way of Annapolis. They paraded to the Capitol, where the 7th camped in the House of Representatives and the 8th in the unfinished Rotunda. Off duty, the men delighted in sitting at congressional desks and holding mock sessions of the legislature. There were good-natured speeches and debates followed by cheers and hoots.

Other units followed and found accommodations where they could. Col. Ambrose E. Burnside commanded the 1st Rhode Island, which settled down among glass cases of models in the Patent Office. (The colonel's scalloped whiskers or "sideburns" would make him immortal.) John Hay, a graduate of Brown University, knew some of the "Rhodian heroes" and estimated that the rich young men of Company C could have taken up the Confederacy's first domestic loan: $15,000,000.

The 5th Massachusetts camped in the Treasury Building, cooking and eating in the courtyard. There were regiments sleeping in warehouses, in the Center Market, and in the Palace of Aladdin behind City Hall. The 71st New York was sent to the Navy Yard, and huts were built for the 12th New York in Franklin Square.

Every day there were parades along Pennsylvania Avenue as more troops kept arriving. A full brigade of 3,200 men from New Jersey came in. Units arrived at such a continuous pace that they formed a procession stretching from 6th to 15th Streets.

The Irishmen of the 69th New York, emerald colors flying, marched to the grounds of Georgetown College. Troops from Maine and New York camped on the spacious grounds of Columbian College. New Jersey outfits camped on Meridian Hill. Dragoons (mounted infantry) from the Regular Army were sent out the 7th Street Pike. The 1st and 2nd Connecticut camped at Glenwood, the home of banker William Corcoran, and Rhode Island troops occupied huts near Glenwood Cemetery.

Pvt. Joseph G. Green, 14th New York Regiment, wrote: "When I started from home I thought I was agoing to see something when I seen Washington but I do not think much of it. I think it is a little better than a country town." The next day Green's brother, a member of the same outfit, wrote: "Washington is not such a grand place after all; take the government buildings out of it and it would be nothing.... but a mere hole."

The most colorful troops to arrive in Washington were the 11th New York Fire Zouaves. These men, recruited by Col. Elmer Ellsworth, were rough-and-tumble firemen from New York City. Their uniforms, based on a French style, were red trousers topped with a red fez. They were quartered in the House Chamber and Statuary Hall in the Capitol. The Zouaves had little respect for law and order. They would take food and merchandise from the markets or order dinners at the finest restaurants and hotels and say "Charge it to Uncle Sam," or "Send the bill to Jeff Davis." They practiced fire drills with ropes hanging from cornices of the Rotunda, to the amazement of spectators. Generally they caused havoc in the city.

Some of these men distinguished themselves when they put out a fire in a tailor shop adjacent to the Willard Hotel. Called out on emergency duty, they ran from the Capitol to 14th Street. They broke down the door of the

Franklin Engine House to get equipment. They formed a bucket brigade and a human ladder and climbed into windows helping guests to escape. Even though the tailor shop was destroyed, the Zouaves saved the hotel and became instant heroes.

No one in the city was sorry, however, when the Fire Zouaves' camp was moved (many thought it appropriate) to the vicinity of the government insane asylum.

On May 24, Ellsworth's Zouaves crossed the Potomac by steamer from Giesboro Point to Alexandria, Virginia. This was part of an operation to secure the Virginia shore, and it included occupying Arlington Heights (now Arlington National Cemetery). Upon landing at Alexandria, the Zouaves marched up King Street to a hotel called the Marshall House, which was flying a Confederate flag from its roof. This flag was visible with a spyglass from the window of President Lincoln's office. Ellsworth climbed to the roof of the house and tore down the flag. As he was coming down the stairs, the innkeeper, James Jackson, shot him dead. Pvt. Francis Brownell instantly killed Jackson. As rage replaced grief, the Fire Zouaves threatened to burn the town of Alexandria, but they were confined for the night on a ship anchored in the middle of the Potomac.

Even though 75,000 troops had been called for, the War Department was not organized to take care of those who reached the capital. There was no system for distributing food, tents, cots, mattresses, blankets, clothing, stoves, and kitchen utensils. There were no means to care for the many cases of accidents and illnesses. Some states had done a better job of mobilization than others. Some regiments arrived with nothing more than the clothing on their backs; others had all sorts of supplies, including tents, bags, haversacks, knapsacks, overcoats, blankets, hammocks, pipes, tobacco, Bibles, books, magazines, towels, soap, slippers, and portable writing desks.

Before long, loads of freight were arriving by rail and ship. Rail service remained unbroken, but the Potomac was closed to Union ships from the fall of 1861, when the Confederates set up artillery batteries downriver, until March

1862, when they abandoned them to concentrate all their strength near Richmond. In the spring and summer of 1861, before the Confederate blockade, the Navy Yard was filled with steamers, schooners, and tugs carrying thousands of blankets and tons of coal, bread, and foodstuffs. The area around the unfinished Washington Monument was transformed into a great cattle pen. Ships landed cattle at the 7th Street wharves, and the cattle were then driven through the streets to the Monument grounds where they were slaughtered. Army butchers cut up and dressed the beef for distribution. Also near the Monument grounds were horse stables with sheds for hay and grain. Nearby Foggy Bottom was crowded with wagon sheds, corrals for 30,000 horses and mules, and extensive barracks. At Giesboro Point, the army set up a cavalry depot that shipped more than 20,000 tons of hay and grain. The new Quartermaster General, Montgomery Meigs, set up his headquarters at the Corcoran Gallery of Art (now the Renwick Gallery) at 17th Street and Pennsylvania Avenue.

The presence of thousands of soldiers added pleasures and pressures to daily life in Washington. Military bands played on the lawn south of the White House and at the Navy Yard, and there were parades up and down Pennsylvania Avenue and on the level ground east of the Capitol. Fourteenth Street saw its share of promenading as carriages and horsemen rode out to meet the troops camped at Meridian Hill.

The military presence also created new nuisances. Irresponsible soldiers fired their weapons daily in every direction. Quiet neighborhoods were disturbed by constant drilling, with bugle calls sounding the orders. The encampment in Franklin Square made the neighborhood so unpleasant that Secretary of War Edwin M. Stanton, who replaced Simon Cameron in January 1862, was forced to move his family out of their house on K Street.

While most of the troops conducted themselves properly, there were enough drunken soldiers who engaged in brawling to keep the provost guard busy. During the course of the war more than 200 gambling houses opened where games of faro, keno, and poker were popular. Approximately 2,000 bars were opened to entice the soldiers, and efforts to regulate their trade never succeeded completely. In 1864, a veteran learned that the "hot lemonade" available in the back room of a general store was really whiskey and that a deep cellar under a Pennsylvania Avenue sidewalk would serve a soldier anything he ordered. Officers, of course, indulged at their own discretion.

Many of the troops showed antagonism towards the residents of the city and vice versa. The soldiers thought of themselves as liberators, while the pro-Southern residents looked upon the soldiers with contempt and hatred. Waldo Denny of the 6th Massachusetts Regiment wrote in his diary: "Our Regiment marched up Penn. Avenue .... Some of the crowd hissed us—others called us Yankee S.O.B.'s a very favorite appellation with the Chivalry. Some cheered Jeff Davis, and some cheered us, but most of the loyal people remained silent."

The men who answered Lincoln's first call were militia, usually with elected officers. Typically, these units were social clubs that practiced their drill as a hobby and enjoyed parading in uniform on national holidays. Now, instead of catered meals at holiday encampments, they got salted beef or pork and hardtack—big crackers that tested their jaws. At best they showed little discipline, and they were ill prepared to fight, but the administration felt compelled to use them before their three months of service were up. As William Howard Russell noted, "General Scott is urged ... to get into Richmond before they are disbanded."

Newspapers in the North were predicting a quick Union victory. The hastily formed regiments had been organized into brigades and divisions and put under the command of Brig. Gen. Irvin McDowell. By July, after weeks of drill in Washington, the troops were looking for a fight. McDowell managed to get about 28,500 men to the vicinity of Manassas, Virginia, and the banks of Bull Run on July 21. They met a slightly larger Confederate force and suffered a humiliating defeat.

The rout at First Manassas showed the Northern public as well as the government that the war was not to be a short and splendid one. Now preparations were made for a long and hard-fought contest. Volunteers were recruited for three years, and serious efforts were made to find officers of ability and military experience. The scramble for commissions of U.S. Volunteers was all too similar to the struggle for civilian patronage jobs. Foreign observers remarked that the enlisted men were better than their officers, and many of the men expressed a similar opinion.

An extensive system of fortifications was planned to extend completely around Washington, including the Virginia shore. By the war's end in 1865, the city was guarded by 68 enclosed forts and batteries, which were supported by 93 small batteries for field guns. Approximately 1,400 gun emplacements had been constructed, and 1,807 cannon and 98 mortars mounted in them. Twenty miles of rifle pits and thirty miles of military roads encircled the city.

Nevertheless, the capital's security rested on the effectiveness of its armies in the field, and its sense of safety varied according to their success or failure. Stonewall Jackson's campaign in the Shenandoah Valley in the late spring of 1862 made for jangled nerves at Lincoln's War Department, and the Federals' defeat at the Second Battle of Bull Run alarmed the city in late August. Within weeks Lee's army was north of the federal city, only to be turned back at the Battle of Antietam. Lincoln had called for a much larger army that summer, and the volunteers who responded liked to sing a new song with words by James S. Gibbons and music by Stephen Foster: "We Are Coming Father Abraham, 300,000 More." By 1863, the city had settled into wartime habits, and Lee's invasion of Pennsylvania stirred concern but not fluster.

Union fortunes seemed to brighten in July 1864, when Lee sent Lt. Gen. Jubal Early with 14,000 men on a raid into Maryland. By July 11, Early's army was testing the northern defenses of Washington, which were manned by a scratch force of convalescent veterans from the city's hospitals, District volunteers, and civilians clerks of the Quartermaster Corps. Early challenged the defenders at Fort

Stevens, out on the 7th Street Pike, but decided to retreat when he saw that the fort had been reinforced by 6th Corps veterans brought up in the nick of time from the siege lines down at Petersburg. Quartermaster General Meigs noted wryly that his men had helped deter the Rebels by "standing upon the parapets and exposing themselves more than more experienced soldiers would have done."

Despite the strength of its fortifications, the city was fortunate in escaping an all-out Confederate attack. Washingtonians were always aware that their fate was tied to the fortunes of the capital's principal defenders, the Army of the Potomac. Sometimes the streets were filled with marching regiments on their way to or from a battlefield. At other times it was filled with the sick, the wounded, and the dying, who would not be forgotten when the victorious Union armies marched in a "Grand Review" on Pennsylvania Avenue at war's end.

One of the greatest military pageants ever: the Grand Review of the Union armies at Washington, D.C., May 23–24, 1865.

Contrabands

In the spring of 1861, Virginia slaves started their migration into Washington. Many had escaped their bondage; others had been deserted by their owners moving away in hopes of safety. Both the military and the District police detained these slaves, and in most cases, returned them to their masters. Other escaped slaves made themselves useful servants and laborers in the army camps.

Abraham Lincoln had promised the slaveholding states that had not joined the Confederacy that the institution of slavery would be protected as the Constitution required. On July 17, 1861, an army order excluded slaves from the army camps in and around Washington. Lincoln's oath of office committed him to the preservation of the Union under the Constitution, and he distinguished his official duty from his personal desire that everyone should be free. Slavery in itself was not yet an issue.

Most of the Union soldiers had not enlisted to right the wrongs of slavery. Although there were regiments in which abolition sentiment was strong, most of the men were accustomed to tolerating slavery as legal and had a low opinion of blacks, slave or free.

Even with this strong feeling running against them, slaves crossed the Potomac to seek their freedom. The laws of the District concerning slavery were the so-called Black Code, derived from 18th-century Maryland law. Slaves who were arrested as runaways and not claimed could be sold to pay the costs of keeping them in jail. No free person of color was safe from arrest without a certificate of freedom to be shown on demand. The city police and the District marshals would hunt and seize black people as circumstances permitted. Lincoln had made his friend Ward

Hill Lamon the U.S. marshal for the District. Lamon assumed that the fugitives really belonged to loyal masters. (Critics said he wanted a cut from the subsistence allowance for jail inmates—21 cents per person per day.)

Maj. Gen. Benjamin Butler, who commanded volunteers at Fort Monroe, set some of the runaways to work for his quartermaster instead of returning them. A lawyer in civil life, he declared that the slaves—like the South's horses, mules, foodstuffs, and sundry equipment—were "contraband of war," enemy property subject to lawful seizure.

The term "contraband" caught on and was used throughout the war to cover all slaves who fled from or were abandoned by their owners. Lincoln found it a handy element in his strategy of appeasing the border states. In Washington, contrabands were put under the protection of the military's provost guard. At first they were housed at the old "Brick Capitol" on 1st Street. In 1862, some 400 lived at Duff Green's Row on East Capitol Street (where the Folger Shakespeare Library now stands).

As the black fieldhands streamed across the Long Bridge (site of the present-day 14th Street Bridge) day after day, they brought new problems for the District. They were used to supervision and unprepared to fend for themselves in the city. Many needed help to find housing, work, clothing, and food. Their health had to be monitored, not only for their own sake but also for fear of spreading disease. A relief association, the first of many, was formed in March 1862, with Vice President Hannibal Hamlin as its head.

In April Congress emancipated the approximately 8,100 slaves owned by District citizens. The owners received compensation based on the value of the slave. This law also included a provision for aiding the freed persons who might wish to go abroad and settle in colonies of their own. Many whites thought colonization the only path to racial peace, but few persons of color chose to leave America. Weeks after Congress took action, Washington repealed its municipal Black Code.

"Contrabands" on their way to a day's work.

The city's established black community saw the contrabands with mixed emotions. They did not want bondage for anyone, but would the new arrivals threaten their own hard-won place? In some cases, charity prevailed. "We see them in droves every day perambulating the streets of Washington, homeless, shoeless, dressless, and moneyless," declared the Reverend Henry M. Turner, pastor of Israel Bethel Church, an African Methodist Episcopal congregation on South Capitol Street. "Every man of us now, who has a speck of grace or bit of sympathy," should "extend a hand of mercy." His church formed a relief association, drew up a constitution for it, and appealed to freed slaves in the North for bedding, clothes, money, and food.

A skilled professional dressmaker, Elizabeth Keckley, had already taken action on a similar plan, thinking, "Why should not the well-to-do colored people go to work to do something for the benefit of the suffering blacks?" Mrs. Keckley had already become a friend as well as a modiste to Mrs. Lincoln, who gave her $200 for the cause. The First Lady's patronage gave Mrs. Keckley access to contributors in New York and to white philanthropists in Boston.

Yet another group under white auspices listed education among its goals: to teach the contrabands "to read and write, and bring them under moral influences." One of its leaders was a city official named Sayles J. Bowen, who later served as mayor and enjoyed black support.

The Military District of Washington established a Contraband Department with headquarters at 12th and O Streets. Contrabands registered and received passes to ensure military protection. The army furnished them rations and employed able-bodied men at 40 cents per day at the corrals and hospitals.

In September 1862, after the Army of the Potomac checked Lee's invasion of Maryland at the Battle of Antietam, President Lincoln issued his Preliminary Emancipation Proclamation, which took effect on January 1, 1863. The proclamation declared that the slaves of persons in rebellion were to be "then, thence-forward, and forever free." By the spring of 1863, almost 10,000 such free persons had gathered in Washington. The government opened a contraband camp called Freedman's Village across the Potomac on the confiscated estate called Arlington, formerly the home of Robert E. Lee.

Another camp was on Analostan (Mason's) Island in the Potomac near Georgetown. Settlements in Washington were Camp Barker at Vermont Avenue and 12th Street (the present site of Howard University), and on 11th Street near the Navy Yard. On camp farms, the freed residents worked from sunrise to sundown. They raised vegetables for the army and for the city hospitals, cut wood for fuel, and made clothing for themselves and for the soldiers.

Most of the former slaves, however, found places for themselves in Washington. Some moved across the Anacostia River into an undeveloped area now called Hillsdale. Some settled in a neighborhood called Fredericksburg in the southern section of the city. Fredericksburg was remarkably orderly and industrious, and there were other black neighborhoods almost as respectable. But many newcomers lived in crowded blocks that soon were overcrowded. Diseases—notably, smallpox—spread easily and rapidly. The scale of the problems outran measures of aid. By the end of the war almost 40,000 former slaves, men, women and children, had made their way into the city.

In March 1865, the superintendent of the metropolitan police force, A. C. Richards, described with grim eloquence the conditions for some of these settlers in a horrendous slum called Murder Bay. This slum was located by the foul Washington Canal, bounded on the north and south by Pennsylvania and Constitution Avenues and lying between 13th and 14th Streets (now the site of the Federal Triangle). Its shanties were pieced together from scrap lumber, tarpaper, and bits of junk. In Richards's words:

> *Here crime, filth, and poverty seem to vie with each other in a career of degradation and death. Whole families, consisting of fathers, mothers, children, uncles, and aunts, according to their own statement, are crowded into mere apologies for shanties, which are without light or ventilation. During the storms of rain or snow their roofs afford but slight protection, while from beneath a few rough boards used for floors the miasmatic effluvia from the most disgustingly filthy and stagnant water, mingled with the exhalations from the uncleansed bodies of numerous inmates, render the atmosphere within these hovels stifling and sickening in the extreme. Their rooms are usually not more than six or eight feet square, with not a window or even an opening (except a door) for admission of light. Some of the rooms are entirely surrounded by other rooms, so that no light at all reaches where persons live and spend their days and nights. In a space about fifty yards square, I found about one hundred families, composed of from three to ten persons each living in shanties one story in height except in a few instances where tenements are actually built on the tops of others. There is a distance of only three or four feet separating these buildings from each other—not even as convenient as an ordinary three-feet alley. These openings lead in so devious a course that one with difficulty finds his way out again. Thus pent up, not even these paths are purified by currents of fresh air .... It was found that from five to eight dollars per month are paid for the rent of these miserable shanties, except in some instances, where a ground rent of*

three dollars per month is paid for a little spot covering a few feet square.

Escape through education would not come quickly or easily for the slum-dwellers. An Act of Congress passed in May 1862 required the District to open public schools for black children, but did not supply funds. The "colored schools" would be funded by 10 percent of taxes paid by the blacks themselves, and for the fiscal year 1862-1863, this amounted to $246. The first such school opened in March 1864 in the Ebenezer United Methodist Church at 4th and D Streets SE. Private benefactors did what they could; the National Freedmen's Relief Association opened two evening schools on the Island south of the canal.

The necessities of war would work changes for many of the freedmen and freeborn. In July 1862, Congress provided that the president would have the power to employ "persons of African descent" at his discretion, "for any military or naval service for which they may be found competent." Lincoln chose to use this power. By now recruiters in the loyal states were having trouble filling their quotas for white volunteers and were offering new inducements to blacks. Massachusetts gave her "colored" infantry her standard enlistment bonus of $50 and mustering-out bonus of $100. The federal government, however, did not deal as well with its "U.S. Colored Troops" (USCT). For too long it offered inferior pay. A white private earned $13 per month, with an issue of clothing; a black private earned $10 (a laborer's pay) with $3 deducted for clothing. Congress did not equalize these pay scales until March 1865. Nevertheless, volunteers of African descent came forward.

In the District, the black recruit had to fear not only the fury of Confederates in the field but also the open hostility of local civilians. To avoid trouble the recruits were taken to Analostan Island to receive their uniforms and guns. Once properly outfitted, these soldiers encountered less taunting from passersby. "They make a good show," noted Walt Whitman, and "are often seen in the streets of Washington in squads. Since they have begun to carry arms, the Secesh here and in Georgetown are not insulting to them as formerly."

Although officers in the USCT were almost all white, at least eight highly qualified physicians of African descent received commissions. One was Dr. Alexander T. Augusta of Baltimore, trained in Canada as a surgeon, who had charge of the Freedmen's Hospital at 13th and R Streets.

Major Augusta figured in a discrimination incident that caused a stir in Congress. The Washington and Georgetown Street Railroad Company, the District's first horse-drawn streetcar line, had a policy of forbidding black people to ride inside the cars. One rainy day in 1864, Dr. Augusta was refused admission into a car, and when he refused to ride outside, he was forced to get off. He had to walk through rain and mud, and his errand was serious. He was on his way to testify as the star witness at the court martial of a private named George Taylor, accused of causing the death of a black man in Freedmen's Hospital. Major Augusta was considerably late. As a result of this incident, Senator Charles Sumner of Massachusetts introduced legislation "that the Committee on the District of Columbia be directed to consider the expediency of further providing by law against the exclusion of colored persons from the equal enjoyment of all railroad privileges in the District of Columbia."

In March 1865, President Lincoln signed into law the creation of a new War Department agency, the Bureau of Refugees, Freedmen, and Abandoned Lands (known to history as the Freedmen's Bureau). This agency was designed to protect, aid, and educate the freed Americans until they could provide for themselves. Maj. Gen. Oliver Otis Howard, a West Point graduate from Maine, was appointed its commissioner and allotted the help of ten clerks. Howard University, chartered by Congress in 1866, still honors his name.

The most adaptable, persevering, and lucky former contrabands would make successful new lives in Washington, but their achievements would not be the common experience.

Washington's Wounded

Following the early defeats of the Army of the Potomac in 1861 and 1862, Washington was turned into one vast hospital complex with more than 20,000 wounded troops. Sanitary conditions were minimal by modern standards. Nobody understood how microbes transmit infections. Many men died of minor wounds, and disease killed twice as many victims as combat did.

The only hospital at the beginning of the war in the District was the E Street Infirmary, with staff doctors from the medical school faculty of Columbian College. It was a three-story brick building located on E Street behind the Court House on Judiciary Square. The structure was originally erected as a jail and dated from 1804. Wounded of the 6th Massachusetts Regiment were taken there after their battle with the Baltimore mob in April 1861.

In the fall of 1861, the E Street Infirmary was destroyed by a fire, but it was soon replaced by the new Judiciary Square Hospital. Also erected was Stanton Barracks Hospital at New Jersey Avenue and I Street. The former mansions of Senator Stephen A. Douglas of Illinois, Senator Henry Rice of Minnesota, and Vice President John C. Breckinridge of Kentucky—known as Minnesota Row—became Douglas Hospital, located on the north side of I Street near 6th Street.

Lincoln Barracks and Emory General Hospitals were erected on the flat plains east of the Capitol. These hospitals were located between Congressional Cemetery and the Alms House. Armory Square Hospital was erected near the Washington Canal and 7th Street. It was directed by Dr. D. Willard Bliss, a surgeon from Michigan who was to gain fame in 1881 as the attending surgeon of President

James Garfield, who died a lingering death from an assassin's bullet.

In what was then a suburb, Cliffburne Hospital occupied ground just to the west of Columbia Road. Nearby, on the Holmead estate in Mount Pleasant, was the Mount Pleasant Hospital.

On the 7th Street Pike, on the farm of banker and financier William Corcoran (a Southern sympathizer who had left the United States in 1862 and stayed in Europe for the duration of the war), sat Harewood Hospital, a makeshift complex of frame wards and canvas tents.

Providence Hospital was located at the corner of 2nd and D streets SE. It was run by the black-robed Sisters of Charity "who did not gossip or fuss." Campbell Hospital was located on Boundary Street between 5th and 6th Streets. In July 1865, the buildings were transferred to the Freedmen's Bureau and reopened as Freedmen's Hospital. Columbian College Hospital located on Meridian Hill took its name from the college on whose grounds the hospital was located. The old Barlow mansion called Kalorama (beautiful view) became a hospital for smallpox and other eruptive diseases.

Many public buildings were converted to hospitals. The northwest wing of the Patent Office was taken over and called, naturally, the Patent Office Hospital. When other facilities overflowed between August and November 1862 and after the Battle of Gettysburg in 1863, wards were improvised within the marble halls of the Capitol. Even the White House grounds were used: Reynolds Barracks Hospital was located on what is now the South Lawn.

As the demands of war increased, many private buildings were also taken over for use as hospitals. One was Desmarre's Eye and Ear Hospital, on the northwest corner of Massachusetts Avenue and 14th Street. Hotels and boarding schools were rented. In Georgetown, the Union Hotel, at Bridge and M Streets, became the Union Hotel Hospital. The owner agreed to a rental fee of $500 a month, which the authorities soon reduced to $200. The well-appointed premises of Miss Lydia English's Female

Seminary at the northwest corner of Washington and Gay Streets brought $300 a month. As Seminary Hospital it housed 150 invalid officers.

Religious congregations offered their buildings in the emergency. Plank floors were laid on top of the pews, with church furniture stored below the flooring. Georgetown churches adapted in this way were the Presbyterian Church on Bridge Street and Trinity Roman Catholic Church on Lingan Street. Most of the Washington sanctuaries were in Northwest. They included Ascension, on the south side of H between 9th and 10th; the Methodist Episcopal Church on 8th between H and I; Epiphany (Episcopal) on G between 13th and 14th; the Unitarian Church (which became Cranch Hospital) at 6th and D; Union Methodist Episcopal on 20th between Pennsylvania Avenue and H Street; Trinity Episcopal at 3rd and C; and Fourth Presbyterian at 9th and G. In Southwest, there were Ebenezer United Methodist Church on 4th Street and Ryland Methodist Episcopal on the Island at 10th and D.

At regular hospitals or converted ones, security was lax. All kinds of people wandered in and out. Family members came from distant states looking for loved ones, and religious zealots preached to soldiers too ill to move. Many patients grew tired of being questioned by the curious. The more presentable patients were given food and other gifts to the exclusion of less appealing wounded and sick.

Generally the buildings were neither heated nor ventilated well enough for hospital purposes. Sanitation was often subpar and asepsis was unthought of. Used bandages might be dropped on the floor to lie there until somebody gathered them up. Instruments were not sterilized, even if the surgeon whetted his knife on the sole of his boot. When he needed to close a wound or incision, he wet the tip of his silk thread with saliva to thread the needle easily. Wounds were doused with unsterilized cold water to relieve a sense of burning. Blood poisoning, tetanus, and gangrene were all too common. Mercifully, chloroform was available for operations and laudanum or morphine for unbearable pain.

The wounded were transported to Washington from the nearby battlefields and field hospitals in Virginia or Maryland in all sorts of conveyances. When the war broke out, the standard army ambulance was a two-wheeled cart, lightly built and poorly balanced. On rutted roads and potholed streets, this unstable vehicle rocked from side to side. Men lying inside were thrown against each other or dashed against the sides. By the end of 1862, a larger, steadier four-wheeled model came into use, but rickety substitutes might be pressed into emergency service.

Railroads provided speed if not comfort in relaying the wounded. Special trains pulled boxcars loaded with men lying on hard floors, sometimes on loose straw or thin mattresses. Flatcars exposed the wounded to the elements—blazing sun, wind, rain, or sleet. Sophisticated cars eventually came into use, with stretchers suspended by rubber to absorb movement, but there were never enough. Whatever their makeup, trains arrived at the Maryland Avenue depot, where ambulances waited to transfer the patients to hospitals. Sometimes no vehicles were on hand when a train came in, and local residents treated the patients with food and drink, medicine, and bandages from their homes.

Slower but probably more comfortable than trains, ships came to the 6th and 7th Street wharves to unload the wounded. Eventually, specialized hospital vessels performed most of this work.

From the first call to the colors, civilians at home were eager to send supplies and comforts to the troops. Some were useless, such as the headgear called havelocks, which were too hot to wear; and some spoiled in transit, such as homebaked cakes; but good sense soon prevailed. As early as April 29, 1861, 3,000 women met in New York City to form the Women's Central Association of Relief, coordinating local efforts and eventually setting up a training program for the nurses.

At that point, the army's medical branch had lost 24 surgeons—Southerners or sympathizers who resigned—of a roster of 115. The 80-year-old surgeon general died in

May, but many of his subordinates were also elderly and resources were obviously inadequate. Civilian organizations came to the rescue.

The U.S. Sanitary Commission was organized in June 1861 to conduct inquiries and give advice in light of the best medical sciences of the day. Its specialists studied standards of examination for prospective recruits, the best means of assuring hygiene in service, and proper standards for hospitals. Dr. Henry W. Bellows, pastor of All Souls Unitarian Church in New York City, was chosen president of the commission, and the other directors were men of high professional standing as well. Their ultimate purpose was "neither humanity nor charity" but "to economize ... the life and strength of the National soldier," and they went about their work with cool efficiency.

They provided not only advice but also well-informed political pressure as needed. They supplied nursing and hospital services, including hospital ships, and bought and distributed supplies. Their agents also performed individual services such as sending telegrams to relatives of the very sick and helping discharged soldiers with their pension claims.

The commission's members donated their services and goods, but paid their field agents and professional fundraisers. Funds came from private gifts and from so-called sanitary fairs; women did much of the work organizing these events. The fairs entertained citizens with exhibits, parades, and auctions of donated merchandise ranging from farm machinery to turnips and handmade lace. President Lincoln donated a draft of the Emancipation Proclamation. Mr. T. B. Bryan of Illinois purchased the document for $3,000 and then donated it to the Chicago Soldiers' Home.

To run its Washington headquarters, the commission chose the versatile superintendent of New York City's Central Park, Frederick Law Olmsted, who had published vivid accounts of travels in the South in the 1850s. His office was at the Adams House, 244 F Street. Soon the commission was managing "lodges," shelters for troops who needed care but weren't ill enough to warrant a hospital bed. One lodge (Lodge No. 6) was on Maryland Avenue near the depot, terminus for trains that crossed the Long Bridge from Virginia; others were at 374 North Capitol Street (Lodge No. 1), H and 18th (Lodge No. 4), and the 6th Street wharf (Lodge No. 5), with two more across the river at Alexandria.

Service to the wounded was part of the work of the U.S. Christian Commission, organized in New York City in November 1861 by the Young Men's Christian Association and recognized by the government. It sought the "spiritual good" and "intellectual improvement" of the men as well as physical comfort. Many of its delegates served in camps and hospitals. Often they worked with volunteers of the Sanitary Commission, with physicians, and with chaplains. They established hospital reading rooms and stocked them

Washington became one vast hospital complex serving more than 20,000 troops.

not only with Bibles and other religious items but also with newspapers from home. They brought whatever seemed needed to the bedside: towels, food, writing paper, reading matter, prayers. The Washington office was originally housed at 344 Pennsylvania on the south side between 6th and 7th. Later it moved to 500 H Street at the corner of 8th.

Among the first to offer help for the wounded was Dorothea Dix, a lifelong crusader for medical reform. On April 23, 1861, the War Department announced that she would help organize military hospitals, supply nurses, receive and control gifts for the comfort of the soldiers, and draw on army stores with the approval of the acting surgeon general. On May 1, the latter officer asked that all ladies volunteering as nurses or donating supplies notify Miss Dix at 505 12th Street, between E and F. On May 20 she was made general superintendent of nurses in the vicinity of Washington. In June, a general order announced that Miss Dix would authorize the service of women nurses who could present certificates of character from two physicians and two clergymen.

Almost 60 years old herself, Miss Dix turned away many would-be nurses because they were too young. She looked for women "plain almost to repulsion in dress," and permitted no hoop skirts on duty. She wanted women strong enough to turn a patient in bed and disciplined enough to do menial tasks.

Like England's Florence Nightingale, she had irreproachable character and self-dedication and interceded for her nurses when they needed help with uncooperative doctors. Unfortunately, she lacked Miss Nightingale's talent for administration and her tact. One lady called her Dragon Dix. A volunteer noted in her journal that Miss Dix was "a kind old soul, but very queer, fussy and arbitrary, no one likes her and I don't wonder."

The writer was Louisa May Alcott, a novelist without training as a nurse. She joined the Union Hotel Hospital in Georgetown in late December 1862 and spent about three arduous weeks on a ward of ten patients. She scrubbed layers of mud from survivors of the Battle of Fredericksburg, dressed wounds, fed men too weak to feed themselves, and supervised patients well enough to help with tasks no gentlewoman could perform. She sang lullabies, held hands, and consoled the wounded. In free hours she wrote detailed letters to her family in Massachusetts, describing the cold, damp, filthy conditions in the hospital. Indifferent nurses and surgeons and women who were temperamentally unsuited for hospital work were favorite targets of criticism. The "vile odors from wounds, kitchens, wash rooms, and stables" tormented her as well as her patients. She became known as the "Nurse with the Bottle" because she sprinkled herself and her surroundings with lavender water to combat the stench.

Nurse Alcott was only too accurate when she called the hospital "a perfect pestilence box." In January she fell ill. The doctors diagnosed her case as typhoid pneumonia—typhoid is a disease linked with poor sanitation—and prescribed calomel, considered something of a cure-all. This drug contained mercury, and lavish doses left many patients lifelong victims of mercury poisoning. Her father arrived to take her home to a slow, incomplete convalescence. Her letters, published in 1863 as *Hospital Sketches,* attracted much attention and remain as one of the most vivid portrayals of Civil War hospital life. They are as enduring as her best novels.

A woman who made her own place in caring for the wounded was a shy, middle-aged spinster named Clara Barton. When the war broke out, she was working as a clerk in the Patent Office—an unusual job for a woman—and earning a man's pay of $1,400 a year. She was at the depot when the 6th Massachusetts arrived and made handkerchief bandages for the wounded. Before long she was organizing a relief program.

When she learned that many of the wounded from Bull Run had suffered from a shortage of medical supplies, she advertised for donations in the *Worcester Spy,* a Massachusetts journal, and made herself the distributing agent. Eventually the surgeon general, Dr. William Hammond, granted her a general pass to travel on campaign with her own wagons for "the purpose of distributing comforts for the sick and wound, and nursing them."

By the end of the war, Clara Barton had performed most of the services that would later be associated with the American Red Cross, which she founded in 1881. She lived in several residences in Washington over the years, including 488 1/2 7th Street NW and 482 11th Street SE.

Most eloquent of the untrained volunteers who cared for Washington's wounded was Walt Whitman. He was working as a journalist from Brooklyn, New York, when he traveled to Virginia to find his wounded brother George, a captain with the 51st New York and a survivor of the carnage at Fredericksburg. Finding George safe and recovering, he remained in the area, both fascinated and appalled by the sights and the sounds of an army in the field. He spent much of his time visiting the field hospitals and talking to the patients, and when he left for Washington, he was placed in charge of a trainload of wounded men. Back in the capital, he rented a room at 394 L Street for $7 a month and got a part-time job as a copy clerk in the paymaster general's office. (This greatly expanded service had been installed in the five-story office building at 15th and F Streets.) His real reason for remaining was to follow his new vocation of sympathetic visitor to the sick and wounded.

During the next three years, Walt Whitman made approximately 600 visits to the hospitals, comforting between 80,000 and 100,000 dying or convalescing soldiers. He worked alone, paying for gifts from his own pocket: cool drinks, fruit, preserves, tobacco, pens and paper, a toothpick, or a comb. Once he found a German Lutheran clergyman for a German-speaking patient dying of tuberculosis. He did not ignore the surly or unattractive and was always tactful. Like mothers turned nurses, he believed in the curative properties of affection. His poem "The Wound Dresser" declares, "many a soldier's kiss dwells on these bearded lips."

As a wound dresser, Whitman was a witness to the most intense drama the war had to offer. He made this clear in March 1863, when he wrote to two friends to say why he spent so much time with the wounded:

> *These thousands, and tens and twenties of thousands of American young men, badly wounded, all sorts of wounds, operated on, pallid with diarrhea, languishing, dying with fever, pneumonia, &c open a new world somehow to me, giving closer insights, new things, exploring deeper mines than any yet, showing our humanity, (I sometimes put myself in fancy in the cot, with typhoid, or under the knife), tried by terrible fearfulest tests, probed deepest, the living soul's, the body's tragedies, bursting the peddy [*sic*] bonds of art. To these, what are your dramas and poems, even the oldest and tearfulest?*

Whitman's hospital experiences inspired his collection of poems *Drum-Taps* (1865) and a prose work, *Memoranda During the War* (1875).

As the war progressed, the army's medical department was restructured and greatly improved. Dr. Jonathan Letterman, chief medical officer for the Army of the Potomac, developed a model ambulance service, and the skills of hospital staffs improved. Even so, one of the mainstay cure-alls was alcohol, usually administered as whiskey or brandy. Working with limited knowledge of medical and sanitary science, Civil War hospitals—in Washington and elsewhere—may have killed as many soldiers as they saved.

Part Two

Tour of Washington

Georgetown

At the beginning of the Civil War, Georgetown was a separate tobacco port and not considered part of Washington, D.C. It had its own locally elected mayor and government and competed economically with the capital city. Georgetown was politically and socially independent from the District of Columbia. The first white inhabitants were Scottish tobacco traders who settled in the area in the 1750s. They built warehouses and other ancillary buildings to support their trade. By the 1780s, the town was granted a charter by the Maryland legislature, and a mayor was elected. George Washington was named president of the Patowmack Company, which intended to open up trade to the Ohio Valley by way of a canal that would bypass the Potomac River. However, by the 1830s, Georgetown lost most of its tobacco and commercial trade to Alexandria and to Washington, D.C. The Long Bridge, built in 1809 at the site of the present-day 14th Street Bridge, carried Virginia traffic to Washington at the expense of Georgetown. Its construction caused silt and mud to block the shipping channel. The idea of a waterway to the Ohio Valley was revived; by 1850, the new C & O Canal was completed to Cumberland, Maryland. An aqueduct bridge was built between 1833 and 1843 that connected Georgetown and Virginia. A channel on the bridge allowed the canal boats to cross the Potomac and unload their cargos for sailing ships moored in Alexandria. During the Civil War, the bridge was drained by the federal government, and a roadway was placed in the bottom of the trough. Prior to the war, Georgetown was a shipping center for coal, lumber, and wheat.

In 1861, Georgetown was Southern in its population and social patterns. The population was approximately 8,800 people, including 600 slaves. Blacks lived southeast of 28th and P Streets, in an area called Herring Hill, and on the west side of Wisconsin Avenue west of 33rd Street. The northernmost limit was R Street, where Oak Hill Cemetery stood on the heights overlooking the Potomac

River. Diverging loyalties sent family members to serve in both the Confederate and Union forces. Government clerks moved south, and many houses remained empty during the war. John H. Bocock, pastor of the Bridge Street Presbyterian Church, gave a tearful sermon on May 4, 1861, and then left for Virginia the following day. Many Georgetown residents formed several companies of soldiers, including the Anderson Rifles, the Carrington Home Guards, and the Potomac Light Infantry Batallion. After the battle at Bull Run in 1861, thousands of troops streamed into Georgetown. Many private homes, churches, and public buildings were converted into makeshift hospitals to care for the wounded. From that point on, the fortunes of Georgetown were tied into Washington's. In 1871 Congress made Georgetown part of Washington, D.C., with one territorial government. The Georgetown street names and numbers were changed to coincide with the names and numbers of the Washington streets.

Civil War Name	Current Name
Bridge Street	M Street
High Street	Wisconsin Avenue
Monroe Street	27th Street
Montgomery Street	28th Street
Greene Street	29th Street
Washington Street	30th Street
Congress Street	31st Street
Market Street	33rd Street
Frederick Street	34th Street
Fayette Street	35th Street
Lingan Street	36th Street
Warren Street	37th Street
1st Street	N Street
2nd Street	O Street
3rd Street	P Street
4th Street	Volta Place
5th Street	Q Street
6th Street	Dent Place
7th Street	Reservoir Road
8th Street	R Street

West Georgetown

Site 1—3350 M Street

Forrest Marbury House

This was the Revolutionary War home of Col. Uriah Forrest, who later became mayor of Georgetown. George Washington met here with the District of Columbia commissioners and Georgetown landowners. In hopes of raising money to build the new capital city, Washington tried to persuade the landowners to donate land for an auction. During the Civil War, the house belonged to John Marbury (son of lawyer William Marbury of the famous *Marbury* v. *Madison* case), who bought the house from Forrest. He was a Southern sympathizer, and after the Battle of First Manassas (or Bull Run), he shut his windows so his wife and daughters would not see and feel sympathy for the wounded soldiers who were making their way back to Washington via the Aqueduct Bridge.

Site 2—1256 Wisconsin Avenue

Forrest Hall

Forrest Hall was owned by Bladen Forrest, one of the wealthiest inhabitants of Georgetown. This hall served as a temporary hospital and as a jail for bounty jumpers and deserters. It was also an armory for the 1st Georgetown Battalion and Washington Light Infantry, who signed up for three months, and the U.S. 2nd Infantry. Forrest complained about the dirt and filth caused by prisoners and soldiers. All of the woodwork was covered by tobacco juice and grease, and much of it was used for kindling. The provost marshal Major Littler had the prisoners clean the walls and scrub the floors, and if any prisoner stuck his head out of a window, a bullet was fired past his nose.

Site 3—3400 Prospect Street

Halcyon House

Halcyon House was originally built in 1783 by Benjamin Stoddert, John Adams's first secretary of the navy. The halcyon was a fabled bird whose nest floated on the sea; it had the power to calm the wind and the waves. "Halcyon" in modern times means tranquil, happy, and prosperous. In the early 1800s, the Templeman family owned most of the land in this part of Georgetown known as Pretty Prospect, and Capt. George Templeman and his family lived here until the beginning of the Civil War. After Templeman moved out, Halcyon was owned by John Kidwell, a rich pharmacist who owned the entire block between 34th and 35th Streets and M and Prospect.

Site 4—3508 Prospect Street

Prospect House

From 1862 until 1865, Daniel Craig McCallum boarded here. An architect and railroad engineer, he was appointed in 1862 as director of all military railroads in the United States with the rank of a brevet (or honorary) brigadier general. The owner of the house was William Whiton who, like McCallum, was a railroad engineer. They were together in the final year of the Civil War, following General Sherman on his march from Atlanta to the sea. In 1868, the house was sold to Franklin Steele, a local merchant. His daughter, Mary Chase Steele, married George Upham Morris who, when only a lieutenant, was left in charge of the USS *Cumberland* during its doomed battle with the Confederate ironclad *Virginia* (converted from the hull of the USS *Merrimack*). The *Cumberland* was a wooden ship whose guns had no effect on the *Virginia*. The Rebel ship rammed the *Cumberland*, opening a large hole in the hull. In response to a demand to surrender, Lieutenant Morris defiantly shouted, "Never. I'll sink alongside." He survived the battle, returned to Prospect House, and eventually reached the rank of commodore after the war.

Site 5—3425 Prospect Street

The house was built by John Thomson Mason in 1798. He was the son of George Mason of Gunston Hall, the Revolutionary statesman remembered as the man who inspired the Bill of Rights by drafting the Virginia Declaration of

Rights. That document was something of a model for the first ten amendments to the U.S. Constitution. James Murray Mason, also a descendant of George Mason and a Virginia congressman, was the Confederate agent who was taken off the British mail ship *Trent* along with John Slidell.

Site 6—37th and O Streets

Georgetown University

The university was founded in 1789 as Georgetown College. It is the oldest Roman Catholic institution of higher learning in the United States. More than a hundred students left the college at the beginning of the war, many of them to enlist in the Confederate army. Northern families, not knowing what to expect, also pulled their sons out of school. In May 1861, the 79th New York arrived. The soldiers broke banisters; spilled grease on the floors; stole guitars, violins, and umbrellas; damaged pillows and mattresses; ripped out door frames; and used the dining tables as butchers' blocks. A bill was sent to Quartermaster General Montgomery Meigs asking that the government replace the broken and stolen items and that the 79th New York be transferred to some other place. Meigs replied that the college enjoyed its property on a tax-free basis, but he would move the 79th New York camp elsewhere. After the Battle of First Manassas the buildings were used as temporary hospitals for the wounded. Buildings still in existence from the time of the Civil War include Old North, Maguire, Gervase, and Mulledy.

Site 7—36th and O Streets

Trinity Church

Trinity Church is the oldest church for Catholic worship in the District of Columbia. The church was used as a hospital from October 1862 until January 1863 for wounded soldiers brought from the Bull Run area. After the second battle there, in late August, a deadhouse was constructed behind the church to house the bodies of the soldiers who died while in the temporary hospital.

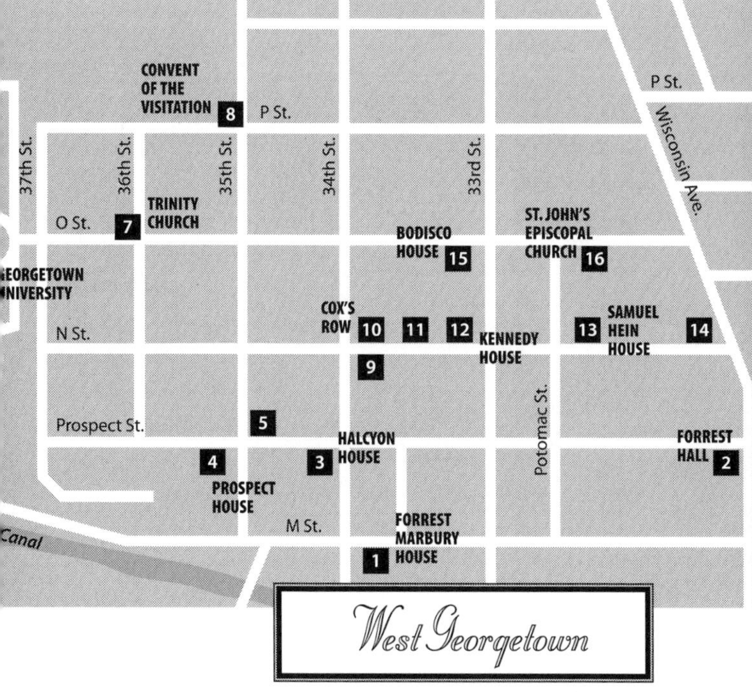

Site 8—35th and P Streets

Convent of the Visitation

The sisters of the Poor Clares ran this convent for girls. Lt. Gen. Winfield Scott had a daughter who had become a nun in the order, and upon her death she was buried on the grounds. When the government wanted to use the convent as a temporary hospital, Scott intervened, calling it "a place made sacred by the grave of my child." The sisters agreed that they would never discuss the war among themselves and that Southern nuns would care for Confederates if needed, while nuns from the North would care for Union soldiers if needed. However, Scott's request was honored by the government, and the convent was never used as a hospital.

Site 9—3340 N Street

John Crumbaugh, a butcher who moved to Georgetown from Loudoun County, Virginia, owned the house. He

Quarters of the New York militia at Georgetown College.

bought a wood and fuel business that had a wharf at the foot of 33rd Street and used the canalboats to smuggle medical supplies across the Potomac River. In February 1863, Col. Lafayette Baker, chief detective in the provost marshal's office, caught Crumbaugh with $14,000 worth of quinine, morphine, and nitrate of silver hidden in crates marked "Apples and Potatoes" in the cellar of this house.

Site 10—3327-3339 N Street

Cox's Row

John Cox, mayor of Georgetown from 1823 until 1845, built these houses. Bladen Forrest, who owned Forrest Hall, lived with his wife, nine children, a governess, and four slaves at 3339 N Street. At 3337 lived William Ridgley, owner of a stone quarry. At 3335 lived E. D. Hartley, who was a commission merchant; and Henry Clay Addison, mayor of Georgetown, lived at 3331. William Hunter, chief clerk of the State Department, lived at 3327.

Site 11—3311 N Street

Charles Slemmer, a post office employee, lived here until after the Battle of First Manassas. He returned home to Pennsylvania, and in 1864, he sold his house to Dr. Charles H. Laub, an army surgeon.

Site 12—3307 N Street

Kennedy House

During the Civil War, the Reverend Nicholas P. Tillinghast, rector of St. John's Episcopal Church, lived here. This house was rented by the vestry for $200 from Mrs. Vincent Taylor, who owned the property and who took her family to Philadelphia for the duration of the war. John F. Kennedy purchased this house in 1957 when he was a senator from Massachusetts.

Site 13—3249 N Street

Samuel Hein House

Samuel Hein was chief clerk of the Coast and Geodetic Survey. A pro-Union man in a Southern town, Hein flew a huge American flag from the entrance of his house. The neighbors who favored the South had to step into the muddy street to avoid walking under the flag. After the Battle of First Manassas, Hein maintained a soup kitchen in his backyard for the Union troops as they returned from the battlefield.

Site 14—NW corner of N Street and Wisconsin Avenue

William Wilson Corcoran started his career in this building in 1815. At age 17, he became a clerk in a dry goods store owned by his brothers, James and Thomas, and they bought him his own store at this location.

Site 15—3322 O Street

Bodisco House

In the 1840s and 1850s, this was the home of Baron Alexander Bodisco, minister from Russia. The house served as the Russian Legation during this period. It was bought by Abraham Herr, who had extensive commercial holdings on Virginius Island near Harpers Ferry, where he owned a four-story cotton factory, frame sawmill, flour mill, granary, brick foundry, and wheelwright shop. Herr was arrested by the Confederates for his pro-Union sympathies. When Union troops reoccupied Harpers Ferry, they destroyed his businesses so that the holdings would not fall into Confederate hands again. In 1862 Herr purchased a large mill in Georgetown but lived in Baltimore. His flour was exported to the West Indies and Brazil. The house served as the headquarters for the officers of the 2nd U.S. Regiment, whose enlisted men were quartered in Forrest Hall.

Site 16—3240 O Street

St. John's Episcopal Church

Unlike most churches in Georgetown before the war, St. John's congregation contained a mixture of blue-collar workers and foreign immigrants. It attracted people of Union sympathy. Its most prominent parishioner was Henry Cooke, a banker from Philadelphia and a member of the vestry. The Reverend Nicholas Tillinghast became rector in 1848 and remained until 1866. In 1864 a school for former slave children was opened in the basement of the church.

East Georgetown

Site 1—3238 R Street

Scott Grant House

Known as The Heights, the south side of R Street was the northern boundary for Georgetown. Built in the 1850s, this house was owned by Mrs. Alfred Vernon Scott of Alabama. She returned to Alabama at the beginning of the Civil War and advertised her house for rent. Maj. Gen. Henry Halleck, named general-in-chief of the land forces in July 1862, rented the mansion. A guardhouse and barracks, which housed a company of soldiers, were erected in the rear of the house. After the war and prior to his presidency, Lt. Gen. Ulysses S. Grant spent several summers in this house.

Site 2—3101 R Street

Dumbarton Oaks

Originally known as The Oaks, this house was built in the early 1800s. Among the early owners of the house were James Calhoun of South Carolina, who loaned the house to his famous brother, Senator John C. Calhoun, and Edward Linthicum, a wealthy Georgetown merchant. During the Civil War it belonged to Josiah Dent, who married the adopted daughter of Edward Linthicum.

Site 3—30th Street

Oak Hill Cemetery

See description on page 170.

Site 4—1623 28th Street

Evermay

This house was owned by Charles Dodge, one of the six sons of Francis Dodge, and his wife Elizabeth. For much of the Civil War, Evermay remained empty, but in 1864 it was rented to the correspondent of the *New York Herald.* Pressed for money, the Dodges lived in a small house on P Street.

Site 5—2715 Q Street

Dumbarton House

Currently the headquarters of the National Society of the Colonial Dames of America, this house was called Bellevue for more than a hundred years. The land on which the house stands was part of the original 795-acre tract granted to Ninian Beall, called the Rock of Dumbarton, which was the first parcel of land granted in Georgetown in 1703. Among the famous people who visited this historic house were Thomas Jefferson, James Madison, James Monroe, John Quincy Adams, and Dolley Madison. Here Dolley Madison planned her escape from the city after the Battle of Bladensburg as the British were marching on Washington. Prior to the Civil War, Sarah Whitall married a Mr. Rittenhouse from Philadelphia. The Rittenhouses lived in the house during the war.

Site 6—1524 28th Street

Robert Dodge rented this house to Edmund Cummins and his family in 1861. Cummins left to join the Confederate army, serving as a captain and a signal officer who fought at Shiloh. At the end of the war, Cummins returned home and sought amnesty. Mayor Henry Addison endorsed his petition, and it was granted in 1866. Cummins began teaching and continued to live at this address.

Site 7—1534 28th Street

Robert Dodge Mansion

This was the Italianate villa of Robert Dodge, one of the six sons of Francis Dodge. Robert owned the Columbia Flour Mill. He shut down the mill and was commissioned a major and a Union army paymaster on June 17, 1861. It was Dodge who, as administrator for Vincent Taylor's estate, rented the widowed Mrs. Taylor's house at 3307 N Street to the Reverend Mr. Tillinghast of St. John's Episcopal Church. In 1862, Dodge sold the Columbia Flour Mill to Abraham Herr, who had recently come to Washington from Harpers Ferry, West Virginia, and bought the Bodisco House.

Site 8—1633 29th Street

Louis Mackall House

This was the home of Louis Mackall, who left Georgetown and spent the war living in Prince Georges County, Maryland. His son, a prominent Georgetown doctor also named Louis Mackall, rented this house as a boardinghouse.

Site 9—1517 30th Street

This house was owned by Francis Dodge, the richest man in Georgetown when he died in 1851. He was worth $300,000, and he left his six sons and four daughters 11 waterfront properties and several large farms in Montgomery and Prince Georges Counties. His son, Francis Jr., lived in this house. Francis Jr. and his brothers lost their fortune in the Panic of 1857. Walter Taylor, who was chief of the claims division, rented this house from Dodge. Just before Abraham Lincoln was sworn in as president, Taylor resigned his position and became second auditor of the Confederate government. In 1864, the house was sold for $25,000 to Henry Cooke, a banker from Philadelphia, who

opened and operated the office of Jay Cooke and Company. Cooke later became a personal friend of President Grant. He also built Cooke Row (3007-3027 Q Street).

Site 10—1644 31st Street

Tudor Place

This house was owned by Britannia Peter Kennon. She was the widow of Comdr. Beverley Kennon, who was killed when a gun exploded on the USS *Princeton* during a pleasure cruise on the Potomac in 1844. Mrs. Kennon was the great-granddaughter of Martha Washington and a first cousin of Mrs. Robert E. Lee. During the war, she rented the house to Union officers, among others. She did not allow any "war talk" at the dinner table. Mrs. Kennon recorded that Mrs. Henry Lee, the widow of "Light-Horse" Harry Lee and the mother of Robert E. Lee, visited Tudor Place.

Site 11—3116 P Street

George Shoemaker, Georgetown's flour inspector and a Quaker, came to Georgetown in 1817 and lived in this house. In 1857 when the Dodge brothers declared bankruptcy, Shoemaker, who was a clerk in their flour mill, was owed $171.53. In 1865 he examined flour from more than 212,000 barrels in Georgetown mills.

Site 12—2819 P Street

This was the home of Alexander Hamilton Dodge, one of the six sons of Francis Dodge. Alexander and his brothers, Francis and Robert, retained the noted British architect Calvert Vaux to design Italianate villas for them. Alexander and Francis continued to operate the import-export business their father had left them under the name F. & A. H. Dodge. During the Panic of 1857, Alexander and his brothers were bankrupted. His sisters helped him financially, and Alexander Dodge became a third-class clerk in the State Department. He later became president of the Georgetown Gas Light Company.

Site 13—2805 P Street

This house, along with 2803 and 2811 P Street, was owned by Reuben Daw, a Georgetown locksmith. He purchased surplus gunbarrels from the U.S. government that were made for use during the Mexican War (1846-1848). By adding spikes to the muzzles, he made a "gunbarrel fence" around his property. Henry Brewer, a clerk in the third auditor's office, was renting this house at the beginning of the Civil War. He resigned from his job to join the Confederate government.

Site 14—3127 Dumbarton Street

Methodist Episcopal Church

This church, built in 1849, served as an army hospital from the late summer of 1861 until January 1863. Usually, boards were laid over the pews and a new temporary floor was used for the wounded soldiers. In this church, however, the galleries were so low that very little space would be left for the wounded. Instead, the pews were removed and the congregation used the Customs House for their services. Abraham Lincoln visited the church/hospital to comfort the wounded. On March 8, 1863, the pews were restored, and the congregation was again able to use the church. Lincoln attended the services, and a plaque is attached to the third pew from the front on the right side of the church to commemorate the visit.

Site 15—2808 N Street

John Haw House

This house was built in 1815 by John Stoddert Haw, nephew of Benjamin Stoddert who was President John Adams's first secretary of the navy. In the 1860s, the house belonged to Haw's daughters, Mrs. Henry Matthews and Mrs. Philip Berry. The women rented the house to a former clerk, William Rind, who went south and served in the quartermaster general's office. The house stood empty for almost two years after Rind left until 1863 when Lydia English moved in. This was one of the houses that she lived in until she could reopen her Georgetown Female Seminary at the end of the Civil War.

Site 16—2812 N Street

Riley Shinn House

This house was the home of Mrs. Stephen Decatur, who moved here in 1820 from her mansion on Lafayette Park after her husband was killed in a duel. After Lydia English rented her seminary to the federal government in July 1861,

Many buildings in Washington, including Lydia English's Female Seminary, were pressed into service as hospitals.

she moved around the corner to this rented house. Miss English advertised that she would take a limited number of pupils at her new address. In November 1863, Riley Shinn, a bottling manufacturer who was also one of the richest men in Georgetown, purchased the house. Shinn sold carbonated liquor, malt drinks, beer, and ale to the residents of Washington and Georgetown. He earned more than $28,000 in 1864. Only banker Henry Cooke earned more than Shinn.

Site 17—1311 30th Street

Lydia English's Georgetown Female Seminary

Lydia English personified the genteel Southern society. Rich Southerners and their sympathizers sent their daughters to her seminary, which began operating at this location in 1826. The school consisted of three floors containing 19 bedrooms, a music room, several parlors, schoolrooms, and a large library. Hot-water pipes served the upper floors. Miss English leased the seminary to the government as a hospital and convalescent home for officers. In July 1861, 150 patients occupied the building, and Lydia English moved around the corner to 2812 N Street. The building is now the Colonial Apartments.

Site 18—1300 30th Street

Grafton Tyler House

Before Dr. Grafton Tyler purchased the house, it belonged to George Riggs, partner of William Corcoran. Dr. Tyler was a prominent Georgetown physician and a Southern sympathizer. When the government took over Lydia English's school, the Tylers, who lived across the street, closed their shutters so that they would be unable to see the American flag draped from the seminary. Dr. Tyler was president of the vestry of Christ Episcopal Church, which had many Southern sympathizers as members of the congregation. When Lincoln was assassinated, however, the vestry passed a resolution condemning the assassination and ordering the church bell to toll on the day of the funeral. The church was draped in black mourning cloth for the next 30 days.

Site 19—3017 N Street

Jacqueline Kennedy House

This house was purchased in 1834 by William Redin, an Englishman who had come to America in 1817. He was a prominent attorney and a Union supporter. In 1863, he refused to take the chief justiceship of a new appellate court of the District from his friend and neighbor, Judge James Dunlop. Instead, he became the court's first auditor. During World War I, Secretary of War Newton Baker lived here. More recently, Jacqueline Kennedy lived in this house after the assassination of President John F. Kennedy.

Site 20—3033 N Street

Robert Dick, a first cousin of Britannia Peter Kennon, lived in this house. Even though he lived in Georgetown for almost 50 years, he still considered himself a citizen of Maryland. Dick was a bachelor and the grandson of one of the founders of Georgetown. He had two cousins who served in the Confederacy, Col. William Orton Williams and Lt. Walter Gibson Peter. They were hanged as spies in Franklin, Tennessee, in June 1863 and were eventually buried in Oak Hill Cemetery.

Site 21—3038 N Street

This was the Civil War home of prominent Georgetown doctor Joshua Riley. It is currently the home of Pamela Harriman, ambassador to France and widow of governor and ambassador Averill Harriman.

Site 22—3043 N Street

Wheatley Row

William A. Gordon, chief clerk of the Quartermaster Corps, rented this house from Francis Wheatley. Gordon was a graduate of West Point. He had a son, William Jr., who fought with the Confederacy and was pardoned in 1865. The father remained loyal to the Union and was cited by his corps as being "one of the oldest and most valuable of government employees."

Site 23—1215 31st Street

Customs House

At the height of Georgetown's international trade in the 1850s, many ships lined the waterfront. Francis Dodge had established a successful import-export business, and a customs house was built. Before 1871, the building also served as the city hall and housed the mayor's office. Georgetown mayor Henry Addison had his office in the southwest corner of the second floor. During the war, the Customs House was used as a church and Sunday school by several of the congregations whose churches were taken over for use as hospitals. The ceilings in the building were 18 feet high.

Site 24—30th Street

Chesapeake & Ohio Canal

The canal reached its westernmost point at Cumberland, Maryland. Grist and cotton mills powered by waterwheels sprang up alongside it. Canalboats arrived in Georgetown carrying coal, hay, furs, lumber, and grain. In 1861, the residents complained that the troops stationed in Georgetown bathed in the canal at all hours, day and night. Soldiers lounged on the bank wearing little (if anything at all), and their immodesty embarrassed residents, who wrote letters to the *National Intelligencer* or *Evening Star.* Graver troubles followed. Confederate raiders caused havoc on the economic life of the canal. Col. John Mosby used every tactic to reduce its trade: he and his men burned and sank bridges, destroyed locks and aqueducts, and stole mules and livestock. Every threat or rumor of a raid was enough to keep the boats and barges in Georgetown.

Site 25—Wisconsin Avenue and Water Street

Dodge Warehouse

This warehouse is the last remnant of a once-thriving business along the Georgetown waterfront. As late as 1864, the port was booming with trade. Every month approximately 600 vessels would arrive. Brick wharves, warehouses, and countinghouses lined K Street, and goods such as lumber, coal, flour, grain, potatoes, and cheese passed through them. After 1871, however, the competition of the railroads put an end to the importance of Georgetown as a port. Unlike many streets above M Street that have remained untouched since the 18th century, the waterfront has been completely transformed by modern construction.

Foggy Bottom

The settlement known as Foggy Bottom was founded in 1765 by a German immigrant named Jacob Funk. Later, Funkstown or Hamburg, as the area was called, was roughly bounded on the north by Pennsylvania Avenue, on the south by the Potomac River, on the east by 19th Street, and on the west by Rock Creek. The area was sparsely settled with few permanent houses. Much of the land near the river was swampy and subject to fog—hence the name. When Pierre L'Enfant laid out the city, he inserted a circle, now known as Washington Circle, and designed the hilly area near the Potomac known as Camp Hill. Several people, including Thomas Jefferson, wanted to build the Capitol on Camp Hill. During the 1840s, the Naval Observatory was built on this site. Today, this vicinity is the home of the Naval Medical Command.

Wharves and warehouses were built along the riverbank here, and a blue-collar waterfront community had developed by 1850. A canal connecting the C & O Canal with the Washington Canal was built. In 1856, the Washington Gas Light Company built a gas storage tank at Virginia and New Hampshire Avenues.

Simon Newcomb, an astronomer at the Naval Observatory who later became its superintendent, wrote in *The Reminiscences of An Astronomer:*

> *No houses were provided for the astronomers, and the observatory itself was situated in one of the most unhealthy parts of the city. On two sides it was bounded by the Potomac, then pregnant with malaria, and on the other two for nearly half a mile was found little but frame buildings filled with quartermaster's stores and here and there a few negro huts. After a rain, especially during winter and spring, some of the streets were much like shallow canals. Under the attrition of the iron-bound wheels the water and clay were ground into mud, which at first was almost liquid. It grew thicker as it dried up, until perhaps another rainstorm reduced it once more to a liquid condition. Whichever road you take, before you get halfway there you'll wish you had taken the other. By night swarms of rats, of a size proportional to their ample food supply, disputed the right of way with the pedestrian.*

During the Civil War, the federal government established Camp Fry (at the present site of George Washington University) as the home for the Invalid Corps who were quartered at the Martindale Barracks. The corps was authorized in April 1863, to consist of officers and men who were unfit for combat but who could perform garrison duty. Those still able to handle a musket or sword served as guards (1st Battalion had muskets and 2nd and 3rd Battalions—one-armed or one-legged men—got swords). Those who were more disabled were put to work as nurses and cooks in hospitals. By December more than 20,000 men were on the Invalid Corps roster. Although they served the valuable purpose of freeing able-bodied men for combat, the invalids took some cruel taunting. Much was made of the corps' initials, I.C., which in other army usage stood for the inscription stamped on worthless equipment: "Inspected—Condemned." In March 1864, the invalids were given a more dignified designation, the Veteran Reserve Corps.

Camp Fuller, adjacent to Camp Fry, was established as a base of supplies for horses and livestock. In December 1861, there was a fire in the stables, and more than 200 horses were "literally smothered or burned at the stake." Soldiers ran into the wooden stable and cut more than 1,000 horses free. The horses galloped off to every part of the city, including the Capitol. It was even said years later that one was found in the Treasury Building. As a result of this incident the cavalry depot was moved across the Anacostia (Eastern Branch) River to Giesboro Point.

Pennsylvania and New Hampshire Aves., K and 23rd Sts.

Washington Circle

The formal circle that L'Enfant proposed in his plans became the northern boundary of Foggy Bottom. In many Civil War pictures of Camp Fry, men of the Veteran Reserve Corps can be seen standing in formation on 23rd Street just south of Washington Circle.

Site 4—23rd and E Streets

Naval Observatory

The Naval Observatory was the first scientific building built by the federal government. It was constructed in 1844 on the high ground known as Camp Hill. Matthew Fontaine Maury of Virginia was its first superintendent. He was known as the "Pathfinder of the Seas" for his work on oceanography, notably his charts to indicate ocean winds and currents. He served at sea 23 years but was injured and had to spend the rest of his career on shore. Maury was assigned to the Navy Department's Depot of Charts and Instruments, and he devoted himself to meteorologic and oceanographic studies. At the beginning of the Civil War, he joined the Confederacy. During the war years, Lt. James M. Gilliss served as superintendent. Gilliss stressed astronomy instead of oceanographic studies, using the telescope in the 22-foot revolving dome. A black ball was suspended from a pole on top of the dome. Each day at noon, the ball slid down the pole, and Washingtonians set their watches. The original Naval Observatory is now the Naval Medical Command, Building Two. (For the Naval Observatory location, See Site 4, The Mall map, pages 102–103.)

Site 5—The Mall at 23rd Street

Lincoln Memorial

At the time of the Civil War, the Potomac River was much wider. The foot of 23rd Street had wharves and warehouses, and men and material were shipped to Camp Fry to be used in the war effort. Later the malarious tidal flats were filled in, and part of that land was set aside for the Memorial. Completed in 1922, the marble temple was not the first proposed monument to Abraham Lincoln. (One suggestion was for a highway linking Gettysburg, Pennsylvania, with Washington, D.C., to be called the Lincoln Highway.) The 36 columns around the Memorial represent each state in the Union when Lincoln was assassinated in 1865. (For the Lincoln Memorial location, see Site 5, The Mall map, pages 102–103.)

Site 6—SW corner of 17th St. and Constitution Ave.

Lock Keepers House

During the Civil War, Constitution Avenue was the Washington Canal. The canal, a continuation of Tiber Creek, connected the C & O Canal with the wharves and warehouses on the Anacostia River. The Washington Canal ran almost the length of Constitution Avenue and then cut in front of the Capitol, terminating at the Anacostia River. Even though the gradient was, in fact, almost flat in this section of the city, probably the only lock on the canal was situated on this site. A description of the canal at the time of the Civil War stated:

> *The Washington Canal is nothing more than an open sewer,*

constantly generating noxious gases, which are most deleterious to those not only residing immediately along its banks, but to the inhabitants of the entire city. It is the main artery of the sewerage of the largest part of the city, it being the receptacle not only of the excrement and sediment of the sewers, but also of the surface drainage.

(For the Lock Keepers House location, see Site 6, The Mall map, pages 102–103.)

White House Area

The White House area at the time of the Civil War was predominantly residential. Because the White House, State Department, Treasury Department, and War Department were all clustered in this area, most of the Cabinet members and influential citizens lived near Lafayette Square.

Security at the White House was strengthened when the war broke out. Armed sentries guarded the gates and every outside door but the north entrance. City policemen dressed in baggy pants masqueraded as visitors. Still, President Lincoln wanted to make sure that the average citizen had access to him. He never thought of closing the White House. Instead, he had weekly receptions of the citizenry and entertained them on weekends with Marine Band concerts on the grounds.

The Lincoln children, Tad and Willie (Robert was enrolled at Harvard for most of the war), would ride their ponies on the White House grounds, and many people would stop and gawk at them. They stared in sympathy at the black-draped house when Willie died in February 1862. The nature of the war meant that the White House was always lit at night to receive messengers and communications, as were the homes of the neighboring government officials and military officers. Depending upon the outcome of a battle, loyal citizens would congregate outside the iron fences to cheer or hold solemn observances.

Starting in the summer of 1862, the Lincolns spent much time at the Soldiers' Home, escaping the heat and the public. Mrs. Lincoln stayed there while the president rode back and forth almost daily to the White House. Often Lincoln would take carriage rides unaccompanied by any military guards. He and his wife liked to visit the many military hospitals and talk with the young soldiers.

Site 1—1799 New York Avenue

Octagon House

Designed by William Thornton, the house was originally the Washington home of John Tayloe, a tobacco planter and a breeder of race horses in Virginia. Tayloe's other commercial properties included Fuller's City Hotel on Pennsylvania Avenue, which was sold to the Willard brothers and became the Willard Hotel. During the War of 1812, the British marched into Washington and burned most of the government buildings. The French minister Louis Sérurier was staying at the Octagon House and asked that it be spared because of its diplomatic status. The treaty that ended the War of 1812 had been signed in Europe at Ghent on December 24, 1814, but needed to be approved by the U.S. Senate and signed by the president. President Madison signed the document on February 17, 1815, in the Octagon House.

At the beginning of the Civil War, the Octagon was leased to the Reverend Charles White, pastor of St. Matthew's Church, for use by St. Rose's Technical Institute, a girls' school. The lease included an agreement that Tayloe "repair such plaster as may have fallen, such roofs as require it, sash cords where they have failed, windows where broken and restore such woodwork as may have become decayed." At the end of the war, the house was being rented by the government for the Hydrographic Office.

There are numerous ghost stories connected to the house. One of them tells about the spirits of two of Tayloe's daughters who fell or jumped to their deaths from the third-floor stairway; another story tells about the spirit of a female slave said to be entombed in the walls of the house.

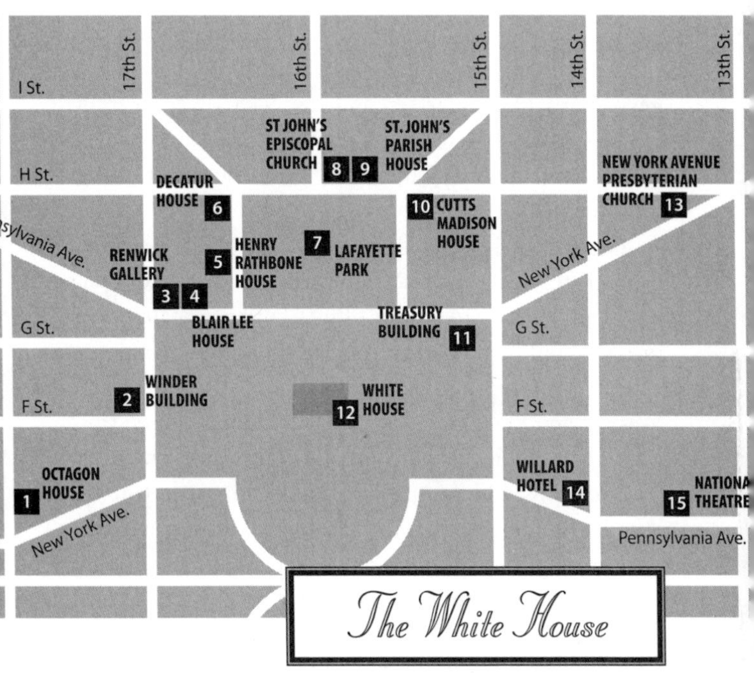

Site 2—600 17th Street

Winder Building

The building was named for Gen. William Winder, who commanded the American forces at the Battle of Bladensburg during the War of 1812. He was not successful. The British force marched into Washington and burned most of the government buildings. Completed in 1848, Winder's structure provided office space for the Navy and the War Departments. Also housed in this building at the time was the Pension Office (sometimes the building was referred to in guidebooks as the Old Pension Office). Winder wanted to sell the building to the government, and he forced their hand by threatening to double the rent as the lease expired in 1854. Secretary of War Jefferson Davis, designated agent for the government's interests, agreed to purchase the building for $200,000. A rarity among antebellum government offices, it had gas lighting and marbled wallpaper.

Government offices during the Civil War included those of the Topographical Engineers' Corps, the Second

Auditor of the Treasury, the Commissioner of Pensions, the Surgeon General and the Bureau of Medicine and Surgery, Army Headquarters, and the Navy's Engineer-in-Chief Office. In 1861, the Office of the Quartermaster General and the Navy's Bureaus of Ordnance and Hydrography moved in.

Legends and stories about the building have been told through the years that have no basis in fact. Lincoln may have had occasion to visit its offices, but he probably never reviewed military parades from its wrought-iron balcony. On the Winder roof in 1865 was a signal station of the Washington detachment of the U.S. Signal Corps, from which communications by signal flags could go out to the fortifications and camps around Washington. But the Winder Building was not the terminal of the wartime military telegraph. That service did not even have a line to the building. No Southern prisoners were ever proven to have been incarcerated in its basement. From time to time, civilian suspects were questioned there, but only civilians. As headquarters for the Bureau of Military Justice under Judge-Advocate-General Joseph Holt, the Winder Building did serve as the center of operations during the search for President Lincoln's assassins. Once the conspirators were caught, evidence for their trial was stored in the building.

Site 3—NE corner of Pennsylvania Avenue and 17th Street

Renwick Gallery

William Corcoran had been collecting prints and other works of art during his European travels. In 1859, he commissioned James Renwick to design a building to house his collection. It was just nearing completion when the Civil War began, and it was taken over by the government to be used as the headquarters of Quartermaster General Montgomery Meigs's department. Warehouses located behind the gallery on 17th Street dispensed thousands of uniforms, tents, and other supplies the soldiers needed as they advanced south into Virginia. After the war, the government gave Corcoran $125,000 as payment for back rent. The

Corcoran Gallery of Art finally opened in 1871 with a grand ball attended by more than 2,000 guests. Its name was changed to the Renwick Gallery in 1965 when it was taken over by the Smithsonian.

Site 4—1650 Pennsylvania Avenue

Blair Lee House

Francis Preston Blair, formerly a famous newspaper editor and a member of President Andrew Jackson's "Kitchen Cabinet," bought this house from the army's first surgeon general, Dr. Joseph Lovell, in 1836. On Thursday morning, April 18, 1861, Col. Robert E. Lee met with Blair in this yellow house, now belonging to Blair's son Montgomery. Montgomery Blair was Lincoln's postmaster general and had been an attorney for Dred Scott. Lee was offered command of the Union Army. Previously, Lee had met with Lt. Gen. Winfield Scott, who had offered him the same position. Pressed by President Lincoln, Blair again offered Lee command. Even though Lee could see no good in secession, he could not draw a sword against his native Virginia.

The Lee House was built in 1858. It was the home of Cdr. Samuel Phillips Lee, a cousin of Robert E. Lee, and his wife Elizabeth Blair Lee, the daughter of Francis Preston Blair. Lee commanded the North Atlantic Blockading Squadron from September 1862 to October 1864. The two houses were combined in 1943 to become the president's guest house.

Site 5—712 Jackson Place

Maj. Henry Rathbone House

After others, including Lt. Gen. and Mrs. Ulysses S. Grant, declined President Lincoln's invitation to attend Ford's Theatre on the night of April 14, 1865, Maj. Henry Rathbone and his fiancée, Clara Harris, accepted. Both were in the President's box when John Wilkes Booth entered and shot Lincoln. Rathbone, who was sitting approximately eight feet away from the President, jumped up and struggled with Booth, who inflicted a knife wound on Rathbone's left forearm. Rathbone helped Mrs. Lincoln across the street to the Petersen House and then fainted from a loss of blood. In 1887, President Grover Cleveland appointed Rathbone consul in Hanover, Germany. Rathbone had become mentally ill—many say as a result of being unable to stop the assassin Booth; he murdered his wife, Clara. German authorities convicted him of murder and committed him to an asylum for the criminally insane, where he died in 1911.

Site 6—748 Jackson Place

Decatur House

Designed by Benjamin Henry Latrobe, Decatur House was the first private residence on Lafayette Square. The Decaturs lived on Lafayette Square only 14 months. Cdre. Stephen Decatur, hero of the war with the Barbary pirates, was killed in a duel with Cdre. James Barron on March 20, 1820.

Prior to the Civil War, Judah P. Benjamin, a senator from Louisiana, lived in the house. After several years of marriage, his wife had left him and gone to live in Paris. He hoped to lure her back and rented Decatur House filling it with costly furnishings. His efforts worked, and the flagrantly immoral Mrs. Benjamin reappeared in the social whirl of Washington, although she was not welcomed by ladies of character. She lived at Decatur House awhile, and then in the middle of the night, she stole away once again to Paris. Benjamin never divorced her.

As the Civil War approached, he resigned from the Senate. On February 4, 1861, in the midst of the secession controversy, he made his farewell speech. His friend Jefferson Davis appointed him Confederate secretary of war and then secretary of state. He was known as the "Brains of the Confederacy." While Benjamin served the South, the U.S. War Department rented Decatur House as the headquarters of the commissary general.

Site 7—Pa. Ave. between Madison and Jackson Pls.

Lafayette Park

Originally, this area was a barren piece of land. In the

1790s, a race track was laid out on the west side of the park extending to what is now 20th Street. This common was also known as President's Park. Clark Mills's statue of Jackson spurred efforts to formally landscape the area in the 1850s. For decades Lafayette Park was the center of social life in Washington. Prominent citizens such as William Corcoran, Charles Sumner, Charles Glover, Schuyler Colfax, Daniel Sickles, William Seward, Henry Adams, George McClellan, and Charles Wilkes lived around the park. Prior to the Civil War, John C. Calhoun, Daniel Webster, Henry Clay, and James and Dolley Madison called this section of Washington home. Once the war started, Lafayette Park was the scene of military activity. The federal government took over Decatur House, the Dolley Madison house, and others, using them as military headquarters or offices. Soldiers guarding the White House camped in the park, trampled the flower beds, and hung their laundry from the statue of Andrew Jackson.

Site 8—1525 H Street

St. John's Episcopal Church

Designed by Benjamin Latrobe and built in 1816, St. John's Church is known as the "Church of the Presidents." Pew 54 has been set aside for them. Abraham Lincoln's first Sunday service after he arrived in Washington in 1861 was in St. John's. He walked across from his room at the Willard Hotel with Senator William Seward and sat in Seward's pew near the altar. Dr. Pyne, the rector, did not recognize Lincoln. The newspaper reporters who accompanied him described the president-elect as "dressed in plain black clothes with black whiskers and hair well trimmed, recognized as a different man entirely from the hard-looking pictorial representations seen of him. Some of the ladies say that in fact he is almost good-looking."

Site 9—1525 H Street

St. John's Parish House

Also known as the Ashburton House, the parish house was the site of the signing of the Webster-Ashburton Treaty, which established the boundary between the United States and Canada. During the Civil War, it was the home of the British Legation headed by Lord Lyon. There was a great deal of activity at the house in the early days of 1862. Capt. Charles Wilkes, commander of the USS *San Jacinto*, had forcibly—and illegally—removed Confederate envoys James Mason and John Slidell from the Royal Mail steamer *Trent*. Britain did not take the offense lightly and was preparing to send soldiers to Canada. Tensions were high, and the threat of war with England seemed real. Fortunately, Mason and Slidell were released, and the U.S. government apologized to the British government. Ironically, Wilkes lived on Lafayette Square and returned to his home in December 1861 to cheers and serenades: he was hailed as "the hero of the *Trent*" within sight of the British Legation. Before the war, Senator John Slidell also lived on Lafayette Park at 1607 H Street, in a house long since demolished.

Site 10—1520 H Street

Cutts Madison House

This house was built by Richard Cutts, the brother-in-law of Dolley Madison, in 1818. When Dolley Madison lived here after the death of her husband, her home was the center of the best society. Officials as well as private citizens always stopped by to pay their respects after social functions at the White House. Maj. Gen. George McClellan used this house as his residence when he was given command of the Army of the Potomac. Cdre. Charles Wilkes also lived in this house.

Site 11—Pennsylvania Avenue and 15th Street

Treasury Building

Flanking the White House on the east, this building was built from 1838 to 1842. According to legend, President Jackson, impatient to have a Treasury Building built, walked out of the White House and tapping his cane on the ground exclaimed, "Right here is where I want the cornerstone." Pierre L'Enfant's idea of a sweeping vista down

Pennsylvania Avenue from the White House to the Capitol was nullified.

When President Lincoln called for 75,000 militia to march to support the government, the 5th Massachusetts answered the call. They encamped at the Treasury, cooking and eating in the courtyard. If the Confederates attacked Washington, Lincoln and his Cabinet planned to take up quarters in the Treasury Building. The basement was strongly barricaded, and munitions, food, and water were stored there. The office of the secretary was placed at the disposal of the president in case of invasion, and adjoining rooms on the second floor of the building were arranged for the Cabinet. As the need to finance the war forced the department to enlarge its staff, the Treasury Department employed more and more women and girls as clerks in clerical jobs. These "government girls" caused much discussion of appropriate female roles.

Site 12—Pennsylvania Avenue and 16th Street

White House

In the 1860s, the building was called the Executive Mansion or President's House. The current East and West Wings of the White House did not exist; in their places stood sheds and a handsome conservatory, with a stable 200 yards to the south. The president and his wife occupied adjoining bedrooms on the second floor. Across the hall was the children's room. The northwest corner suite held the State Bedroom, which was called the Prince of Wales Room after its royal occupant during President Buchanan's administration. The rooms had running river water for washing.

An iron fence enclosed the house on the Pennsylvania Avenue side and on the South Lawn side. A statue of Thomas Jefferson stood in the circle at the entrance on Pennsylvania Avenue. Near the south lawn was marshland that opened into the Washington Canal. Interior paths crisscrossed the grounds, connecting the State Department on the east and the Navy and War Departments on the west.

Lincoln at home with son Tad.

There was no telegraph at the White House, and almost nightly, President Lincoln would cross the lawn to the War Department to examine and answer telegrams and to talk with the young telegraph operators.

Lincoln's secretaries, John George Nicolay and John Hay, lived in the White House but ate their meals out. Office seekers, inventors, citizens looking for information about soldiers, and general sightseers crowded into the house when the doors were opened at 9 a.m. on weekdays. No room, even the President's private office, was free from the continual noise and commotion. Doormen and ushers were badgered with requests for drinks of water and use of the water closets. Lincoln could have closed the White House, but the symbolic gesture of being accessible to the people was important to him.

In the first emergency of 1861, guards slept on the carpeted floor of the East Room. Soldiers marched and drilled on the White House grounds and added to the noisy, seemingly undisciplined hustle and bustle of everyday activity. Lincoln's younger sons, Willie and Tad (nicknamed at birth Tadpole because he looked like one), often annoyed visitors by pulling on their beards. Tad set up a lemonade stand in the hall. The boys were privately tutored by a Treasury Department clerk named Alexander Williamson and attended meetings with government officials. Even when his sons misbehaved, Lincoln never punished them, to the dismay of important visitors.

Willie Lincoln died February 20, 1862. He and Tad were both sick with what was then called a "bilious fever," probably typhoid. Willie died in the Prince of Wales Room in the great state bed. Tad survived his illness, and he and his father became inseparable. Crowds of people stood waiting to look at the two as they walked hand in hand to the War Department for the latest news.

On December 10, 1864, the White House stables caught fire. Lincoln raced from the White House to try to save Willie's pony. Even though some carriage horses were killed as well as horses belonging to Hay and Nicolay, Lincoln grieved that his late son's pony was destroyed. Today the most popular ghost in the White House is that of Lincoln, reportedly seen numerous times in the Lincoln Bedroom, once Lincoln's study.

Site 13—New York Avenue and H Street

New York Avenue Presbyterian Church

The Lincoln family attended this church while they were in Washington. In 1859, the congregation of the old F Street Presbyterian Church, which was the building that became Willard Hall (site of the Peace Convention), joined the Second Presbyterian Church to form the New York Avenue Presbyterian Church. The Reverend Phineas Gurley was the pastor, and he had the sad duty of presiding over the funeral services for both Willie and Abraham Lincoln. Dr. Gurley was in the Petersen House at Lincoln's bedside when the president died. On April 19, 1865, Lincoln's body, clad in the suit bought for his second inauguration, was laid in a $1,500 open casket in the East Room of the White House. Dr. Gurley preached the funeral sermon there.

The original New York Avenue Presbyterian Church was torn down in 1950 and a larger reproduction was built.

Site 14—1401 Pennsylvania Avenue

Willard Hotel

The most famous of all the hotels in Washington was the Willard. The Willard brothers, Joseph and Henry, had enlarged and redecorated the old Fuller's City Hotel. Politicians, entertainers, society figures, and diplomats, all at one time or another, stayed at the Willard. During the early months of the war, the Willard escaped a spectacular fire that made national headlines. It broke out in a tailor shop next to the Willard. Some of Ellsworth's Fire Zouaves, who were quartered at the Capitol, ran down Pennsylvania Avenue to the Willard. They formed human ladders and bucket brigades and climbed into windows. One man was suspended upside down from the roof to reach the hose line.

In the latter part of 1861, a writer named Julia Ward Howe came to Washington from Boston. At the Willard she wrote new words to the tune of "John Brown's Body." The new song became known as "The Battle Hymn of the Republic."

Site 15—1321 Pennsylvania Avenue

National Theatre

The National Theatre is Washington's oldest. It is also one of the oldest theaters in the United States. Six buildings have occupied this site since 1835. During the Civil War it was known as Grover's National. Along with Ford's, the National Theatre was one of the major sources of entertainment in Washington. President Lincoln liked to attend plays and had a lower box in the lower tier. John Wilkes Booth played the lead role here in *Richard III.* Lincoln's son Tad was attending a performance of *Aladdin,* also called *The Wonderful Lamp,* the night that the president was assassinated. Mrs. Lincoln had given her ticket to her son because she planned to go to Ford's Theatre with her husband. There is a story that Booth was in theater owner Leonard Grover's office on Friday morning when he heard that Mrs. Lincoln was not going to accept Grover's invitation but had decided to go to Ford's to see the famous actress Laura Keene.

Downtown/Commercial District

Downtown is a general term that refers to the part of the city that is north of the Mall between the White House and the Capitol. The main commercial street in this area was 7th Street, then known as the 7th Street Pike, that ran from the rural Maryland farmland into the city and south to the waterfront. The Center Market (site of the National Archives) was the destination for the farmers. During the war, more than a hundred businesses operated in the market. The open area around the Central Market was known as Market Square, and many more vendors operated from pushcarts and stalls in the square. Pennsylvania Avenue was the main road that farmers east of the city used to bring in produce and goods to sell. Many of the merchants lived near their businesses. Several blocks north of Market Square, the government had its Patent Office and Post Office (now the National Portrait Gallery and the National Museum of American Art). Rooming houses sheltered government clerks and secretaries. F and 11th Streets were upper-class residential streets. Here were the homes of many members of Congress as well as wealthy merchants. Many of the area's businessmen had immigrated from Germany and Austria. The Irish poor had settled in the area known as Swampoodle, northeast of Massachusetts and New Jersey Avenues.

Site 1—511 10th Street

Ford's Theatre

Originally, John Wilkes Booth had planned to kidnap Lincoln as the president rode to the Soldiers' Home and take him to Richmond, where the hostage would be exchanged for Confederate prisoners. By the time Booth enlisted enough men for his scheme, Lincoln was no longer traveling regularly to the Soldiers' Home. After the fall of Richmond, Booth decided to kill the president as well as Vice President Andrew Johnson and Secretary of State William Seward.

On April 14, 1865, Booth reserved a box at Grover's

National Theatre in case the Lincolns would accept an invitation from theater owner Leonard Grover. In the late morning, Booth was told the Lincolns would be attending Ford's Theatre. The theater had previously been a Baptist church, which was bought by John Ford after a fire destroyed his previous theater, Ford's Atheneum, in 1863. The theatre could hold 1,700 people. On April 14, 1965, the Lincolns would see Miss Laura Keene in her last performance of *Our American Cousin.* The play revolved around Asa Trenchard, an American country bumpkin who goes to England to claim an inheritance from Mark Trenchard, an English nobleman.

After Booth picked up his mail, he went up to the box that John Ford was going to use for his honored patron. He drilled a small peephole in the door of the box. That evening, Booth made several trips into the theater. Several people saw him drinking in Peter Taltavull's Star Saloon next door. After leaving the saloon, he went into the alley behind the theater and asked Edman Spangler, a scene changer, to hold his horse. Spangler gave the job to "Peanuts John" Burroughs.

The Lincolns arrived after the play had started. Once the chief executive's presence was known, the audience stood and applauded. Lincoln slowly bowed and then sat down in a rocking chair. His guests that evening were Maj. Henry Rathbone and his fiancée, Clara Harris, daughter of Senator Harris of New York. Booth, meanwhile, approached the president's box and encountered no trouble from Lincoln's guard, metropolitan policeman John Parker, who apparently left the door unguarded to watch the play. Booth knew the lines to *Our American Cousin* well and knew at what point he was going to shoot the president. Actor Harry Hawk as Asa Trenchard was saying, "Well, I guess I know enough to turn you inside out, old gal—you sockdologizing old mantrap." Booth stepped into the box and fired his pistol. The bullet entered Lincoln's head about three inches behind his left ear and traveled diagonally through his brain, stopping behind his right eye. Major Rathbone, who had his back to the door, jumped up and

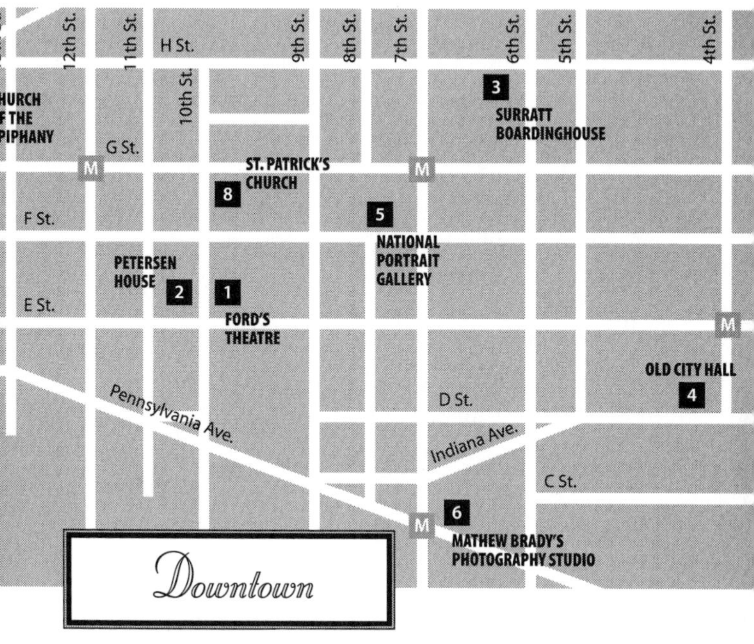

turned around at the sound. Booth pulled a knife and slashed Rathbone along his left arm between the elbow and shoulder. Booth then jumped over the railing to the stage ten feet below. He caught his spur on a U.S. Treasury Guard flag and fractured the fibula of his left leg just above the ankle. Most members of the audience thought that the shot was part of the play. Despite his injury, Booth was on his feet almost instantly, shouted *"Sic semper tyrannis"* (thus ever to tyrants) and ran offstage. He ran out to the alley, jumped on the horse that Peanuts John was holding, and headed toward the Navy Yard Bridge. After a moment of silence, the audience started to scream and shout.

The first person to enter the president's box was Dr. Charles Leale, a 23-year-old army surgeon. Leale originally thought Lincoln had been stabbed. When he found no stab wound, he lifted the president's eyelids and saw evidence of brain damage. He then quickly found the head wound and administered artificial respiration. Laura Keene reportedly brought water to the dying president and held his head in her lap. Leale had been joined by surgeons Charles Taft and Albert King; they all wanted to move the president to the nearest house, because they thought he would not survive the seven-block trip over the rough streets to the White House. Soldiers assisted the doctors in carrying the president across the street to the Petersen House. Several witnesses claimed that Lincoln was carried across the street on a shutter or on a stretcher improvised from the partition dividing the Presidential Box.

After Lincoln was assassinated, Secretary of War Edwin Stanton had guards placed at the theater. He did not want it to open again. When Ford announced plans to reopen in June, the government rented the building at $1,500 a month. It later purchased the building for $100,000 and converted it into a three-story office building that held the Record and Pension Bureau of the War Department. In 1893, a fire destroyed the interior of the building, killing 22 people.

Site 2—516 10th Street

Petersen House

After Abraham Lincoln was shot, he was carried across the street to this boardinghouse owned by a Swedish tailor named William Petersen. Lincoln was carried into a small bedroom at the rear of the first floor. The room was only 9 1/2 feet wide and 17 1/2 feet long. It was rented by William Clark, a member of the District of Columbia Infantry who was detailed as a clerk at the headquarters of Maj. Gen. Christopher Columbus Augur, commander of the Department of Washington.

Because of his height, the president was laid in a diagonal position on the bed with his feet toward the wall and his head toward the entrance. No one in the room knew it at the time, but the bed on which Lincoln lay dying was once occupied by John Wilkes Booth—Booth had rented the room during the 1864-1865 winter. Secretary Stanton set up a headquarters in the back parlor of an adjoining suite and started to send messages to Cabinet officers, military leaders, and other government officials.

Mrs. Lincoln, Tad, and Robert went into the back bedroom several times during the night. Mrs. Lincoln's emotional outbursts caused Stanton to order that she not be brought back into the room. Meanwhile, General Augur went out on the steps of the house and called for someone able to take shorthand. Cpl. James Tanner, a wounded veteran boarding next door who had attended business school, spent the night recording the testimony of witnesses and making his own observations on the comings and goings in the back bedroom.

Possibly as many as 65 people were in and out of the bedroom that night, but there is controversy as to the number of people present when Lincoln died on the morning of April 15 at 7:21 a.m. Artists have painted pictures that incorrectly show people present who were not actually there, like Tad Lincoln and Vice President Andrew Johnson. Based on the small size of the room and on the testimony and observations of Tanner and other people present, probably only 14 people witnessed the death of President Lincoln. Dr. Gurley, Lincoln's pastor at the New York Avenue Presbyterian Church, offered a prayer. After the prayer, Secretary Stanton, tears streaming down his cheeks, sobbed the words that were to become immortal: "Now he belongs to the ages" or "Now he belongs to the angels."

Site 3—604 H Street

Surratt Boardinghouse

Mary Surratt leased her tavern and farm in Surrattsville, Maryland, and operated an eight-room boardinghouse in Washington. Her son John was an active member of John Wilkes Booth's group of conspirators. It was in her boardinghouse that much of the planning and plotting to assassinate Lincoln took place. Even though Mary Surratt was a Southern sympathizer and had blockade runners among her patrons, there is controversy about what she knew or did not know about the plot to kill President Lincoln. George Atzerodt had stayed at this house, and Lewis Powell and John Wilkes Booth made several visits—John Surratt had invited them over to discuss plans for kidnapping Lincoln.

Mary Surratt's boardinghouse.

Three days after the assassination, Mrs. Surratt and her entire household of boarders were arrested. As the police officers were making arrangements to transport Mrs. Surratt, Lewis Powell appeared at her front door dressed as a workman, wearing a cloth cap and carrying a pickax. He claimed Mrs. Surratt had hired him to dig a gutter. She swore she did not know him. Powell, too, was arrested. Mrs. Surratt was taken to the Old Capitol Prison and was transferred eventually to an isolated cell in the arsenal prison. She was found guilty and was sentenced to hang. On the day of her execution, a relay of horses was set up to carry any clemency order from the White House to the prison. President Johnson refused to see Mrs. Surratt's daughter, Anna, who had hoped to plead for mercy. On July 7, 1865, Mary Surratt was hanged.

Site 4—4th and D Streets

Old City Hall

English architect George Hadfield designed the building.

Congress contributed $10,000 on the condition that the federal government be allowed to use one wing. The building was completed in 1853, and housed the U.S. district courts. Early in the war, it was used as a temporary hospital.

When President Lincoln signed into law on April 16, 1862, the act prohibiting slavery in the District of Columbia, Old City Hall was invaded by former slaveholders. Under the law, Washington became the only city in the United States to have compensated emancipation. By provisions of the law, slaveowners were to free their slaves and to be duly paid for their property. A commission was appointed; former Mayor James Berret was offered a seat as a commissioner (he refused), and a Baltimore slave dealer was hired to appraise the value of each slave. The law provided for an average payment of approximately $300 per slave.

More than 1,000 people presented claims for 3,128 slaves. When the claimants reached City Hall and the grand jury room, they faced the three commissioners, a marshal, a clerk, and the slave dealer. Almost every owner claimed that his or her slave was in the best moral and physical health. The highest-priced slave earned almost $1,700 for his former master, and the lowest were babies who were priced at only $50.

Site 5—F Street between 7th and 9th Streets

National Portrait Gallery

Known during the Civil War as the Patent Office, this building is the third oldest government building in Washington (after the White House and the Capitol). The Patent Office displayed patent models and designs, natural history specimens, and "curiosities from around the world."

At the beginning of the war, President Lincoln raised a giant flag over the building. Later, more than 2,000 beds were brought in and set up on the marble floors between the display cases and in the gallery above the hall. Clara Barton and Walt Whitman made visits to this temporary hospital.

On the evening of March 6, 1865, the building was the site of the inaugural ball and banquet for the second term of President Lincoln. Any gentleman who paid $10 could bring one or more ladies of his choice. The proceeds benefitted needy families of soldiers in the field. According to the *National Intelligencer,* more than 4,000 guests thronged into the building.

Shortly after midnight the presidential party was escorted to the supper room followed by the guests. Mounted on 250-foot tables were sugar models of the Capitol and Admiral Farragut's flagship with the admiral tied high on the mast as a lookout as in his great victory at Mobile Bay. The buffet menu included oyster stew, terrapin stew, pickled oysters, beef, veal, turkey, chicken, grouse, pheasant, quail, venison, duck, lobster and chicken salads, cakes, tarts, jellies, and creams.

Site 6—633 Pennsylvania Avenue

Mathew Brady's Photography Studio

To supplement the prestige and profits of his New York studio, Mathew Brady opened a Washington branch above Gilman's Drugstore to photograph presidents, statesmen, generals, actors, and members of society. He learned the complex new glass-plate process that brought him national recognition. Brady did not work full time in Washington until the 1870s, but left his studio in the care of a number of assistants.

The first floor of the studio was a reception room; a showcase of photographs was provided to entertain guests while they waited. The second floor was a finishing and mounting room, and the camera operators worked on the third floor. When Brady first opened his studio, he added sidewalls and a skylight to admit the sunlight essential to taking his photographs.

At the beginning of the war, he and his assistants accompanied Federal troops into the field and recorded their camp scenes. Brady's assistants—Alexander Gardner, Timothy O'Sullivan, and James Gibson—took most of the photographs, but the credit went to Brady. His assistants resented not being given credit for their work and quit to start their own firms.

Site 7—1317 G Street

Church of the Epiphany

Among the church's early parishioners were President Buchanan, Jefferson Davis, Edwin M. Stanton, and Lord Ashburton, British envoy. The rector, the Reverend Charles Hall, was from South Carolina and came under suspicion as a Southern sympathizer. When Jefferson Davis was a parishioner, the Reverend Hall promised Davis that his nameplate would be left on his pew. This was done in spite of criticism from the congregation, but the plate was stolen during the war and never replaced. When Hall was informed that the federal government considered him a secessionist at heart, he went to Secretary of War Edwin Stanton and explained that although he sympathized with the Southerners being killed, he was still loyal to the Union. Stanton had so much confidence in Hall's loyalty that he joined the congregation. Ironically, Stanton chose Jefferson Davis's pew as his own.

Site 8—SE corner of 10th and G Streets

St. Patrick's Church

Although this building was not standing in the 1860s, an interesting story is attached to the church. The present building was constructed in 1872 on the same site as the church that had served as a temporary military hospital. Mary Surratt was one of the members of the congregation. Father Walter, the priest and a longtime friend of Mrs. Surratt, believed that she was innocent. Secretary of War Stanton notified the priest that he would not be granted permission to visit Mrs. Surratt unless he promised to remain silent regarding her case for 25 years. Not wanting her to die without the sacraments, Father Walter agreed. Twenty-five years later, he published a pamphlet stating the reasons for his belief that Mrs. Surratt was innocent.

The Mall

Prior to the construction of the privately financed Washington Monument (begun in 1848) and the building of the Smithsonian Institution in 1849, the Mall was used as grazing and agricultural land. In 1850, Andrew Jackson Downing, America's pioneer landscape gardener, was invited by President Millard Fillmore to design the grounds on the Mall. Downing tried to create an area of trees and shrubs linked by curving walks and drives. In 1861, Downing's plan met with financial obstacles. Most of the land on the Mall was not developed, and the only area to benefit was the grounds of the Smithsonian. Since gang members frequented the Mall, people did not feel safe walking alone on Downing's curved paths and drives, especially at night.

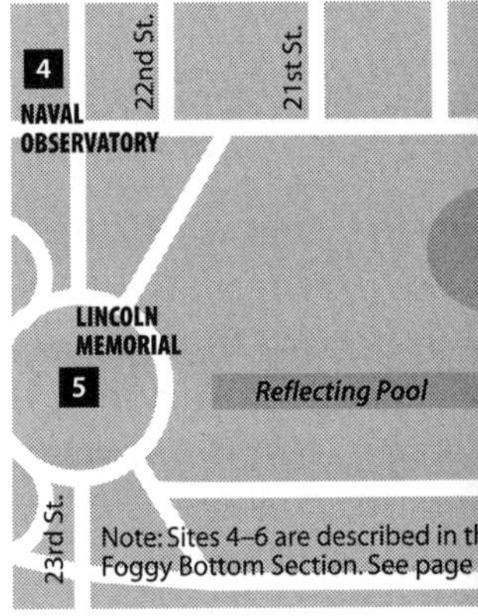

Site 1—The Mall between 15th and 17th Streets

Washington Monument

Construction of the Monument, begun in 1848, was stopped in 1855 due to lack of money and arguments about control of the records of the Washington Monument Society. The shaft was only 154 feet above the ground. Today, different-colored stone easily identifies the height of the Monument during the Civil War. To reach the shaft of the Washington Monument, a person had to cross the foul-smelling Washington Canal, which was spanned at intervals by iron bridges. Cattle were fenced in here during the war, waiting to be slaughtered at an abattoir built nearby. Citizens complained about the offensive and malodorous smells coming from the site.

Site 2—1000 Jefferson Drive

Smithsonian Building

James Smithson, the founder of the Smithsonian Institution, was an Englishman who had never visited the United States. His will left almost $500,000 "to found at Washington, under the name of the Smithsonian Institution, an establishment for the increase and diffusion of knowledge

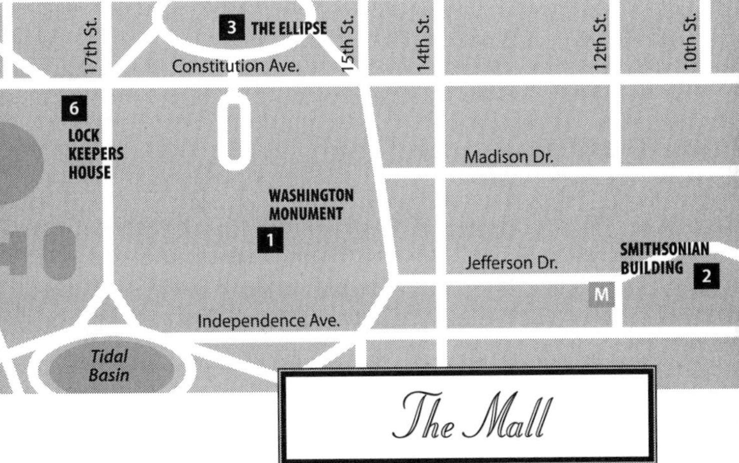

among men." Former President John Quincy Adams suggested an astronomical observatory. Others argued for a library, a research laboratory, or a meteorological bureau. Congress decided to establish an institution that would include a museum, an art gallery, a chemical laboratory, and a library.

The man selected to be the Smithsonian's first secretary was Joseph Henry, then America's most distinguished scientist. Henry felt that the Smithsonian should promote science in every way possible, especially original research. In 1855 Henry and his staff moved into the red-brown castle building. During the Civil War, the Smithsonian sponsored lectures in its lecture hall. Speakers included abolitionists Henry Ward Beecher, Horace Greeley, and Wendell Phillips. After he was criticized by the Washington press for these controversial lecturers, Henry insisted the speakers mention that what they said was not the responsibility of the Smithsonian.

The museum also sponsored Thaddeus S. C. Lowe, an aeronaut. Lowe inflated a hydrogen balloon that was tethered to the ground near the Armory on the Mall. He tried to impress President Lincoln by reporting on what he saw from the air with a telegraph key that was attached to the ground. Lowe claimed to have ascended more than 500 feet. In January 1865, a fire destroyed a large part of the Smithsonian collection.

Site 3—Constitution Ave., E Street, 17th to 15th Streets

The Ellipse

This large grassy area was known during the Civil War as the White Lot, because it was enclosed by a wooden fence painted white. Lincoln was the only president to hold a patent (on a device to float a boat run aground in shallow water). He took an interest in technology and encouraged inventors to come to the White House. Early in the war, Lincoln would frequently be seen in the White Lot trying out new inventions, including a breech-loading rifle and a "coffee mill" gun, a hand-cranked forerunner of machine guns.

Capitol Hill

Pierre L'Enfant, in his plan for Washington, put the House of Congress on Jenkins Hill, "which stands as a pedestal waiting for a monument." Because of the new occupant on this rise of land east of the Tiber Creek, the area became known as Capitol Hill. Around the Capitol, homes were built to serve Congress, its employees, and construction workers. Boardinghouses sprang up to provide temporary homes for members of Congress. Carroll Row, which stood on the site of the Library of Congress's present Jefferson Building, was one of the most fashionable areas. Abraham Lincoln, as a congressman from Illinois, boarded with a Mrs. Sprigg in her boardinghouse on Carroll Row. The Hill had taverns and hotels to accommodate the visitors who came to the area during sessions of Congress. Providence Hospital opened in a large mansion at 2nd and D Streets SE.

The old "Brick Capitol" located on the present site of the Supreme Court Building at 1st and East Capitol Streets was built in 1815 as a temporary meeting site for Congress after the British burned the Capitol. The building was the home of Congress for four years. Later it was a boardinghouse for members of Congress, and Senator John C. Calhoun of South Carolina died in his room in this building in 1850. During the war, the building was used as a prison (Old Capitol Prison), housing political prisoners, Confederate spies, local prostitutes, and "contraband" slaves. Probably the most famous prisoners were Mrs. Rose O'Neal Greenhow and Belle Boyd, Confederate spies, and former mayor James Berret, who refused to take the loyalty oath. On November 10, 1865, the superintendent of Andersonville Prison, Capt. Henry Wirz, was hanged in the rear courtyard. He was the only man formally executed for war crimes during the Civil War.

The bakery in the basement of the Capitol.

In 1862, Washington's first horse-drawn streetcars linked Capitol Hill to the Navy Yard, White House, and Georgetown. Temporary military hospitals and troops were quartered in the Capitol along with sessions of Congress, and rallies gave the Hill a constantly noisy and bustling character that was missing before the war.

Site 1—1st and East Capitol Streets

The Capitol

When Abraham Lincoln took the oath of office at the East Front of the Capitol, the new dome was unfinished. Lincoln wanted construction to continue in order to show the country that the business of the government would go on. Prior to his swearing in, President-elect Lincoln went with President Buchanan into the Senate Chamber to witness the swearing in of Hannibal Hamlin of Maine as vice president.

Some of the first troops in Washington were quartered in the Capitol. Their officers used the Speaker's Room, staff members occupied committee rooms, and the men were assigned to the floor, galleries, and lobbies. The soldiers barricaded the doors and windows with lumber and barrels of cement and even used the iron plates intended for the construction of the dome. The statues and pictures were protected by wooden planking. Troops from New York's 7th Regiment and Massachusetts's 6th were quartered in the House of Representatives. For amusement they held mock sessions of Congress. A soldier would rap the gavel, the "House" would come to order, and "members" would rise to debate the most incredible points of order. The "session" would usually end with all of the soldiers laughing.

Ellsworth's Fire Zouaves were quartered in the Rotunda. They were a noisy and aggressive group. For exercise, the men slid down ropes attached to the Rotunda walls. On April 30, 1861, the *Daily Intelligencer* described the Zouaves:

> *We saw one of the Zouaves, a mere boy, swing from the cornice in the interior of the new dome on a rope, and let himself down to the floor of the Rotunda—a distance of nearly 100 feet with apparent ease and in an incredible short space of time, checking his speed as he reached the floor to light easy. It did not seem to be a novel feat to the others, as they noticed it no more than any ordinary occurrence. We saw one of the boys with bare legs and feet, in the open space below the building on the west side with a hose pipe in his hand and a full head of Potomac water on, washing the pavement, and he seemed to enjoy the accustomed sport hugely, making the water fly at a great rate, and occasionally squirting his comrades. These men are generally of Herculean proportions, with massive shoulders and chests, and will be effective soldiers, no doubt.*

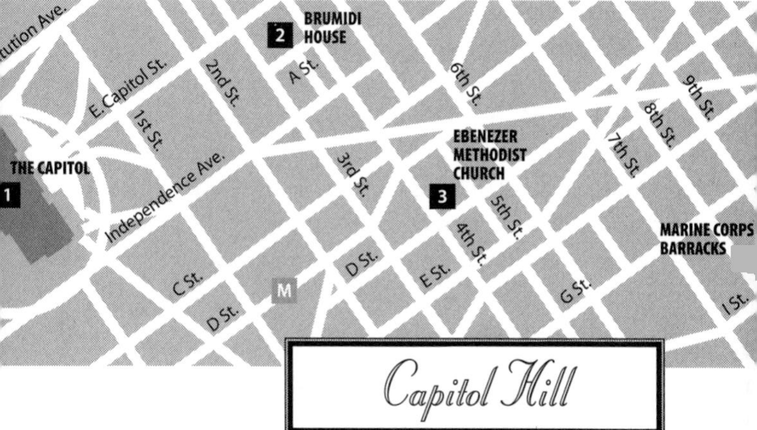

Capitol Hill

An employee of the Senate, upon entering the chamber, once -heard a great noise and the sound of splitting wood. As he ran over, he discovered a number of Zouaves with their bayonets, stabbing and splitting one of the desks. He shouted, "Stop that, stop that, what are you doing?" "We are cutting that damn traitor's desk to pieces," shouted one of the soldiers. The employee responded that it was not Jeff Davis's desk, it belonged to the government of the United States: "You were sent here to protect government property, not to destroy it."

In April 1861, the army issued orders to build bake ovens in the Capitol basement. The entire west basement was used by the bakeries. In 1862, a reporter for *Harper's Weekly* stated that there were 14 ovens baking 200 loaves a day and 6 or 7 ovens baking 800 loaves a day. This amount of bread required 250 barrels of flour and 1,900 gallons of yeast daily. The flour was stored in the Capitol's cellars. Each loaf was approximately 12 ounces, the amount for an individual ration. The ovens, located under the Bulfinch terraces, operated from April 1861 until October 1862. Beef, pork, and ham were also stored in the cellars.

Abraham Lincoln was the first person to lie in state in the Rotunda of the Capitol. His coffin was placed on a catafalque on April 19, and in the early morning of April 22, was carried from the Capitol to the Baltimore & Ohio Railroad Station for the long trip back to Springfield, Illinois.

In August 1865, Capt. Henry Wirz, the superintendent of Andersonville Prison, was tried on charges of murder and conspiring with Confederate President Jefferson Davis to commit murder. The trial took place in the U.S. Court of Claims Chamber in the Capitol. The courtroom—then a large single room—was the area known today as Rooms S-151 and S-152, which are now occupied by the Joint Committee on Printing. Captain Wirz was convicted of murder by a U.S. military court and was hanged at the Old Capitol Prison in November 1865.

Site 2—326 A Street SE

Constantino Brumidi House

Known as the "Michelangelo of the Capitol" for painting the dome of the Rotunda while lying on his back, Brumidi came to the United States when he was almost 50 years old. A plaque at his grave in Glenwood Cemetery tells of his plans and dreams: "My one ambition and my daily prayer is that I may live long enough to make beautiful the Capitol of the one country on earth in which there is liberty." Brumidi painted the walls and ceilings of the Capitol from 1855 until his death in 1880.

Site 3—4th and D Streets SE

Ebenezer United Methodist Church

In March 1864 this church opened the first colored public school in Washington. One hundred adults and children tried to enroll. Since the school had only one teacher and an inexperienced assistant, some people were turned away. The teacher was paid $400 per year by the District of Columbia.

Site 4—8th Street between G and I Streets

Marine Corps Barracks

Established in 1801, the Marine Barracks is the oldest Marine post as well as the official residence of the commandant of the corps. The Commandant's House at the north end of the barracks was completed in 1805 and is the only original building still standing, as well as the oldest public building in continuous use in Washington. On October 18, 1859, 90 marines under the command of 1st Lt. Israel Greene traveled by rail to Harpers Ferry and reported to the senior officer present, Col. Robert E. Lee of the army. Their mission was to capture abolitionist John Brown. The Marines stormed the engine house where Brown and his followers maintained their stronghold. Greene wounded Brown with his sword while overpowering him. Ten of Brown's followers were killed and four were taken prisoner. Lee's second in command at Harpers Ferry was Lt. J. E. B. Stuart, who would become a legend in 1862 as a commander of Confederate cavalry.

The barracks was home for a small group of Marines during the Civil War. Residents from the neighborhood would watch the marines parade on a daily basis. The Marine Band, also called "The President's Own," performed regularly on the White House lawn under the direction of Bandmaster Francis Scala. After Willie Lincoln died, Mrs. Lincoln did not allow music in the White House or on the grounds of the White House. The citizens objected, and the concerts were performed at another site.

At the end of the Civil War, Confederate Rear Adm. Raphael Semmes was held prisoner in the barracks' Center House (no longer standing). He had been commander of the commerce raider CSS *Alabama*. He was imprisoned for four months while the federal government tried to find a way to charge him with treason and piracy. He was never tried and was set free.

Anacostia

Anacostia—or Uniontown—was originally an isolated village on the far side of the Anacostia (Eastern Branch) River. It became an important suburb for Washington in 1846 with the rebuilding of the Navy Yard Bridge (now 11th Street Bridge). With the completion of the bridge, people living in Anacostia had access to employment opportunities at the Navy Yard.

In 1852, Dorothea Lynde Dix, the defender of the rights

of the mentally ill, urged President Millard Fillmore to purchase part of the old St. Elizabeth's Tract on a plateau overlooking the Anacostia River, "commanding a grand panorama of nature and of art." The site was owned by Thomas Blagden who, at the urging of Miss Dix, sold his farm to the U.S. government for $27,000. A building was constructed that originally housed 90 patients. This government insane asylum also provided local employment for the residents of Anacostia.

In 1854, the Union Land Association purchased and developed 240 acres near the asylum. This was the earliest suburban development in Washington. In addition to prohibiting black and Irish buyers, it allowed no pigs or soap boiling.

The plateau of Anacostia afforded a strategic and commanding view of the Potomac River and Giesboro Point (site of a Civil War cavalry depot and now Bolling Air Force Base). The federal government built Fort Carroll here.

Immediately after the war, the Bureau of Refugees, Freedmen, and Abandoned Lands—or Freedmen's Bureau—bought 370 acres from James Barry. This land was converted to house some of the thousands of former slaves who came to Washington during and after the war.

In 1877, Frederick Douglass purchased Cedar Hill on 14th and W Streets. In 1886, Congress passed legislation that officially changed the name of the area to Anacostia because Uniontown was chosen by many communities after the Civil War.

2700 Martin Luther King Jr. Avenue SE

St. Elizabeths Hospital

Directions—Take Pennsylvania Avenue east past the Capitol and across the John Philip Sousa Bridge. Bear right and get onto Route 295 going South. Stay in right lane and exit at Portland Street. Make a left turn at Portland Street (entrance to Bolling Air Force Base is on your right) to Martin Luther King Jr. Avenue. Make a left turn at Martin Luther King Jr. Avenue. Go approximately one mile to Gate I on your left. Center Building is the original hospital, and it is directly in front of you.

To get to Civil War Cemetery, follow road around Center Building. Bear right to warehouse and laundry area. Follow road past baseball diamond on left. Follow road into wooded area. Approximately 50 yards farther there is a dirt road to your left. Make a left turn and follow road approximately 100 yards to cemetery parking area. This gives a magnificent view of Washington, the Potomac River, and Bolling Air Force Base.

The hospital has not always been known as St. Elizabeths. In the 1840s and 1850s, when Dorothea Dix was crusading on behalf of the mentally ill, she badgered the U.S. Congress into making an appropriation for a "government hospital for the insane." Her objective was to give "the most humane care and enlightened curative treatment of the insane."

Land known as the St. Elizabeth's tract was selected for the government hospital. This tract was granted to John Charmes "in the name of St. Elizabeth of Hungary, patron saint of the lepers and the insane." In the 1850s, the asylums for the insane were small. The policy was that a hospital should be small enough to let the superintendent greet every patient personally every day.

The first building, now called the Center Building, was built in what architects called Collegiate Gothic, a castle style complete with battlements and buttresses. The red bricks with which the first building was built were made from the soil of the land. Lumber came from the trees of the surrounding forest. Center Building housed the entire hospital—wards, kitchen, chapel, and an apartment for the superintendent. Transportation at the time was such that guests who came to the hospital often had to stay overnight, so seven bedrooms were provided. One room, known as Miss Dix's Room, contained the large bed in which she slept. The Director's Room, which was part of the superintendent's apartment (now called the staff lounge), contains the desk on which Miss Dix wrote the basic plan adopted by Congress for the organization of the hospital.

Dr. Charles Henry Nichols was appointed superintendent of the Government Hospital for the Insane and served from 1852 until 1877. At the onset of the Civil War, a portion of the Center Building was extended, and 250 beds were set aside as a general hospital for the army. This area was called St. Elizabeth's Hospital. Another building was set aside for the sick and wounded of the Navy's Potomac Flotilla.

The minie bullet, the standard bullet in use during the war, was mainly responsible for the large number of battle casualties. The bullets shattered bones so completely that they could not be set, so limbs were often amputated on the battlefield. Many of the patients who survived were sent to the Government Hospital for the Insane, so a small factory for making artificial limbs was established on the grounds. When the amputees were ready for them, the artificial limbs were fitted. The men who were at the hospital for an extended time refused to write home saying that they were in a hospital for the insane. They simply wrote that they were at "the St. Elizabeth's Hospital." The name was used so frequently that in 1916 Congress officially changed it to St. Elizabeth's Hospital, and later the apostrophe was dropped, as in many place names.

Among the soldiers who were treated here was Maj. Gen. Joseph Hooker. He commanded the 1st Corps at Antietam, where he was wounded in the foot.

Within the Center Building, in the former quarters of Superintendent Nichols, is a museum that houses artifacts, furnishings, and patient records. The museum consists of ten rooms, including the old staff dining room and conference rooms. Miss Dix's immense bed, desk, and traveling trunk, along with other personal belongings, are on display. Civil War memorabilia and ephemera, and documents bearing Abraham Lincoln's signature, can also be seen. The museum is not open on a regular basis, and an appointment to view the collection must be made in advance.

More than 300 soldier patients who died of their wounds rest at peace at the Civil War Cemetery. It was one of the first cemeteries in which both black and white soldiers were interred. Confederate soldiers are also interred here. The headstones are placed in the form of a cross, and in the winter the white stones can be seen from a distance.

Martin Luther King Jr. Avenue and South Capitol Street SE

Fort Carroll

Directions—Exit Gate I from St. Elizabeths and make a right turn onto Martin Luther King Jr. Avenue. Go approximately one mile to the intersection with South Capitol Street. Prior to intersection, earthwork remains of the fort are visible on the right side of avenue.

Fort Carroll was named for Maj. Gen. Samuel Sprigg Carroll, a native Washingtonian and an 1856 graduate of West Point. Its guns guarded the Navy Yard Bridge, Potomac River, Piscataway Road (Martin Luther King Jr. Avenue), Uniontown, and the cavalry depot at Giesboro Point. The fort became the site of administrative facilities for the area as well as headquarters for other forts in the area. Open areas formerly used for drill were obstructed by hospitals, tents, horses, and cavalry.

Surrounding Neighborhoods

M and 9th Streets SE

Washington Navy Yard

The Washington Navy Yard has several Civil War-era structures: the Commandant's Office; Tingey House, which is supposedly haunted by the ghost of the first commandant, Thomas Tingey; and the Latrobe Gate. There are also numerous Civil War guns and naval cannon on the grounds.

Perhaps the most unusual object of all the Civil War memorabilia found throughout the Navy Yard is the plaque on Building 28. The plaque states: "Within this wall is deposited the leg of Col. Ulric Dahlgren, USV, wounded July 6, 1863, while skirmishing in the streets of Hagerstown with the rebels after the Battle of Gettysburg." On the day that Adm. John Dahlgren, inventor of the Dahlgren gun and then chief of the Bureau of Ordnance, was scheduled to lay the cornerstone of a new foundry at the Navy Yard, his son, Ulric, lay near death from a leg wound received in a fight with Rebel forces. It was decided that in order to save his life, the leg would have to be amputated. Admiral Dahlgren felt that a proper tribute to the bravery and courage exemplified by his young son would be a tablet on the corner of the foundry, where those who built the guns of war would be reminded that through the ages, men had always been willing to fight and sacrifice for what they believed was right.

The leg was brought to the Navy Yard in a flag-draped box and placed beneath the cornerstone of what is now the sheet metal shop, known as Building 28. Dahlgren recovered from the amputation but was killed while leading an attempt to free federal prisoners being held at Libby Prison in Richmond. When the original building was demolished to make way for a new one, the leg could not be found. Some say that Confederate sympathizers opened the wall and removed the leg; other people believe that it was removed and buried with Dahlgren's body after his death.

During the Civil War, President Lincoln frequently came to the Navy Yard. His carriage would come through the Latrobe Gate on its way to Admiral Dahlgren's office. Secretary of the Navy Gideon Welles and Secretary of War Stanton would usually accompany him. Two monitors, USS *Saugus* and USS *Montauk,* were berthed at the Navy Yard at the time of President Lincoln's assassination. Stanton had decided to confine those who might be arrested as suspects on board these vessels. The first person to be incarcerated was Lewis Powell, who was brought to the Navy Yard at midnight in a closed carriage. He was put in double irons and taken aboard the USS *Saugus.* Following him were George Atzerodt, Ned Spangler, Samuel Arnold, and Michael O'Laughlin. Mary Surratt was taken from the Old Capitol Prison and delivered to the USS *Saugus*. Finally David Herold was brought in with John Wilkes Booth's body.

Booth's body was placed on a carpenter's bench on the *Montauk* and securely guarded. Visitors were not allowed on board except with a pass signed jointly by the Secretaries of War and Navy. An autopsy was performed, at which several people were asked to identify the dead actor. John Frederick May, a surgeon who had removed a growth from Booth's neck, was only able to identify him by the surgical scar. May said two years later: "To my great astonishment it revealed a body in whose lineaments there was to me no resemblance to the man I had known in life. My surprise was so great that I at once said to General Barnes, 'There is no resemblance in that corpse to Booth, nor can I believe it to be that of him.'" After the autopsy, Col. Lafayette Baker took possession of the body. He delivered it to the old penitentiary on the arsenal grounds, where it was buried under the floor of a jail cell.

Meanwhile, by Stanton's order, the other conspirators had canvas bags put over their heads and tied around the neck. Each bag had a hole for proper breathing and eating but not for vision. (Mrs. Surratt was spared this ordeal of blindness.) The conspirators were kept on the *Saugus* and then transferred to the penitentiary where they stood trial.

Mary Surratt's son John was brought to the Navy Yard on the warship *Swatara* after his capture in Egypt. It anchored in the Anacostia River, and John was transferred to the Navy Yard by a small boat. He was tried for treason and murder in 1867 in the federal courthouse in the Old City Hall. The jury could not agree on a verdict, and he went free.

4th and P Streets SW

Fort Leslie McNair

Directions—Drive on Maine Avenue until it turns into M Street. At 4th Street (Waterside Mall is on your left) make a right turn. Fourth Street dead-ends at P Street. Make a left turn. Fort McNair is on the right.

On the grounds of Fort McNair are the sites of the U.S. Arsenal and the Washington Penitentiary. This site was selected for its strategic military position at the confluence of the Potomac and Anacostia Rivers. Originally, this land was purchased by the government from Boston entrepreneur James Greenleaf, and the peninsula was called

Greenleaf Point. The Washington Arsenal was a major center for the manufacture of arms and munitions. In 1864, an explosion killed 21 women who were working in a room making rifle cartridges. They were buried in a mass grave in Congressional Cemetery. The funeral was attended by President Lincoln and Secretary of War Stanton. The Armory stood on the present-day site of the Army War College.

The Washington Penitentiary, built in the 1820s, was the oldest federal penitentiary in the United States. It was meant to hold 160 inmates. It stressed isolation; each 2 1/2-feet-by-7-feet cell was built so that only one inmate could occupy it. Three 20-foot-high brick walls enclosed a courtyard. On the fourth side was the penitentiary.

At the time of President Lincoln's assassination, it was closed. The conspirators were first kept shackled on board the *Saugus* anchored off the Washington Navy Yard. They were then brought to the old penitentiary and kept under constant surveillance by heavily armed guards. The body of John Wilkes Booth had been previously brought to the penitentiary and buried under the floor in one of the cells.

The room where the trial took place was at one end of the penitentiary. The conspirators sat along one wall behind a wooden railing. All of the conspirators—Herold, Powell, Atzerodt, O'Laughlin, Spangler, Mudd, and Arnold—had 32-pound iron balls attached to their left legs. They were also handcuffed. The exception was Mrs. Surratt, who was neither handcuffed nor chained. A long table covered with green felt was used by the military judges. In the center of the room was a long table for the press. Near the wall opposite the judges, chairs were set aside for spectators who needed a pass to enter the courtroom. A major question arose as to whether the conspirators should be tried by a military or civilian court. Because Lincoln was commander in chief, it was decided that a military court should try the conspirators. In all, more than 340 witnesses were called to testify. Four of the conspirators—Mrs. Surratt, Herold, Powell, and Atzerodt—were sentenced to be hanged; the others were given prison sentences.

The day of the executions was hot and muggy, a typical summer day in Washington. Mrs. Surratt had to be half carried to the scaffold, and a chair was placed for her while her hands and feet were bound. Powell appeared bold and defiant. When the noose was put around his muscular neck, the executioner said to him, "I hope you die quick." Herold seemed thoroughly dazed, and Atzerodt was quaking with fear. Everyone expected a reprieve for Mrs. Surratt, and the spectators kept turning their heads as if expecting to see a messenger with a stay of execution for her. At 1:26 p.m. on July 7, 1865, the trap was sprung, and the four bodies dropped. Just before the trap was sprung, Atzerodt cried out, "Gentlemen take war." He probably intended to say "take warning," but the sentence was finished in eternity. The bodies remained suspended for 30 minutes and then were cut down. Like Booth, they were buried under the floor of a cell. The conspirators' bodies, along with Booth's body, were disinterred in 1869 and given to their families for private burial.

The buff-colored building near the tennis courts is what remains of the penitentiary. It was in this building that Mary Surratt's cell was located. The building is now used as officers' quarters and according to legend is haunted by the ghost of Mrs. Surratt.

Florida Avenue and 7th Street NE

Gallaudet University

Directions—Travel north on North Capitol Street. Make a right turn onto Florida Avenue. Drive to 7th Street. Entrance to the university is on the left.

This area was the estate of President Andrew Jackson's postmaster general, Amos Kendall, and was called Kendall Green. Kendall served as Jackson's major political adviser. He made his money as the business manager to Samuel F. B. Morse, the inventor of the telegraph in the 1840s.

Kendall became a philanthropist and started a school for five deaf mute orphans in 1856. The school was chartered as the Columbian Institution for the Deaf, Dumb, and Blind. During the summer of 1861, Kendall Green became a military camp. Regiments were quartered on the commons, and more than 3,000 soldiers used the well for drinking water. Congressman Thaddeus Stevens of Pennsylvania once visited the college and saw the students working silently in the classrooms. He commented, "Great Heavens! How rapidly one could transact business in the House if half the members were like these children."

13th and Quackenbos Streets

Fort Stevens

Directions—Drive up 7th Street until it becomes Georgia Avenue. Make a left turn at 13th Street. Drive two blocks to Quackenbos Street. An earthwork fort is on the right.

When it was constructed, this fort was called Fort Massachusetts. The government changed the name to Fort Stevens in honor of Brig. Gen. Isaac L. Stevens, killed at Chantilly, Virginia, on September 1, 1862. The fort was located on what was called the 7th Street Pike. It was one of approximately 60 forts that ringed Washington. Along with Forts Slocum and De Russy, it guarded against any Confederate attack from the north down the 7th Street Pike. In July 1864, Confederate Lt. Gen. Jubal Early left the Shenandoah Valley for a raid on Washington. Early was delayed at the Monocacy River just south of Frederick, Maryland, for a little more than 24 hours. That delay bought enough time for combat troops to reinforce Fort Stevens. On July 11, Early's skirmish line was approximately 2,000 yards north of the fort and started to fire at it. On the afternoon of July 12, President and Mrs. Lincoln, along with Secretary of War Stanton, drove out to the fort. Eyewitnesses told of Lincoln climbing the bullet-swept parapet, making himself an easy target. According to legend, a soldier next to him fell wounded, and Capt. Oliver Wendell Holmes yelled to the president, "Get down you damned fool." This story has been exaggerated over the years as to who got the credit for removing Lincoln from the parapet, but the only thing that is certain is that this was the first time in United States history that a president came under fire during battle.

Drive a short distance north on Georgia Avenue to the first gate of Walter Reed Army Medical Center and make a left turn into the first gate. Approximately 100 yards on the right is a small plaque on a rock near ground level—flanked by two cannonballs from the field—that reads: "Lincoln under fire." This plaque marks the spot of a tulip tree, known as the "sharpshooters tree," where Confederate marksmen were firing south into Fort Stevens. Ironically, even though neither person knew it at the time, this battle marked the only time that a president and a former vice president, John Cabell Breckinridge of Kentucky, were on opposite sides in a battle. Breckinridge was Early's second in command. Several blocks north at 6625 Georgia Avenue is Battleground National Cemetery, holding the remains of soldiers killed during the battle at Fort Stevens.

Rock Creek Church Road and Upshur Street NW

United States Soldiers' Home

Directions—Travel north on North Capitol Street approximately two miles. Cross Michigan Avenue. Follow signs on right to Soldiers' and Airmen's Home. Once you exit, make a left turn over North Capitol Street to main gate. Tell the guard that you want to visit Anderson Cottage.

The U.S. Soldiers' (and more recently Airmen's) Home was established by Congress in March 1851 after the Mexican War, due largely to the efforts of Maj. Robert Anderson and Lt. Gen. Winfield Scott. It has served as a residential home to distinguished veterans from five major wars from the Civil War through Vietnam. The home's first lands were a farm purchased from George Riggs, a founder of Riggs National Bank. His original home, now Anderson Cottage, was the summer home for Abraham Lincoln.

Lincoln used Anderson Cottage as his summer White House from 1862 through 1864. His stay usually lasted from late June until early November of each year. In addition to escaping the terrible Washington summer, Mary Todd Lincoln was trying very hard to gain solitude for herself and her husband. Their son Willie had died in 1862, and the loss brought overwhelming grief to the couple.

The tower atop the Scott Building was used as a signal tower during the war, especially during Jubal Early's raid on Washington and the battle at nearby Fort Stevens.

The safety of the president gave Secretary of War Stanton deep concern, and at Stanton's insistence, Lincoln was given a cavalry escort for his trips between the White House and the Soldiers' Home. These troops were apparently not impressive-looking. Walt Whitman, writing for the *New York Times* in the summer of 1863, reported, "I see the president every day. He always has a company of 25 or 30 cavalry, with sabres drawn and held upright over their shoulders. The party makes no great show in uniform or horses."

The most significant association of Lincoln with the home is in his writing of the second draft of the Emancipation Proclamation. Lincoln wrote this document in "the upper corner room with the two big windows under the big gray gable, at the left end of the building."

There was also an attempted assassination of the president near the Soldiers' Home. While riding alone one evening along the 7th Street Pike not far from the main gate, Lincoln heard the sound of a gunshot. Spurring his horse, he rode into the grounds at a full gallop, unharmed but without his stovepipe hat. Several soldiers were sent out to investigate the incident. Upon retrieving the hat, they discovered a bullet hole through the stovepipe.

Lincoln also conducted state business from the Anderson Cottage, and many notables—including Secretaries Stanton and Seward—met with him there.

Part Three

Cemeteries

The Civil War raged near Washington, D.C., and the casualty rate grew. Usually, the dead were interred on the battlefields where they fell. Often the soldiers' remains lay on the field for days before they were removed. The wounded and the reporters who traveled with the armies were critical of burials in the field. By the end of 1861, additional burial sites were needed. In Washington, D.C., the Soldiers' Home National Cemetery filled and in June 1864, Arlington National Cemetery was opened. St. Elizabeths Hospital had its own military cemetery. Many times, military burials were temporary; bodies were taken home for reburial after the war.

Cemeteries listed here contain the remains of military personnel and those of prominent citizens who contributed to the cause in their own way. Some people who are mentioned in this section died before 1861, but they had affected the course of events and are included accordingly.

The listings are not complete and definitive. I take full responsibility for choosing certain people to include, knowing well that there are many other stories and personalities waiting to be discovered.

Arlington National Cemetery

Directions—Cross Memorial Bridge behind the Lincoln Memorial. Continue around grassy traffic circle. Entrance to parking lot and visitors center is 1/4 mile on left.

Arlington was the home of George Washington Parke Custis, the grandson of Martha Washington by her first husband, Daniel Parke Custis, and step-grandson of George Washington. In 1804, Custis married Mary Lee Fitzhugh, who was descended from the Lee, Fitzhugh, and Randolph families of Virginia. He and his wife had one child, a daughter named Mary Ann Randolph Custis. On June 30, 1831, Mary became the wife of Lt. Robert E. Lee, a young West Point graduate. After the death of Mr. and Mrs. Custis, the Arlington estate was bequeathed to their daughter, Mrs. Robert E. Lee, for her lifetime. Upon her death it was to pass to her eldest son George Washington

Custis Lee. It is interesting to note that Robert E. Lee never owned the Arlington estate.

Lee was distressed when news reached him on April 19, 1861, that the Virginia legislature had passed an ordinance of secession. Lee had supported the preservation of the Union that his father, a Revolutionary War hero named "Light-Horse" Harry Lee, and other family members helped to create. Lee had also always disliked slavery, but he remained loyal to his native state. In a letter to his older sister Ann, who was married to a man with Union sympathies, Lee wrote:

> *With all my devotion to the Union and the feeling of loyalty and duty of an American citizen, I have not been able to make up my mind to raise my hand against my relatives, my children, my home. I have therefore resigned my commission, in the Army, and save in defense of my native state, with the sincere hope that my poor services may never be needed, I hope I may never be called upon to draw my sword.*

On April 22, 1861, Robert E. Lee left his Arlington home to accept command of Virginia's military forces in Richmond. He never again returned to Arlington. Shortly after he left, Mrs. Lee was informed that the estate would be occupied by Union forces. She packed as many things as possible but left behind in the attic and cellar many of the relics that her father had brought from Mount Vernon. When Brig. Gen. Irvin McDowell made Arlington his headquarters, he tried to protect the Lees' property but was unsuccessful. Many relics of the Washingtons disappeared. He packed what remained and sent everything to the Patent Office for safekeeping. In May 1861, Lt. Gen. Winfield Scott, U.S.A., ordered Union troops to cross the Potomac River and take possession of Arlington Heights. This measure was simply a military operation for the protection of Washington. The hills of Arlington were well suited for fortifications; once strongly established here, Confederate batteries would have commanded the city.

A ring of forts was built around Washington. Two of these were located on the Arlington property. Fort Whipple stood on the present site of Fort Myer and Fort McPherson on the present site of the Memorial Amphitheater.

In June 1862, Congress passed an "Act for the Collection of Direct Taxes in the Insurrectionary Districts Within the United States." The purpose of this act was to levy and collect taxes on property owned by Southern sympathizers. Commissioners were appointed to carry out the provisions of the act. In the case of default of payment, the commissioners had the power to sell the real estate upon which the taxes were levied. The commissioners established, announced, and uniformly followed a rule under which they refused to receive payment of taxes from anyone other than the owner.

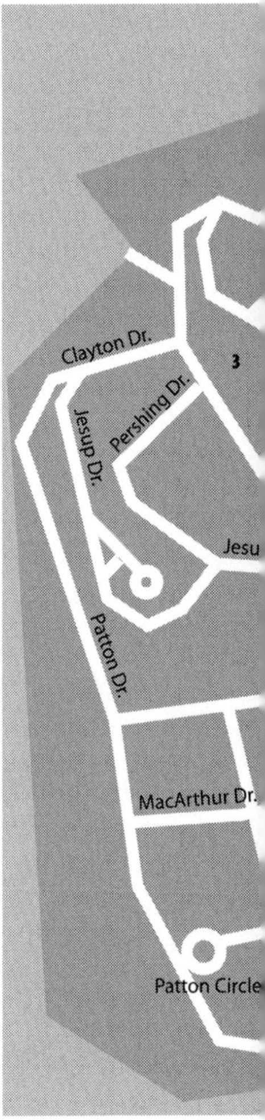

Mrs. Lee was within the military lines of the Confederates and therefore could not go in person to pay the taxes due upon the Arlington property. She sent her agent, a Mr. Fendell, to pay the taxes, interest, and costs that had accrued upon the property. The commissioners refused to receive the money from Fendell and told him that they would not take the money from anyone except Mrs. Lee. On January 11, 1864, the 1,100 acres of the Arlington Estate Plantation were sold "according to law." The commissioners bid $26,800 on behalf of the federal government, seeking the property for "government use for war, military, charitable, and educational purposes." The tax due on the acreage was $92.07.

National cemeteries were established in Alexandria and on the grounds of the Soldiers' Home in Washington. Burial space became increasingly scarce, and there was a constant need for more space to accommodate the dead

from military hospitals and battlefields. In 1864, Secretary of War Edwin M. Stanton ordered Quartermaster General Montgomery Meigs to survey sites that might be used as national cemeteries. Meigs had once been friendly with Lee; they had served together when they were both lieutenants. When Lee resigned his commission and accepted command of the Confederate forces, Meigs considered it an act of treason, and he developed a passionate hatred for his former friend. He became very anti-Southern and disliked all Southerners—including his own brother, who had remained loyal to their native Georgia.

Meigs made no survey of sites. He recommended to Stanton on June 15, 1864, that the Arlington estate be made a national cemetery. On the same day, Stanton formally designated as a military cemetery the Arlington mansion and 200 acres of its surrounding grounds. Meigs ordered the first burials to take place near Mrs. Lee's rose garden, close to the house. The mansion was still being used as headquarters for troops stationed there, and the officers in residence objected and countermanded his order. Meigs was stubborn and wanted to make the mansion uninhabitable for the Lees if they ever wanted to return. The remains of Union troops were disinterred and reinterred in the rose garden and near the mansion. The first military burial at Arlington took place May 13, 1864, more than one month before Stanton's order, when the remains of Pvt. William H. Christman, Company G, 67th Pennsylvania Infantry, were interred.

The original burials in Arlington were those of soldiers who died in the hospitals of Washington and Alexandria. Subsequent interments were those of Union soldiers whose remains were recovered from the battlefields of Manassas, Bristoe Station, Chantilly, and Aldie, Virginia; from abandoned cemeteries in the District of Columbia; from other locations in Maryland and Virginia within a 40-mile radius of Washington; and from the military post cemetery at Point Lookout, Maryland.

There were some wartime interments of Confederate dead, but most of the 500 Confederates now buried in Arlington were veterans who died in Washington after the war was over.

The Arlington estate also was used to house former slaves. Many slaves, former slaves, and runaways flocked to Washington from Virginia and Maryland. Washington became a haven for these fugitives. In 1863, plans were made to relocate some of these people to the Lee estate. Col. Elias M. Green, chief quartermaster of Washington, suggested Arlington in an effort to provide additional housing, increase employment, and lessen the congestion of the city. He felt that "pure country air" would have a positive effect upon the newly freed slaves. Freedman's Village became the name of the camp. The village was initially run by military commanders and special agents of the Treasury Department. The freedmen were taught to be tailors, shoemakers, blacksmiths, and wheelwrights. The majority of the villagers, however, were farmers.

Abbott Hospital, as well as a home for the aged, infirm, and permanently disabled, were established in the village. Many of the villagers worked in Arlington National Cemetery. Freedmen's Village existed for more than 30 years. When the government bought the Arlington estate and turned it into a military reservation, it resulted in the village's demise. On March 23, 1900, Congress appropriated $75,000 to help the villagers resettle in other parts of the Washington area.

There are more than 3,200 graves in Arlington National Cemetery of these former slaves—men, women, and children who died as free people. Many of the stones are marked "unknown citizen" or "unknown civilian." Little is known about them because few records exist to tell who they were. The "contraband" section (section 27) is located near the area where the first recorded military burials took place.

Fred Crayton Ainsworth — Section 3, Grave 1889

As chief of the Record and Pension Office, Brigadier General Ainsworth was responsible for all rulings on applications for veteran pensions. He was also responsible for completing the publication of the official records of the Union and Confederate armies in 1901. Ainsworth was not a veteran of the war.

Christopher Columbus Augur — Section 1, Grave 63

Augur was appointed a brigadier general of U.S. Volunteers in November 1861. He commanded the Department of Washington from 1863 until the end of the war. It was Augur who came out onto the steps of the Petersen House and called for someone able to take shorthand. After Abraham Lincoln was assassinated, Secretary of War Stanton ordered Augur to assign extra police and troops to the Old Capitol Prison, when almost 2,000 people marched on the prison wanting to set it on fire to see the Rebels burn.

Alexander T. Augusta — Section 1, Grave 1-14C

One of the first black surgeons in the Union army, Major Augusta was in charge of the Freedmen's Hospital located at 13th and R Streets, which later moved to 7th and Boundary (now Florida Avenue) Streets.

Romeyn Beck Ayres — Section 1, Grave 12

As an artillery captain, Ayres saw service under Brig. Gen. Irvin McDowell at the Battle of First Manassas. In 1862, he was promoted to brigadier general. He fought at Antietam, Chancellorsville, Gettysburg, the Wilderness, Spotsylvania, and Petersburg. He finished the war with brevets for gallantry as a brigadier and major general in both the Volunteer and the Regular Armies.

William Worth Belknap — Section 1, Grave 132

An Iowa politician, Belknap saw action at Shiloh, Corinth, Vicksburg, the Atlanta Campaign, and General Sherman's march to the sea. He was breveted major general. After the war, he was appointed President Grant's secretary of war. In 1876, Belknap was accused of accepting more than $24,000 in bribes. He was impeached by unanimous vote of the House of Representatives; at Belknap's trial, however, the Senate fell one vote short of conviction.

Hiram Berdan — Section 2, Grave 979

Berdan was an inventor and an expert marksman from New York. He proposed the organization of two regiments of sharpshooters using the best available rifles with telescopic sights. These troops were used primarily as skirmishers. They were known as Berdan's Sharpshooters and were dressed in distinctive green uniforms that blended with their surroundings. Berdan was breveted brigadier and major general for Chancellorsville and Gettysburg, but the highest permanent rank he received was that of colonel.

John Lincoln Clem — Section 2, Grave 993

John Clem ran away from home in May 1861 to join the army. He soon found that the army was not interested in nine-year-old boys. He was turned down several times, but even though he wasn't mustered into service, Clem became the drummer boy for the 22nd Michigan Regiment. He received a soldier's pay of $13 per month, which was donated by the officers. Clem reportedly went into battle at Shiloh and his drum was destroyed. After the battle, he became known as "Johnny Shiloh." At Chickamauga he had a shortened rifle, and he killed a Confederate officer. He was thereafter called "Drummer Boy of Chickamauga." Clem retired from the army in 1916 as a major general.

George Crook — Section 2, Grave 974

Crook fought at South Mountain and at Antietam. He was a cavalry officer at Chickamauga. On the night of February 21, 1865, Crook was captured by Confederate partisan rangers and was sent to Libby Prison in Richmond. He was exchanged, and he participated in the pursuit of General Lee to Appomattox. He was promoted to major general. In postwar years, Crook earned his fame as an Indian fighter in the West.

Edward Doherty — Section 1, Grave 690

Doherty was commander of the cavalry detachment that captured John Wilkes Booth and David Herold. As a reward, the lieutenant was promoted to captain and received $5,250. At Garrett's farm, Booth was shot by Sgt. Boston Corbett after the barn he was hiding in was set on fire. Herold came out with his hands up, and Booth yelled that Herold had nothing to do with the assassination of President Lincoln.

Abner Doubleday — Section 1, Grave 61

A career artillerist, Doubleday fired the first Union shot at

Fort Sumter. He also fought at the Battle of Second Manassas, South Mountain, Antietam, Fredericksburg, and Chancellorsville. At Gettysburg, Doubleday took over command of the 1st Corps upon the death of Maj. Gen. John F. Reynolds. On orders from Meade, he was relieved of command and replaced by Maj Gen. John Newton, his junior—a great humiliation that earned him the epithet "Forty-eight Hours Doubleday." He saw no more active duty for the rest of the war. He is best remembered as the inventor of baseball, even though this fame is mythical.

Sir Moses Ezekial — Section 16, Under Memorial

A Confederate veteran, Ezekial designed the Confederate Memorial. The monument was unveiled on June 4, 1914, on the 106th birthday of Jefferson Davis. The main theme of the memorial is the reconciliation between the North and the South.

John Gibbon — Section 2, Grave 986

Gibbon graduated from West Point in 1847 in the same class with future Union general Ambrose Burnside and Confederate general Ambrose Powell Hill. As a brigadier general, Gibbon was given command of one Indiana regiment and three Wisconsin regiments. He bolstered his men's morale by making them wear distinctive tall hats made of black felt, and his brigade was called "The Black Hat Brigade." Several months later at South Mountain, Maj. Gen. Joseph Hooker referred to them as "The Iron Brigade," an honor that became famous. Gibbon was with Grant at Appomattox to receive the surrender of General Lee's army. After the war, Gibbon fought Indians in the West. He participated in the Little Big Horn Campaign under George Armstrong Custer; he and his men were detached from Custer's force when it was wiped out by the Sioux.

William Alexander Hammond — Section 1, Grave 465

In April 1862, Hammond was appointed surgeon general with the rank of brigadier. He brought reform to the medical service; he tried to bring the ambulance service from the quartermaster's department to his own. He also established the Army Medical Museum (forerunner of the Armed Forces Medical Museum) and collected data that became the basis for the *Medical and Surgical History of the War of the Rebellion.* Secretary of War Stanton disagreed with him about the direction of the medical corps and brought petty charges against him over the distribution of liquor contracts. Hammond was court-martialed and dismissed from the army as of August 18, 1864.

William Selby Harney — Section 1, Grave 117

Harney, as brigadier, was one of only four general officers at the beginning of the Civil War. The Lincoln administration officials watched him closely, however, because they were suspicious of his loyalties; he was from Tennessee and married into a St. Louis, Missouri, family. Harney retired from military duty August 1, 1863, and was breveted major general for his limited war service as commander of the Department of the West.

William Babcock Hazen — Section 1, Grave 15

Hazen was a brigadier general in the Army of the Ohio in November 1861. He had a distinguished military career, serving at Stones River, Shiloh, Chickamauga, Chattanooga, Missionary Ridge, Savannah, and Sherman's march to the sea. He was a brigadier general, chief signal officer, and brevet major general. In the latter part of 1863, survivors of Stones River erected the oldest known Civil War battlefield monument near Round Forest in memory of Hazen's brigade. He had lost almost one-third of his force at the site on December 31, 1862.

Charles Heywood — Section 2, Grave 1115

During the Civil War Heywood served on the USS *Cumberland* during her fight with the CSS *Virginia* (the former *Merrimack*) and received a brevet promotion for his services during this engagement. Heywood also served on the USS *Hartford* in the Battle of Mobile Bay, where he received the brevet rank of lieutenant colonel. Later in his career, Heywood was the ninth commandant of the U.S. Marine Corps from June 30, 1891, until October 2, 1903.

Oliver Wendell Holmes — Section 5, Grave 7004

In the Battle of Antietam in 1862, Holmes was wounded so severely that he was left for dead. He survived, however, and according to legend, the future associate justice of the Supreme Court yelled to President Lincoln to "get down, you damn fool," when Lincoln stood on the parapet at Fort Stevens in 1864 to observe the action. After the war, he returned to Harvard and graduated from the law school in 1866. His combat experience shaped his pattern of thought thereafter.

Juliet Opie Hopkins — Section 1, Grave 12

At the outbreak of the war, Mrs. Hopkins offered her services to the Confederacy, and she was put in charge of the Alabama section of Chimborazo Hospital in Richmond. In addition to staffing and supplying base and field hospitals, she also went on the battlefield to help treat the wounded. She has been called the "Florence Nightingale of the South." Her portrait was put on the $100 note issued by the Confederate state of Alabama. She is buried with her son-in-law, Col. Romeyn Ayres.

Rufus Ingalls — Section 1, Grave 101

Ingalls was made chief quartermaster of the Army of the Potomac in September 1861. In 1864, Lt. Gen. Ulysses S. Grant placed Ingalls in charge of supplying all of the armies operating against Richmond. He built up a huge supply depot at City Point, Virginia. Ingalls was breveted major general in the Volunteer and Regular Armies in 1865.

Philip Kearny — Section 2, Under Statue

Kearny was a professional soldier who studied cavalry tactics at the French Cavalry School at Saumur. He served in Napoleon III's Imperial Guard in the Italian War and won the Legion of Merit; he had also served in the Mexican

War, where a battle wound caused him to lose his arm. When the Civil War broke out, Kearney was appointed brigadier general of volunteers and saw action during the Peninsula Campaign. After Second Manassas, he was promoted to major general. During the action at Chantilly, Kearny was killed when he accidentally rode into a party of rebels at twilight. The New Jersey town where he lived was renamed in his honor. Also in his honor, a medal and cross called the Kearny Medal and the Kearny Cross were given to officers and men who distinguished themselves in battle.

Jonathan Letterman — Section 3, Grave 1869

Letterman was appointed medical director of the Army of the Potomac on April 16, 1862. He set up a system of battlefield care for the wounded by establishing an ambulance corps and divisional hospitals close to the front. Sanitary and nutritional standards were improved under his direction. Letterman resigned from the army on December 22, 1864, and left the East to practice medicine in California.

Robert Todd Lincoln — Section 31, Grave 13

Robert Lincoln was the oldest son of Abraham and Mary Lincoln, and the only one to reach adulthood. At the outbreak of the war, he was at Harvard, and his mother requested that he finish his studies. When the draft law was enacted, newspapers were critical of the Lincolns for keeping Robert out of the army. In February 1865, General Grant appointed him to his staff with the rank of captain and assistant adjutant general of volunteers. Robert declined to attend Ford's Theatre with his parents, a decision he never forgave himself for. In the 1870s, he had his mother declared insane and committed to an asylum. He served as secretary of war in the administrations of Presidents Garfield and Arthur.

Arthur MacArthur — Section 2, Grave 856A

MacArthur was awarded the Medal of Honor for seizing the colors of his regiment, the 24th Wisconsin, at a critical moment and planting them on the captured works on the crest of Missionary Ridge. He was the father of Gen. Douglas MacArthur of World War II fame.

John Rodgers Meigs — Section 1, Grave 1

After his death, Meigs became a controversial figure. He was the son of Quartermaster General Montgomery Meigs and the grandson of Cdre. John Rodgers, a Navy hero. He saw action in the Shenandoah Valley as a member of General Sheridan's staff. On October 3, 1864, Meigs and two Union soldiers encountered three Confederates on the Swift Run Gap Road in the Shenandoah Valley. Meigs was shot and killed. One Union soldier was captured and the other escaped. The survivor told Sheridan that Meigs was murdered in cold blood by Confederate partisans. General Sheridan ordered that the town of Dayton, Virginia, be burned to the ground in retaliation. The town was spared, but other homes in the area were burned. After the war, Lt. Gen. Jubal Early claimed that young Meigs had offered resistance. He also said that the Confederates were in uniform and were regular soldiers, not partisans. The monument to Meigs shows him in the position in which his body was found.

Montgomery Cunningham Meigs — Section 1, Grave 1

Before the Civil War, Meigs was an accomplished engineer who worked on the new Senate wing of the Capitol and the Potomac Aqueduct. Throughout the war, he served as quartermaster general of the Union army. His responsibilities included providing all necessary supplies to the armies in the field, as well as transportation by rail, wagon, and ship of men and matériel. By the end of the hostilities, Meigs had dispensed over $1 billion and had accounted for every penny. In 1864, the Soldiers' Home Cemetery was full, and Meigs was responsible for the establishment of Arlington National Cemetery on the former Lee estate. After the war, he designed the Pension Building in Washington to hold the pension records of war veterans.

Nelson Appleton Miles — Section 3, Grave 1873

At the outbreak of the war, Miles recruited a hundred volunteers for the 22nd Massachusetts Regiment. Too young to command, he served on the staff of Brig. Gen. Oliver O. Howard during the Peninsula Campaign. He also served at Fredericksburg and Chancellorsville, where he was awarded the Medal of Honor and breveted brigadier general. He fought at the Wilderness, Spotsylvania, Cold Harbor, and Petersburg. At the end of the war, he commanded Fort Monroe and was the jailer for Jefferson Davis when the former Confederate president was imprisoned there. Later he saw service in the West and was involved in the capture of the Apache chief Geronimo.

Edward Otho Cresap Ord — Section 2, Grave 982

Ord was involved in the campaign that captured John Brown at Harpers Ferry, Virginia, in 1859. At the outbreak of the Civil War, he was appointed a brigadier general of volunteers. He saw service at Iuka, Corinth, Vicksburg, Richmond, Petersburg, and the final campaign against General Lee at Appomattox. He was present at Lee's surrender on April 9, 1865.

David Dixon Porter — Section 2, Grave S5

The Porter family name is one of the most famous in U.S. military history. His father, David Porter, commanded the *Essex* in the War of 1812. His brother was William D. (Dirty Bill) Porter, his brother by adoption was Adm. David G. Farragut, and a cousin of his was Maj. Gen. Fitz John Porter. In 1862, Porter took command of the Western Flotilla and assumed responsibility for operations on the Mississippi. His gunboats saw action at Vicksburg and in the aborted Red River Campaign. In 1863, he was promoted to rear admiral. In the assault at Fort Fisher in 1864, Porter commanded the largest American fleet assembled to that time. At the end of the war, he became superintendent of the U.S. Naval Academy.

John Wesley Powell — Section 1, Grave 408

Powell was commissioned second lieutenant at the outbreak of the Civil War, and at the Battle of Shiloh he received a wound that resulted in the loss of his right arm. He was discharged January 14, 1865, with the rank of major of artillery. Powell is best known for his accomplishments after the Civil War as the first white explorer of the entire Colorado River, including the Grand Canyon. He rafted almost 900 miles down some of the most treacherous rapids in the world.

John Aaron Rawlins — Section 2, Grave 1007

Rawlins was a politician from Illinois who nominated Senator Stephen A. Douglas for the presidency. He joined Ulysses S. Grant's staff and served as his aide throughout the war. On August 11, 1863, Rawlins was promoted to brigadier general and given the title of Grant's chief of staff. Rawlins did not have much formal education, and Grant usually drafted orders and had Rawlins sign them—a reverse of the standard procedure. Rawlins became head of Grant's military household, and he boasted that he helped Grant control his drinking problem, a claim on which a debate has lasted many years. When Grant was elected president, he appointed Rawlins secretary of war. Rawlins's appointment was more of a reward for loyalty than a recognition of his ability.

Vinnie Ream Hoxie — Section 3, Grave 1876

As a 17-year-old girl, Vinnie Ream was able to get President Lincoln to sit for her portrait sketches. After Lincoln died, she was awarded $10,000 for a sculpture of Lincoln that was placed in the Rotunda of the Capitol. She was the first woman ever awarded a government contract. Miss Ream also sculpted the statue of Adm. David G. Farragut that stands in Farragut Square.

James Brewerton Ricketts — Section 1, Grave 17

Ricketts commanded an artillery battery at the Battle of First Manassas. He was shot four times during the battle and taken prisoner by the Confederates. In January 1862, he was exchanged and received his commission as brigadier general of volunteers. He fought at Cedar Mountain, Second Manassas, and Antietam, where he was again seriously injured when his horse fell on top of him after being shot. Ricketts served on the court-martial that forced Maj. Gen. Fitz John Porter out of the army for his actions at the Battle of Second Manassas. In 1864, at the Battle of Monocacy, Ricketts joined forces with Maj. Gen. Lew Wallace to delay the Confederate advance on Washington. At Cedar Creek, he again received a serious chest wound. Ricketts was breveted a major general in the Regular Army.

John Rodgers — Section 1, Grave 130

Rodgers was the son of John Rodgers, a naval hero of the War of 1812. He commanded the ironclad *Galena* and the monitor USS *Weehawken,* on which he captured the Confederate ironclad CSS *Atlanta* on June 17, 1863. He was promoted to commodore and spent 1864 and 1865 in administrative duties.

William Starke Rosecrans — Section 3, Grave 1862

A West Point graduate, Rosecrans was commissioned a brigadier general in the Regular Army in May 1861. He took charge of the Department of the Cumberland in October 1862 and commanded its namesake army at the Battle of Stones River. At Chickamauga he mistakenly opened a hole in his line, and Confederates under James Longstreet attacked and almost routed the entire Union force. In October 1864, Rosecrans was relieved of command; he was reassigned to duty in Missouri in January 1865.

After the war, Rosecrans repeatedly turned down requests to run for Congress and became known as the Great Decliner. Rosecrans finally did serve as a member of Congress and was appointed by President Johnson as minister to Mexico.

Lovell Harrison Rousseau — Section 2, Grave 1047

As an elected politician from Kentucky, Rousseau raised

troops for the Union at the outbreak of war. He was promoted to brigadier general and fought at Shiloh and Perryville. Later he was promoted to major general, but he resigned from the army on November 10, 1865, after his election to Congress as a Radical Republican. He quickly moderated his views, however, and became a supporter of President Johnson. Shortly after Rousseau resumed his political career, he was forced to resign his seat when he lost his temper and beat Congressman Josiah Grinnell of Iowa with a cane (reminiscent of the notorious beating given to Senator Charles Sumner by Congressman Preston Brooks of South Carolina). Kentucky voters continued to support him; they reelected him to Congress, where he served until July 1866. Rousseau then reentered the army and served in Alaska, taking formal possession of Seward's Folly from the Russians.

Daniel Rucker — Section 1, Grave 74

Rucker served under Montgomery Meigs and commanded the quartermaster depot in Washington, D.C. He was promoted to brigadier general of volunteers in the spring of 1863.

William Thomas Sampson — Section 21, Grave S9

In 1862, Sampson was an instructor at the U.S. Naval Academy, which was temporarily moved to Newport, Rhode Island. In 1864, he was the executive officer aboard the ironclad USS *Patapsco* of the South Atlantic Blockading Squadron. During the Spanish-American War, Sampson was credited with destroying the Spanish fleet at Santiago, Cuba.

John McAllister Schofield — Section 2, Grave 1108

As a staff officer to Brig. Gen. Nathaniel Lyons, Schofield took part in the Union disaster at Wilson's Creek, where Lyons was killed. Schofield received the Medal of Honor for his actions. On May 12, 1863, he was promoted to major general and commanded the Department and Army of the Ohio. He fought under General Sherman at Atlanta and under George H. Thomas at Franklin and Nashville. After the war, he served as superintendent at West Point, and in 1888 Schofield succeeded General Sheridan as general-in-chief of the army.

Philip Henry Sheridan — Section 2, Grave S 1

At the beginning of the Civil War, Sheridan was a second lieutenant. By the end of the war, he was a major general. When Grant was promoted to lieutenant general, he gave Sheridan command of the cavalry in the Army of the Potomac. Sheridan's troopers were responsible for the death of the irreplaceable Confederate cavalryman J. E. B. Stuart at Yellow Tavern. "Little Phil" was very aggressive, and he was made commander of the Army of the Shenandoah on August 1. On October 19, Jubal Early surprised Sheridan's troops at Cedar Creek while Sheridan was meeting with Grant at Winchester. He made his famous ride to the front and rallied his troops, turning near-defeat into victory. Sheridan's horse, Rienzi (his name was changed after the battle to Winchester), is stuffed and on display at the Smithsonian's Museum of American History. For this campaign, Sheridan was named major general in the Regular Army and received the thanks of Congress. Sheridan and his men were at Appomattox when General Lee surrendered his army. In 1883, Sheridan became general-in-chief of the army. He was the son-in-law of Quartermaster General Daniel Rucker.

Daniel Edgar Sickles — Section 3, Grave 1906

Sickles was first thrust upon the national scene in a spectacular trial in Washington, D.C., in 1859. As a congressman from New York, he shot to death attorney Philip Barton Key, Francis Scott Key's son, who was having an affair with Sickles's wife. The defense attorney was future secretary of war Edwin M. Stanton. Sickles was acquitted of all charges; for the first time in American jurisprudence, he pleaded "temporary insanity."

As a politician, he supported Abraham Lincoln and was rewarded a generalship for raising a brigade of soldiers from New York. At Chancellorsville, Sickles advanced his troops after Stonewall Jackson mistakenly believed Sickles was retreating. Jackson's move was actually a flank march that smashed into Sickles's corps and carried the battle. At Gettysburg, Sickles—without the approval of General Meade—moved his corps forward to the Peach Orchard, endangering Little Round Top as well as his own men. He bore the brunt of James Longstreet's assault on his position. Sickles was severely wounded during the fighting, and his right leg was amputated. (A leg bone of his is on display at the Armed Forces Medical Museum at Walter Reed Army Hospital.) He was awarded the Medal of Honor for his actions at Gettysburg, but was denied further field command. He had tried to put the blame on General Meade for the mistake at Gettysburg and a very public controversy ensued. President Grant appointed Sickles minister to Spain, where he became an intimate friend of Isabella, former Queen of Spain.

Julius Stahel — Section 2, Grave 988

Stahel, a Hungarian immigrant, accompanied future general Louis Blenker in raising a regiment (1st German Rifles) from New York. Stahel was commissioned its lieutenant colonel and fought at First Manassas. In November 1861, he was promoted to brigadier general. In March 1863, he was promoted to major general and commanded the cavalry in the defenses of Washington. He was awarded the Medal of Honor for valor in action at Piedmont, West Virginia, where he was severely wounded in 1864.

George Sternberg — Section 2, Grave 994

In 1861, Sternberg was appointed assistant surgeon in the Army Medical Corps. He saw action at First Manassas, Gaines's Mill, and Malvern Hill. After the war, he set up hospitals in New York and Florida to help battle yellow fever. In the 1890s he was named surgeon general of the army.

Samuel Davis Sturgis — Section 2, Grave 1044

At the beginning of the Civil War, Sturgis was stationed in Arkansas. He refused to surrender and marched his troops to Fort Leavenworth, Kansas. He was promoted to brigadier general in March 1862 and commanded a brigade in the defenses of Washington. At the Battle of Second Manassas, while waiting to board a train, Sturgis made the famous remark, "I don't care for John Pope one pinch of owl dung." (Pope was the exceedingly unpopular commander of an improvised Union army.) He fought at South Mountain, Antietam, and Fredericksburg. After being transferred to the western theater, he suffered a major defeat on June 10, 1864, at Brices Cross Roads. Hoping to clear his name, Sturgis asked for a court of inquiry. He was told that it wasn't convenient to assemble one, and he spent the balance of the war awaiting an assignment that never came.

James Tanner — Section 2, Grave 87

Tanner lost both of his legs below the knee when he was struck by a fragment from a bursting shell at the Battle of Second Manassas. When he felt comfortable using artificial limbs, he returned to Syracuse, New York, where he attended a business school. After completing his course, Tanner returned to Washington and became a clerk in the Ordnance Bureau of the War Department. On the night of April 14, 1865, Tanner was attending Grover's National Theatre and had returned to his rented rooms on 10th Street next door to the Petersen House. He answered the summons for a person proficient in shorthand to take testimony and record the events happening next door. During the long night, Tanner took witnesses' statements and recorded his impressions. He saw Mary Lincoln faint and heard her moan, "Oh my God, and I have given my husband to die."

Joseph Rodman West — Section 1, Grave 553

West, who settled in California before the Civil War, was commissioned lieutenant colonel of the 1st California Volunteers and promoted to brigadier general in October 1862. In 1863, West led his troops against the Gila Apache and captured the noted Apache chief Mangas Coloradas. Mangas Coloradas was killed during the night, and it was reported that he was shot trying to escape. A witness claimed that the chief was tortured and that West said "he did not want the Apache alive in the morning." West also commanded the District of Arizona. He finished the war commanding the cavalry in the Department of the Gulf.

Joseph Wheeler — Section 2, Grave 1089

Wheeler was a Confederate general but qualified to be buried in Arlington National Cemetery because of his service as a major general of volunteers in the Spanish-American War. During the Civil War, "Fighting Joe" Wheeler fought at Shiloh. He was commander of the cavalry of the Army of Mississippi. He also fought at Stones River, Chickamauga, Chattanooga, and in the Atlanta Campaign. He was captured in May 1865 in Georgia and was sent to Fort Delaware until June 8. After the war, he served as a congressman from Alabama. During the Spanish-American War, Wheeler again commanded cavalry. He took part in the Battle of San Juan Hill, urging his men on with a shout of "We've got the damned Yankees on the run!"

Charles Wilkes — Section 2, Grave 1164

Wilkes gained his fame as commander of the USS *San Jacinto.* In November 1861, Confederate agents John Slidell and James Mason were taken off the British mail ship *Trent* after it was stopped by Union forces. Wilkes became a hero in the North, even though the incident embarrassed the administration and raised the possibility of an armed confrontation with Great Britain. Slidell and Mason were released. Throughout the next two years, Wilkes continued to harass British shipping, saying that the cargo of their ships was bound for the Confederacy. Even though he was promoted to rear admiral, Wilkes was court-martialed in 1864 and received a public reprimand.

Horatio Gouverneur Wright — Section 45, Grave S4

When Virginia seceded, Wright was the engineering officer in the expedition to destroy the Norfolk Navy Yard.

On September 16, 1861, he was promoted to brigadier general. When Maj. Gen. John Sedgwick was killed by a sniper's bullet at Spotsylvania, Wright assumed command of the 6th Corps and was promoted to major general. In the absence of General Sheridan, Wright was in command at Cedar Creek when General Early's Confederates made a surprise attack. Wright regrouped the troops after Early's initial assault, and Sheridan's return helped to rally the Union troops to victory. Wright was involved in many engineering projects after the war, including the completion of the Washington Monument.

Marcus Joseph Wright **Section 16, Under Memorial**

Wright accepted a commission as a lieutenant colonel in the Confederate army. He was the military governor of Columbus, Kentucky, and fought at Belmont and Shiloh. Promoted to brigadier general, Wright also fought at Chickamauga and Chattanooga. He is best remembered as the collector of Confederate records that were included in the *War of the Rebellion: Official Records of the Union and Confederate Armies.*

Battleground National Cemetery

Directions—6625 Georgia Avenue NW. From the Mall, drive north on 7th Street, which becomes Georgia Avenue.

The grounds of this cemetery of only one acre were established exclusively for the Union soldiers who took part in the action at Fort Stevens. The military graves are arranged in circular fashion, each marked with a small military headstone inscribed with the name of the deceased, the grave number, and the state from which the soldier's unit originated. Located to the east of the graves is a columned marble rostrum from which Memorial Day services are held. Several large monuments, erected by state governments to commemorate those who participated in the battle, are in front. Inscriptions on these monuments list the names of Union soldiers killed in the battle who are not interred here, as well as the names of the wounded. In 1936,

Maj. Edward R. Campbell, the last survivor of the battle, was interred in the cemetery and received special official recognition. There are four civilian interments in the cemetery. These graves belong to family members who cared for the cemetery—the Armbrechts.

Continue traveling north on Georgia Avenue. At the corner of Georgia Avenue and Grace Church Road in Silver Spring (on the right) is a Confederate shaft erected to the memory of 17 unknown Confederate dead who fell in front of Washington, D.C., on July 11 or 12, 1864.

Congressional Cemetery

Directions—1801 E Street SE. Drive east on Independence Avenue past the Capitol. Beyond 1st Street at the James Madison Building of the Library of Congress, Independence Avenue merges with Pennsylvania Avenue. Continue on Pennsylvania Avenue approximately one mile to Potomac Avenue. Make a left turn on Potomac Avenue and continue several blocks to cemetery on right.

Congressional Cemetery was originally known as the Washington Parish Burial Ground. It was established in 1807 by members of Christ Church's Washington Parish (Episcopal) for "all denominations of people" and became indelibly linked to Congress. Benjamin Latrobe designed cenotaphs for members of the House and Senate who died in office, hence the name Congressional Cemetery. A series of congressional appropriations dating from 1823 make it, in the words of a 1939 report, "the first national cemetery created by the government."

Morrison's *Stranger's Guide and Etiquette for Washington City and its Vicinity* (1862) describes "a burying ground beautifully situated on the banks of the Eastern Branch ... with the noble range of forest-clad hills on the opposite side of the beautiful expanse of water."

Because of its convenient location near Capitol Hill and the Navy Yard community, many citizens of Civil War Washington are interred here. Of the more than 70,000 dead, more than half are children. Health conditions in

19th-century Washington, D.C., were far from ideal: smallpox threatened those who had not been vaccinated—and few of the poor had been; defective sanitation created a health hazard that claimed many infants at weaning age.

The 36 acres are flat and easily accessible. Congressional Cemetery houses one of the finest collections of funeral sculpture in the United States. In addition to the remains of Civil War–era residents, there are many thousands of notables at rest here.

Joseph Bell Alexander — Range 30, Site 22

Alexander was co-owner (with Dr. Charles Brown) of the undertaking firm of Brown & Alexander, which prepared Lincoln's body for his funeral tour. The firm was located at 323 D Street.

Dr. Charles E. Allen — Range 12, Site 204

Allen was a Washington physician who testified at Dr. Samuel Mudd's trial that Mudd and several other people stopped at his house on March 23 and stayed until midnight. The government was trying to show that Dr. Mudd was in Washington for a meeting with the conspirators to kill President Lincoln.

John Jay Almy — Range 51, Site 229

Almy was commissioned as a commander in April 1861 and commanded USS *South Carolina* of the South Atlantic squadron under Admiral DuPont, USS *Connecticut* under Admiral Lee, and USS *Juniata* under Admiral Dahlgren.

Arsenal Memorial — Range 97, Site 150

On June 17, 1864, an explosion and fire at the U.S. Arsenal claimed the lives of 21 young women. A large quantity of fireworks was placed in the open next to the building where the women were making cartridges. The heat of the sun set off the fireworks and a burning fuse blew through the open window, igniting the exposed gunpowder where the women were working. The resulting explosion was heard all over

Capitol Hill. The explosion and fire were so great that most of the women were charred beyond recognition. The victims were buried on June 20, 1864. The funeral procession went from the arsenal to Congressional Cemetery. Leading the cortege was a carriage containing President Lincoln and Secretary of War Stanton. Stanton stated that "the funeral and all expenses incident to the interment of the sufferers by the recent catastrophe at the arsenal would be paid by the department. You will not spare any means to express the respect and sympathy of the government for the deceased and their surviving friends." A monument committee was established, composed of representatives of each department or guild at the arsenal, and this committee was authorized to solicit contributions for the purpose of erecting a monument. The monument, standing 30 feet tall, bears the names of the 21 women and the inscription: "Died by an explosion at the U.S. Arsenal, Washington, D.C., June 17, 1864. Erected by public contributions by the citizens of Washington, D.C., June 17, 1867." The monument was designed by sculptor Lot Flannery.

Alexander Dallas Bache — Range 32, Sites 191-196

Bache was the great-grandson of Benjamin Franklin. In 1843, he became the superintendent of the U.S. Coast Survey. Bache founded and was first president of the National Academy of Sciences. During the Civil War, he was an adviser to President Lincoln and was vice president of the Sanitary Commission.

Henry W. Benham — Range 52, Site 249

Benham was appointed chief engineer of the Department of the Ohio. From the spring of 1863 until the end of the war, he commanded the engineer brigade of the Army of the Potomac. Benham was breveted major general in both the Regular and Volunteer Armies.

James G. Berret — Range 48, Site 256

Berret was mayor of Washington from 1858 until 1861. As an ex-officio member of the Metropolitan Police Board,

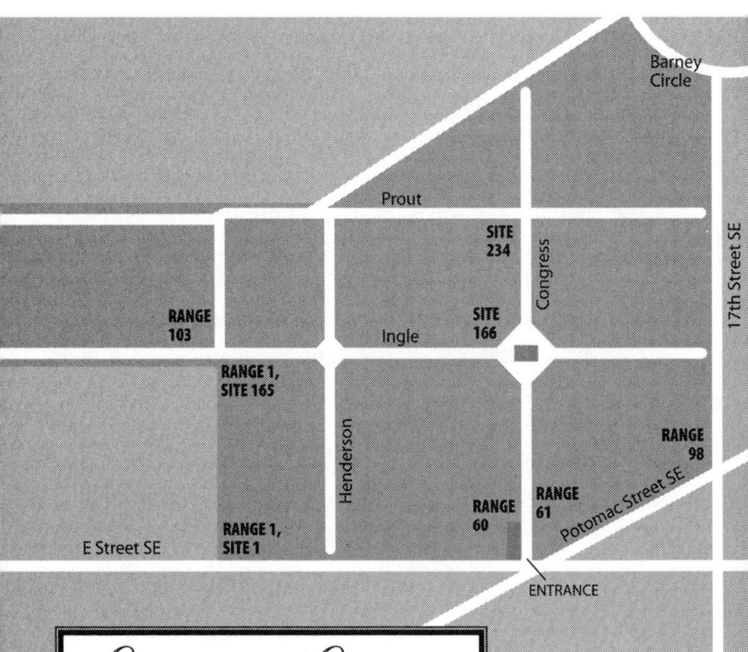

Congressional Cemetery

Berret refused to swear allegiance to the Union, saying that his position was above the oath. He was imprisoned at Fort Lafayette in New York Harbor and was removed from office. No evidence was ever presented that Berret was disloyal to the government. In an attempt to atone to the ex-mayor, President Lincoln offered him a place on the commission to award compensation for the freed slaves in the District of Columbia. Berret refused the appointment.

George A. Bohrer — Range 23, Site 94

Bohrer was a jury member for the trial of John Surratt. Selecting a jury was difficult because many of the prospective jurors had an opinion as to whether Surratt was guilty. Bohrer was chosen from a panel of a hundred men.

Mathew B. Brady — Range 72, Site 120

Brady, a Civil War photographer, took many photographs of Abraham Lincoln. In 1843, he opened a portrait studio in New York City, which attracted thousands of people. In 1850, he published his *Gallery of Illustrious Americans,* which had a considerable circulation. Brady established a studio branch in Washington, and the most prominent Americans sat for him, making him famous as well as prosperous. At the beginning of the war, Brady interested President Lincoln and others—including Allan Pinkerton, the head of the Secret Service—in his proposal to photograph battle and camp scenes, and he received permission for himself and his assistants to accompany the armies. Zealous in their work—often heedless of danger—and at all times handicapped by the difficulties of the photographic process of the day, these men carried their cameras to every scene that promised an interesting picture. More than 3,500 photographs were said to have been taken during the war by Brady and his cameramen.

In 1875, the government purchased for $25,000 a set of 2,000 of Brady's negatives. These have been the basis for many photographic histories of the Civil War. Brady lost money heavily during the war, but continued his career as a photographer.

William A. Browning — Range 37, Site 85

Browning was a private secretary to Vice President Andrew Johnson. On the morning of April 14, Booth left Browning his calling card at the Kirkwood Hotel. Booth wrote on a card: "Don't wish to disturb you: are you at home? J. Wilkes Booth." A hotel clerk placed the card in Browning's mailbox in his absence.

John Edward Buckingham — Range 19, Site 180

Buckingham was the night doorkeeper at Ford's Theatre the night of Lincoln's assassination. He had helped Clay Ford decorate the box that President Lincoln occupied. Buckingham was not at his daytime job at the Navy Yard because it was Good Friday. At approximately 9:40 p.m. Booth came up to Buckingham. Taking hold of two of his fingers, he asked Buckingham the time of night. Several minutes later, Booth again approached Buckingham and asked him for a chew of tobacco. Booth's actions were not strange to Buckingham, who later remembered that the actor was "naturally a nervous man and restless in his movements."

Henry Pratt Cattell — Range 8, Site 61

Cattell was an embalmer for Brown & Alexander and embalmed the body of Abraham Lincoln for the trip back to Springfield, Illinois. Lincoln's blood was drained from his jugular vein. A cut was made on the inside of his thigh, and a chemical preparation was force-pumped into the circulatory system, which soon hardened the body like marble.

John Alexander W. Clarvoe — Range 23, Site 91

Clarvoe was one of four city detectives who went to Mary Surratt's boardinghouse on H Street on the night of April 14 looking for John Wilkes Booth and John Surratt. He told the boarders at the house that Booth had shot the president and that John Surratt had assassinated the secretary of state. Clarvoe then showed them a black scarf saying, "Do you see the blood on that? That is the blood of Abraham Lincoln."

James Croggon — Range 66, Site 273

Croggon was an *Evening Star* reporter who viewed Booth's body at the U.S. Arsenal.

Dr. Charles W. Davis — Range 55, Site 18

Davis was a defense witness for conspirator David Herold. He testified: "I do not know that I can describe his character in better terms than to say that he is a boy; he is trifling, and always has been. There is very little of the man about him .... I should say he is very easily persuaded and led."

William H. Emory — Range 43, Site 37

Emory was a brigadier general who commanded the Cavalry Reserve near Washington. Emory saw service on the Peninsula, in the Red River Campaign where he commanded the 19th Corps, at Fisher's Hill, and at Cedar

Creek. He was breveted major general in 1864. His wife was a great-granddaughter of Benjamin Franklin.

Charles Forbes — Range 34, Site 76

Forbes was President Lincoln's valet. He was called Charlie by President Lincoln and "my friend Charles" by Mrs. Lincoln. Forbes was detailed to the White House as clerk-messenger from the Treasury Department. Because of his discretion and versatility in handling details, he soon became the personal attendant to the president.

Forbes accompanied the Lincolns to Ford's Theatre on the fateful night of April 14. He was sitting in the audience just outside the presidential box as Booth passed him and the unattended post where a policeman was supposed to be stationed. Forbes regretted afterward that possibly there was something he could have done to stop the assassination. Mrs. Lincoln bore him no ill will and showed him only kindness and friendship. She gave Forbes the suit of clothes President Lincoln wore that night.

Dr. Charles Mason Ford — Range 85, Site 98

Ford was an acting assistant surgeon, USA, and he was at Lincoln's deathbed. During the night, a total of 16 doctors attended Lincoln. They would take his pulse, inspect his bulging eye, listen to his hoarse breathing, shake their heads, check their watches, take notes, and record vital signs.

French Forrest — Range 45, Site 42

Forrest was commandant of the Washington Navy Yard from June 1855 until August 1856. During the Civil War, he was a captain in the Confederate Navy, standing third in seniority. As head of the Norfolk Navy Yard, he was in charge of the alterations made on the USS *Merrimack,* and at the Battle of Hampton Roads, he steamed boldly out in the little tug *Harmony* to offer assistance when the Confederate ironclad ran aground.

Benjamin Brown French — Range 63, Site 228

French was commissioner of public buildings. One of his

more pleasant duties was presenting visitors to Mary Lincoln at her many receptions. When Willie Lincoln died, French had the task of making funeral arrangements. After President Lincoln's assassination, French had to make plans for the funeral. Later he had to answer charges that Mary Lincoln had misappropriated public property when she left the White House. He was a Grand Master in an order of Freemasonry and treasurer of the U.S. Agricultural Society. After emancipation, French disapproved of giving African Americans equal rights.

Joseph Gales — Range 55, Site 158

Gales was co-editor of the *National Intelligencer.* In 1807, he traveled to Washington to report congressional proceedings for S. Harrison Smith, editor of the *National Intelligencer.* He sat next to the vice president and shared the snuff box with him from 1807 to 1820. In 1810 he became the sole owner of the newspaper and took his brother-in-law, William W. Seaton, into business with him in 1812. Gales was responsible for most of the editorials in the *Intelligencer.* They were short and compact.

Gales supported President Madison and the War of 1812. (When the British burned Washington in 1814, they destroyed Gales's library and printing equipment.) On December 14, 1813, Gales married Sarah Juliana Maria Lee, the niece of "Light-Horse" Harry Lee. Among the people that he called friends were the Adamses, Websters, and Calhouns. He did not believe in government by the masses and considered the election of Andrew Jackson a national calamity. He gave money to the American Colonization Society. He also served as mayor of Washington from 1827 to 1830.

His most permanent work was the preservation of the proceedings of Congress throughout a considerable period. Although Gales was employing other reporters at the time of the Webster-Hayne Debate, he reported the speeches himself at Webster's request.

Count Adam Gurowski — Range 53, Site 206

Gurowski, a State Department employee, was said to be

the only man President Lincoln feared would attack him. A Polish count with a checkered career leading through Russian prisons and a professorship at a Swiss university, Gurowski had come to the United States in 1849, taking a position with the State Department as a translator.

Gurowski was described as being short in stature, ugly in feature, and disfigured by a pair of green goggles. Known as a rude, rough, Polish bear, he kept a diary in which he ridiculed and abused almost every member of the government. He tried to publish his diary, but the district attorney of Washington had him indicted for libel. Senator Charles Sumner once threw Gurowski out of his house after listening to a torrent of abuse.

Dr. James Crowhill Hall — Range 45, Site 169

Hall was a physician at Lincoln's deathbed. He testified in defense of Lewis Powell by saying that there were "no signs of mental insanity, but of a very feeble inert mind, a deficiency of mind rather than a derangement of it—a very low order of intellect." According to Hall, Powell could not remember his mother's maiden name upon questioning.

Simon P. Hanscom — Range 15, Site 24

Hanscom was the editor of the *Daily National Republican.* This liberal, gossipy newspaper tried to be the president's unofficial paper. Hanscom irritated other editors and reporters by being very ingratiating in his dealings with Lincoln. He was permitted to walk into the president's office without an appointment at any hour, and after small talk with Lincoln, Hanscom would go back to his office and write an entire column on the state of the Union and the conduct of the war. Hanscom also delivered a telegraph message from the War Department to the president's box at Ford's Theater prior to the assassination. The president's valet, Charles Forbes, was sitting against the wall, and Hanscom told him about the sealed message. Forbes waved him inside. The message turned out to be of little importance: it asked for a permit for two former Confederate officials to visit Washington and have a meeting with Lincoln.

Emerick W. Hansell — Range 86, Section D4

Hansell, a State Department messenger, was wounded by Lewis Powell after his attack on Secretary of State Seward. As Powell fled, crying, "I'm mad, I'm mad," he met Hansell, who was coming up the stairs. Powell slashed him with his knife and stabbed him in his right side, inflicting a dangerous wound three inches deep and nearly an inch wide.

Charles P. Henningsen — Range 55, Site 81

Henningsen had a brief career in the Confederate army. A soldier of fortune, he fought in Spain and in Hungary before immigrating to the United States in the early 1850s. He offered his services to the South as a commissioned colonel, 59th Virginia, in August 1861. He served in campaigns on the Peninsula, western Virginia, and North Carolina. In November 1862, when the regiment was reorganized, Henningsen was relieved of his command.

David (Davy) Herold — Range 46, Site 44

Herold was a convicted conspirator in Lincoln's assassination. He was caught with John Wilkes Booth in a barn on the Garrett farm. Herold was the sixth of ten children born to Adam George Herold and Mary Porter Herold. Two brothers died at an early age, so he was the only son raised with seven daughters. The Herolds were respected people in their neighborhood. They lived in a large brick house on the site of 1110 8th Street SE, just outside the main gate of the Navy Yard where Mr. Herold held a job as chief clerk. The family was religious. They attended services regularly at Christ Church, where they met and counted among their friends the family of band leader John Philip Sousa.

David Herold studied pharmacy from October 1855 to April 1858 at Georgetown College. He took a job with a Dr. Bates near the Navy Yard and later worked for William Thompson, who owned a drugstore near the White House. According to one story, Herold delivered a bottle of castor oil to President Lincoln. He never recorded his impressions of the incident. He left Thompson's Drugstore in October 1863, when he began working and living with Dr. Francis

S. Walsh on 8th Street SE. Dr. Walsh liked Herold and would later testify on his behalf. Herold was universally regarded as immature and unreliable; most witnesses agreed that he was more boy than man. Even his father did not trust him. When Adam George Herold died in October 1864, he left a will in which he stipulated that "under no circumstances shall the duty of settling my estate devolve upon my son, David." Still, Davy's familiarity with the roads of southern Maryland and the fact that he claimed to know "almost everyone in Maryland," coupled with his knowledge of drugs, would have been very useful for a plotter.

John Wilkes Booth met Herold while the latter was working at Thompson's Drugstore. Booth had been involved with smuggling quinine to the Confederates. After his arrest, Herold stated that Booth visited him several times each week while he worked at Thompson's. Though he never revealed why Booth came to see him, it is hard to imagine the visits as anything but business. It is unlikely that Booth ever trusted him with a major role in the plot, but there was never any doubt that Herold would guide the escape. Meeting Booth near the present Camp Springs, Maryland, after the murder, Herold stayed with him until they were cornered in Garrett's barn. Once captured, he was taken back to Washington and put aboard the USS *Montauk* where he was interrogated by John Bingham.

Though sometimes described as a mental defective, Herold showed no signs of slowness during this interrogation. Handling himself quite well during the questioning, Herold led Bingham astray on the details of the escape, and he seemed rather adept at evading certain questions.

The deeds of Herold naturally brought great suffering upon his family. A local story related the events of July 7 in the Herold home. The family knew that he was sentenced to die before 2 p.m. that afternoon, and some friends tried to ease Mrs. Herold's agony by stopping all of the clocks in the house so she could not tell when the fateful hour had passed. But at the stroke of the hour, the church bells announced the time, and the plan was foiled. Mrs. Herold broke into tears.

After the hanging, Herold's body, along with the other conspirators' bodies, was put beneath the floorboards of a jail cell in the arsenal. On February 15, 1869, the Reverend J. Vaughn Lewis of St. John's Episcopal Church made application to President Johnson in behalf of Herold's mother and sister to reinter his body. The order to exhume his remains was given to an undertaker named Joseph Gawler, who presented it to the commandant at the arsenal. A detail of men dug to the pine box containing the remains, lying between the coffins of Atzerodt and Powell. The top of the case was found to have decayed and collapsed. The body was removed from the pine case and placed in a fine walnut coffin ornamented with silver handles and screws. A plate over the breast was inscribed, "David Herold, aged 23 years." The flesh had entirely disappeared and only the skeleton remained, but the clothing appeared to be in a fine state of preservation. A vial, containing a parchment slip with the name of the deceased, was found in the coffin and given to his mother.

Andrew A. Humphries — Range 63, Site 184

Humphries entered the war a brigadier general of volunteers and served as chief topographical engineer of the Army of the Potomac. He was a division commander at Antietam, Fredericksburg, Chancellorsville, and Gettysburg. He served as Maj. Gen. George Meade's chief of staff until 1864. Humphries was breveted major general for gallantry at Saylor's Creek.

William Henry Keilholtz — Range 111, Site 191

Keilholtz, a brother-in-law of Davy Herold, testified in his defense, saying that Herold never associated with men but with boys between the ages of 18 and 22 and that he was easily persuaded and influenced.

Horatio King — Range 53, Site 78

In 1839, King received a clerkship at $1,000 per year in the Post Office Department in Washington, D.C. For the next 22 years under Democratic and Whig administrations from

Van Buren to Lincoln, he served in the Post Office Department. King became acting postmaster general. He warned Rep. J. D. Ashmore of South Carolina on January 28, 1861, that his continued use of the franking privilege had to cease when Ashmore resigned his House seat.

Noble D. Larner — Range 27, Site 164

In April 1861, Larner answered President Lincoln's call for troops for 90 days' service. In 1864, along with other citizens, he formed the Third Ward Draft Club. The club's purpose was to raise money to purchase substitutes to relieve those Washington citizens who were drafted but unwilling to serve. President Lincoln wanted to place a substitute for himself from the District of Columbia, so the provost marshal general, Col. James B. Fry, sent for Larner and placed the matter in his hands. Larner secured the enlistment of John Summerfield Staples as Abraham Lincoln's representative recruit. Staples was sworn in, dressed in uniform, and taken to the White House, where Lincoln spoke to him about the duties of a soldier. As payment for the substitute, President Lincoln sent Larner a check for $300 drawn on Riggs Bank.

Dr. Samuel A. H. McKim — Range 70, Site 98

McKim, a physician, testified in defense of Davy Herold. He said Herold was immature and unreliable and that he would never trust him to deliver medicine to any of his patients for fear that Herold might tamper with the prescriptions just for fun.

John G. Merritt — Range 72, Site 359

Merritt was a sergeant in Company K, 1st Minnesota Infantry, who was awarded the Medal of Honor for gallantry in action at the Battle of First Manassas on July 21, 1861. He was wounded while capturing an enemy flag in advance of his regiment. The Medal of Honor is presented to its recipients by a government official "in the name of the Congress of the United States." For this reason, it is often called the Congressional Medal of Honor.

Robert Mills — Range 35, Site 111

Mills was the designer of the Washington Monument, Treasury Building, Patent Office, and Post Office Building. He trained with James Hoban, the designer of the White House, and with Thomas Jefferson, who took him into his home at Monticello. Mills had the benefit of Jefferson's collection of architectural books, then unrivaled in America. Mills also studied under Benjamin Latrobe from 1803 to 1808.

Early in his career, he began to make designs of his own. He designed several buildings in Charleston and in Philadelphia, where he lived until 1817. He won the competition for the first Washington Monument, which stands in Mount Vernon Place in Baltimore. This column was completed in 1829. In 1830, Mills moved to Washington, where he was a supporter of Andrew Jackson. In 1836, he was appointed architect of public buildings, a position that he held for 15 years. During his tenure, he designed three of the principal 19th-century buildings in Washington: the Treasury Building, the Patent Office, and the Post Office.

The crowning success of his life was his victory in competition for the design of the Washington Monument. The Washington National Monument Association solicited design ideas, and funds were obtained by popular subscription. Mills's design proposed an obelisk 600 feet in height, surrounded at the base by a circular colonnaded building, with a portico at the principal face and surmounted by the figure of Washington in a triumphal chariot. Subscriptions came slowly, and the cornerstone was not laid until 1848. The work languished for a lack of funds and was suspended in 1855, the year of Mills's death, when the shaft had reached a height of 154 feet. It was not until 1878, and after much controversy, that Congress made it possible to resume construction. The monument was completed in 1884, at a height of 555 feet, but without Mills's elaborations at the base. In its day, it was the tallest structure in the world.

William George Moore — Range 81, Section D3

Moore, a War Department clerk, attended the inquest on

Booth aboard the USS *Montauk.* The purpose of the inquest was to have Booth's body positively identified. Historians have noted that witnesses had different opinions about Booth's body. India-ink initials tattooed on his hand as a boy and a surgical scar on the back of his neck served as positive identifiers. To this day, there is controversy surrounding the positive identification of Lincoln's assassin.

Frank Munroe — Range 56, Site 169

Munroe took George Atzerodt's confession aboard the USS *Saugus.*

Seaton Munroe — Range 56, Site 168

Munroe attended the inquest on John Wilkes Booth aboard the USS *Montauk.* Seaton was the brother of Frank, and in spite of Secretary of War Stanton's tight security orders, Munroe was able to walk aboard the ship. Munroe's description of Booth's body was far different than the descriptions given by the other witnesses. Munroe stated that Booth's corpse was "unmarred by the agony of death and his handsome countenance also unmarred."

Dr. Charles Henry Nichols — Range 49, Site 175

Nichols was the son-in-law of John Maury, a former mayor of Washington, and the superintendent of the government insane asylum (St. Elizabeths). During the Civil War, he acted as a volunteer surgeon at the asylum's army hospital and he was present as one of General McDowell's staff at the Battle of First Manassas. At the trial for the conspirators in the Lincoln assassination, he testified in defense of Lewis Powell. In 1877, he accepted the position of medical superintendent of the Bloomingdale Asylum in New York City. Nichols was one of the foremost experts in what is now called forensic psychiatry, and he supplied testimony for the defense in the trial of Charles Guiteau, who assassinated President James Garfield.

James Nokes — Range 47, Site 141

Nokes testified in defense of David Herold, calling him "a

light and trifling boy—very little reliability is to be placed in him." According to Nokes, Herold was easily impressed by anyone with whom he associated and who had fascinating qualities. Nokes lived in the Navy Yard section of Washington (the 6th Ward), and he knew Davy Herold and his family.

Joseph T. K. Plant — Range 64, Site 51

Plant testified in defense of Edman Spangler, a stagehand at Ford's Theatre. Plant was a dealer in furniture and a paper-hanger, and had been engaged in cabinetwork at the time of the conspirators' trial. He lived at 350 D Street NW. Plant gave testimony about the condition of the locks on Boxes 7 and 8 in Ford's Theatre, which comprised the Presidential Box. He also testified about the hole in the door of Box 7. There was doubt concerning who made the hole—John Wilkes Booth or Edman Spangler. If Booth had indeed made the hole, the question arose as to whether Spangler had any knowledge of it.

Alfred Pleasonton — Range 42, Site 245

As a brigadier general, Pleasonton helped in the reorganization of the cavalry of the Army of the Potomac. He fought at South Mountain, Antietam, Fredericksburg, and Chancellorsville. He participated in all the operations leading to Gettysburg, and at Brandy Station, in the largest cavalry battle of the war, he surprised Maj. Gen. J. E. B. Stuart. This engagement was touted as the "battle that made the Federal cavalry." Pleasonton was promoted to major general shortly after the battle.

James W. Pumphrey — Range 47, Site 206

Pumphrey was the owner of the livery stable where John Wilkes Booth rented his horse, a small bay mare. Booth had originally wanted a sorrel horse, but it had already been rented. Booth often rented horses from Pumphrey's stable, and on one occasion he showed up at the stable with John Surratt, another of the conspirators.

James Henry St. Clair — **Range 63, Site 58**

St. Clair, a Washington bookbinder, was an usher at Ford's Theatre the night of the assassination.

Frank T. Sands — **Range 84, Site 132**

Sands, a Washington undertaker, provided President Lincoln's coffin and accompanied the funeral train on its trip to Springfield, Illinois.

Francis Maria Scala — **Range 8, Site 9**

Scala served as leader of the U.S. Marine Band that often entertained the Lincoln family. Scala had a close relationship with the president: "Lincoln I always remember with affection. He was so delightfully plain and honest. Old Abe liked music and was my friend. I have many personal souvenirs of him." Scala had conducted the Marine Band in a serenade for Lincoln the evening the president-elect arrived in Washington. He and the Marine Band also accompanied Lincoln to Gettysburg when Lincoln delivered his Gettysburg Address.

Albin F. Schoepf — **Range 84, Site 108**

Schoepf was born in Poland and came to the United States in 1851. While working as a porter in a Washington hotel, he met Joseph Holt, then the commissioner of patents. Schoepf followed Holt to the War Department, where he was given a field command in 1861, brigadier general of volunteers. He served in the Army of the Ohio until he asked to be relieved and was then given command of the federal prison camp at Fort Delaware, near New Castle, where he earned the unpopular nickname "General Terror." The camp, located on a marshy site unsuitable for large numbers of prisoners, housed Confederate political and naval prisoners and had a notorious reputation for overcrowding and mistreatment.

William Winston Seaton — **Range 57, Site 165**

Seaton was both mayor of Washington and co-editor of the *National Intelligencer.* In 1809, he moved to Raleigh, North

Carolina, and became associated with the elder Joseph Gales (he married Gales's daughter, Sarah Weston Gales). In 1812, he joined his brother-in-law, the younger Joseph Gales, as associate editor of the *National Intelligencer* of Washington, D.C. Seaton's policy became conservative, nationalistic, and free from partisanship. His most important work was conducted as a reporter covering Senate debates, while Gales covered the House. Masters of shorthand, the brothers-in-law were the exclusive reporters of Congress from 1812 to 1829.

Seaton served as mayor of Washington from 1840 to 1850 and helped to develop the local educational system. He also led the movement for the Washington Monument. For many years, he was an official in the American Colonization Society. He favored gradual emancipation of slaves and freed his own. He was not an abolitionist, however, and maintained that the national government should not interfere with slavery.

Joseph G. Shelton — Range 96, Site 82

Shelton was a Washington metropolitan policeman who was assigned to guard President Lincoln at the White House.

Ann G. Sprigg — Range 53, Site 41 (no marker)

Mrs. Sprigg was Abraham Lincoln's landlady when he first came to Washington in 1847 to serve in the House of Representatives. The widow of Benjamin Sprigg, she kept a boardinghouse on 1st Street, between A Street South and East Capital Street. Like most congressmen of the time, Lincoln lived in a boardinghouse with colleagues belonging to the same political party—in his case, Whigs.

Peter Taltavull — Range 68, Site 53

Taltavull owned the Star Saloon next door to Ford's Theatre. He testified that he served John Wilkes Booth a drink about ten minutes before Booth shot President Lincoln. Booth usually drank brandy, but Taltavull said that Booth drank whiskey and water before he left the saloon.

William Grenville Temple — **Range 40, Site 53**

Temple first commanded the steamer *Flambeau* trying to intercept blockade runners off Nassau in the Bahamas. Then he commanded USS *Pembina* on the Mobile blockade until November 1863.

Joseph G. Totten — **Range 44, Site 32**

At the beginning of the Civil War, Totten had been the chief engineer of the U.S. Army since 1838. Born in 1788, he was a captain of engineers before most of the Civil War generals were born. In addition to his regular peacetime duties of maintaining harbor channels and lighthouses, Totten was responsible for providing engineering officers to the armies in the field and for providing special supervision for the ring of forts around Washington. He died of pneumonia on April 22, 1864. Upon hearing of Totten's illness, Lincoln forwarded Totten's commission as brevet major general.

Richard Wainwright — **Range 38, Sites 221-226**

Wainwright commanded the *Hartford*, the flagship of Flag Officer David G. Farragut, on the lower Mississippi River.

William P. Wood — **Range 65, Site 248**

Wood, superintendent of Old Capitol Prison, believed Mary Surratt was innocent of the charges brought against her: "This unfortunate lady was as innocent of any connection with the assassination of President Lincoln as any of the officers who sat upon her trial." After the death sentence had been pronounced, Colonel Wood did his best to have it rescinded. He tried to gain access to President Andrew Johnson at the White House but was turned away. Wood claimed that Secretary of War Stanton wanted Mrs. Surratt hanged and had prevented his admission to the White House.

Henry Gaither Worthington — **Range 25, Site 41**

Worthington was elected as a Republican congressman from Nevada to the 38th Congress and served from October 31, 1864, to March 3, 1865. He was a pallbearer at the funeral of President Lincoln.

Glenwood Cemetery

Directions—2219 Lincoln Road NE. Drive north on North Capitol Street toward U.S. Soldiers' and Airmen's Home. Bear right on Lincoln Road. Cross Rhode Island Avenue. Cemetery is on the left.

Glenwood Cemetery was chartered on July 27, 1854, and was located on what was then known as Clover Hill Farm. In the 1850s and 1860s, many churches removed the remains of people buried in the churchyards to Glenwood. In addition to the Civil War soldiers buried here—mostly in private graves—there are thousands of civilians who contributed to the history and lore of Washington, D.C.

Constantino Brumidi — Section Q, Lot 70, Site 6

Brumidi, a political refugee to the United States, is known as the "Michelangelo of the Capitol." For almost 24 years and six administrations—those of Franklin Pierce, James Buchanan, Abraham Lincoln, Andrew Johnson, Ulysses S. Grant, and Rutherford B. Hayes—Brumidi worked on the Capitol. He made frescoed ceilings and wall murals in six committee rooms (five in the Senate extension, and one in the House extension). Brumidi was responsible for the design and execution of the President's Room in the Senate Annex; the Senate Reception Room; and a large mural in the House of Representatives, *Washington at Yorktown*, signed "C. Brumidi, Artist. Citizen of the U.S." He also sketched the 15 scenes of American history for the frieze that encircles the Rotunda 58 feet above the floor. Brumidi's most important work was the huge fresco in the dome of the Rotunda, entitled *The Apotheosis of Washington.* On October 1, 1879, Brumidi was working on *Penn's Treaty with the Indians* on the frieze. He fell from his suspended painting chair and had to hold onto a ladder with his fingertips for 15 minutes until he was rescued. He never returned to the Capitol, and died five months later at his home at 921

G Street SE. Throughout his career painting the Capitol, Brumidi received $8 to $10 dollars a day.

Alexander Gardner — **Section C, Lot 38, Site 8**

Born in Scotland, Gardner came to the United States in 1856 and worked for Mathew Brady in Brady's photographic gallery in New York. In 1858, he became manager of Brady's studio in Washington. Gardner's views of the dead at Antietam, which bore the backstamp of "Brady and Company," shocked the nation. Photos of troops in the field and generals were sold to illustrated news weeklies. All of the credit went to Brady. By 1863, Gardner left Brady's employ and opened his own studio at 7th and D Streets. He advertised himself as "Photographer to the Army of the Potomac." He photographed the executions of the Lincoln assassination conspirators and the execution of Andersonville's Confederate commander Henry Wirz. After the Civil War, Gardner published a *Photographic Sketch Book of the Civil War,* featuring his best work. Unlike Mathew Brady's assistants, all of Gardner's photographers received full credit for their work.

Amos Kendall — **Section B, Lot 176, Site 3**

Kendall studied at Dartmouth College and was employed as a tutor to the family of Henry Clay. As the business manager for Samuel F. B. Morse, the inventor of the telegraph, he became very wealthy and purchased a 103-acre farm north of Boundary Street (Florida Avenue) at 7th Street. This estate was known as Kendall Green. He began a grammar school for five deaf mute orphans, which was chartered in 1857 as the Columbia Institution for the Deaf, Dumb, and Blind. In 1864, the school was expanded to a four-year college, and in 1894, was renamed Gallaudet College after its first teacher, Edward Miner Gallaudet.

Clark Mills — **Section 0, Lot 132, Site 11**

Mills learned the trade of house plasterer in 1830 and soon began to study sculpture. He entered and won a competition for an equestrian statue of Andrew Jackson for Lafayette

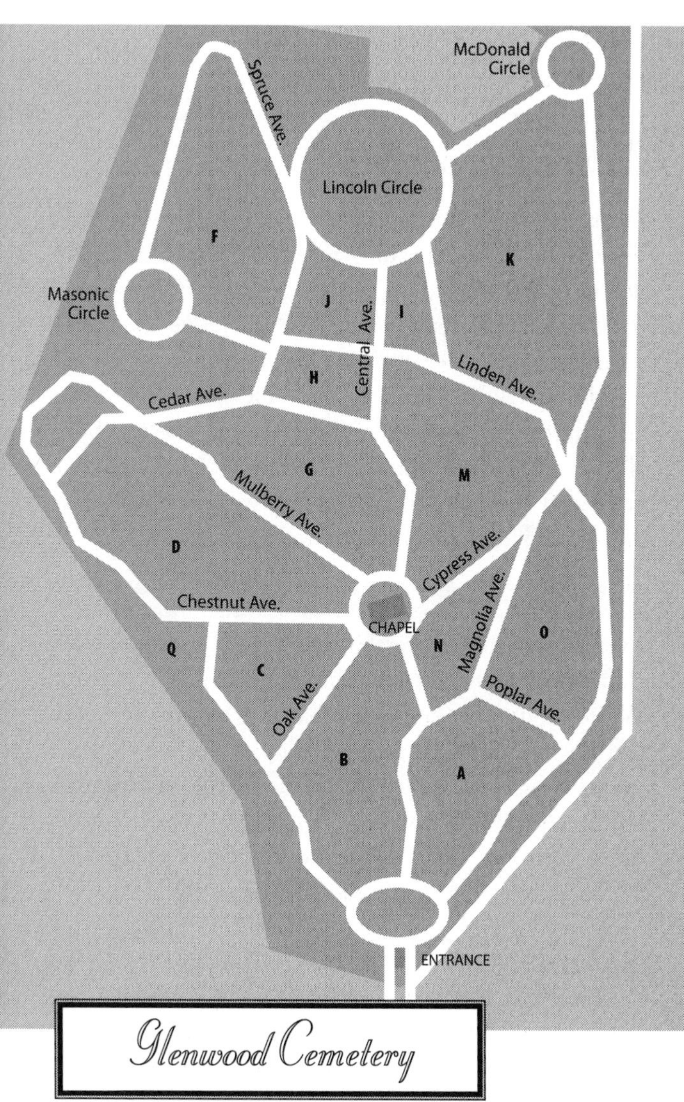

Park. The statue was cast from surplus brass and copper from the Washington Navy Yard. With the money he won, Mills opened an octagonal-shaped foundry on Bladensburg Road. In this foundry, he cast his equestrian statue of George Washington for Washington Circle in 1859. Mills also cast Thomas Crawford's figure of *Freedom* for the top of the new dome of the Capitol in 1862. Mills had two sons whom he sent to Germany to study art during the

Civil War, allegedly to keep them from joining the Confederate army.

Mount Olivet Cemetery

Directions—1300 Bladensburg Road NE. Drive east on New York Avenue, heading toward Annapolis. At Bladensburg Road, make a right turn. At R Street you will see the National Arboretum on the left. Travel one more block to the entrance of the cemetery at a dead end.

Mount Olivet Cemetery is the oldest Catholic cemetery in the metropolitan Washington area. The first burials were in 1858, the year Catholic parishes in Washington purchased Fenwick Farms to comply with an 1852 city ordinance prohibiting burials within city limits.

James Hoban — Section 12

Even though this Irish architect died in 1831, Hoban is included because he designed the President's House, as the White House was known. Hoban was an architect who had practiced for ten years in Charleston and had designed the state capitol in Columbia. He also designed Blodgett's Hotel at 8th and E Streets. (The hotel did not exist at the time of the Civil War.) Hoban was a member of the Washington City Council from 1820 until his death.

William Matthew Merrick — Section 24

William Merrick was the brother of Richard Merrick, one of the attorneys for John Surratt. He was a representative from Maryland and served as an associate judge of the U.S. Circuit Court for the District of Columbia.

William Russell Smith — Section 45

As a representative from Alabama, Smith voted against secession. During the war, however, he fought for the Confederacy as colonel of the 26th Alabama. He was also a representative in the First and Second Confederate Congresses. He was originally buried in Tuscaloosa, Alabama, but his remains were reinterred in Mount Olivet.

To this day, there is a great deal of debate on whether or not Mrs. Surratt was guilty of conspiring to kill President Lincoln. Her husband John, who was deeply in debt when he died, left her a tavern and post office in what was called Surrattsville, Maryland, and a debt-free boardinghouse on H Street in Washington. Lack of income forced the widow to move to Washington on November 1, 1864, where she opened a boardinghouse at 541 (now 604) H Street. The house contained ten rooms. Mrs. Surratt's hospitality was a constant obstacle to the financial success of her boardinghouse. She welcomed her friends who would stop by, and some even boarded there for a length of time, not always paying for their room and board. Mrs. Surratt's son, John, was a Southern sympathizer and had served in the Confederate army. His friends, with whom he met at the boardinghouse to plan a kidnapping of President Lincoln, included John Wilkes Booth, George Atzerodt, and Lewis Powell.

Three days after Lincoln's assassination, Mrs. Surratt was arrested. As the police officers were arranging for her transportation, there was a knock at the door. In walked Lewis Powell, the conspirator who had attacked Secretary of State Seward. Powell had spent three days wandering and hiding in the city and came back to the house where he had been received with hospitality. His coming to the Surratt boardinghouse was hailed as proof of Mrs. Surratt's guilt.

While she was awaiting trial, rumors began to spread that she was being maltreated. No one in authority confirmed or denied these stories, which for many years stirred controversy. Mrs. Surratt was described as "more dead than alive" as she walked to the scaffold. One of two priests attending her had to keep her from falling. The execution was under the direction of General Hancock, who hoped and expected that a reprieve would come for her. Hancock had stationed riders with swift horses between the White House and the arsenal so that if President Johnson did relent, the news would be swiftly known. Nobody really believed that a woman would be hanged. When no orders came, the executions were finally carried out at 1:26 p.m. Mary Surratt's body remained suspended 30 minutes and was then cut down. Like the others, it was buried beneath a cell in the penitentiary and remained there until February 1869, when under an executive order, it was reburied in Mount Olivet Cemetery.

Henry Wirz — Section 27A

Andersonville was the most notorious prison in the Civil War. Captain Wirz was the commander of this prison. The concentration of Union prisoners in Richmond had drained the local food supply, and Confederate soldiers were taken from much-needed duty to guard prisoners. A new prison site of 26 acres was selected in southwestern Georgia between Oglethorpe and Americus. By July 1864, almost 32,000 Union troops were crowded into the prison stockade. Poor shelter, nonexistent sanitary conditions, food shortages, lack of medicine, and poorly trained militia guards (old men and boys) made conditions at the prison intolerable. A stream that flowed through the prison was used for drinking, cooking, and sanitation. A "dead line" ran near the stockade walls, and prisoners crossing it were shot by guards stationed on catwalks. Union prisoners called raiders robbed other prisoners with impunity. By the end of the war, Union dead at Andersonville numbered almost 13,000.

The publicity about the prison made a lasting impression upon America. Wirz was arrested in May 1865 and brought to Washington. He was tried in the Court of Claims Chamber in the U.S. Capitol and found guilty of both impairing the health of prisoners and destroying their lives. He was offered a reprieve in exchange for implicating former Confederate President Jefferson Davis, but he responded, "Davis had no connection with me as to what was done at Andersonville." Wirz was hanged at the Old Capitol Prison on November 10, 1865.

Former Andersonville prisoners were in the crowd at the execution chanting, "Remember Andersonville." Wirz

told the officer who was directing his hanging, "I know what orders are, Major, I am being hung for obeying them." When the trapdoor was sprung, Wirz fell through the floor, and the rope broke. He was promptly walked up the steps of the scaffold again, waited for another rope, and was executed.

Debate today questions whether or not Wirz was physically capable of personally committing atrocities against the prisoners. Questionable Union witnesses testified that they had personally seen Captain Wirz shoot men. They had seen him knock sick and crippled men down and stamp upon them. Witnesses swore that they saw Wirz knock prisoners down with his hands, even though he had received a wound to his right arm during the Battle of Seven Pines that made his right arm useless. Dr. C. M. Ford, acting assistant surgeon in charge of the hospital at the Old Capitol Prison, testified at Wirz's trial that when he examined Wirz, his right arm was swollen and inflamed, ulcerated in three places, and portions of both bones in the arm were dead. He added, "I don't know how much strength he has in the arm, but I should think him incapable of knocking a man down, or lifting a very heavy instrument of any kind, without doing great injury to the arm."

Oak Hill Cemetery

Directions—From M Street in Georgetown: Drive north on Wisconsin Avenue to R Street. Make a right turn on R Street and go on to 30th Street. Cemetery is on the left. If you are traveling south on Wisconsin Avenue, make a left turn onto R Street.

William Corcoran, a banker and founder of the Riggs National Bank, purchased 15 acres along Rock Creek in 1848 from George Corbin Washington, grandnephew of George Washington. This land was contributed to the Cemetery Company, incorporated in 1849. This "natural garden" cemetery is situated on four terraced plateaus accessible by steps cut into the ground. James Renwick, architect of the Smithsonian Castle building and the original Corcoran Gallery of Art (now the Renwick Gallery), designed the Gothic chapel.

Oak Hill was a neighborhood cemetery, and many of the deceased were intimately involved in Georgetown life. It was not used as a military cemetery by the government, but many prominent officers were privately buried here.

Henry Addison — Lot 18

Addison was mayor of Georgetown from 1845 until 1857 and again from 1861 until 1867. He lived at 3331 N Street and had a hardware business at M and 30th Streets. Prior to the war, Addison complained to the Senate Committee on the District of Columbia about how the Long Bridge obstructed Georgetown commerce. After the war, several prominent Georgetowners applied to Mayor Addison for endorsements of good character when they sought a pardon and restoration of citizenship.

Dr. Joseph Barnes — Lot 628

Barnes was the surgeon general of the Union army and was called to Secretary of State William Seward's house on the night of April 14, after Lewis Powell attacked the secretary and severely injured him. Upon learning that Lincoln had been shot, he hurried to the White House, thinking the president would be there. Barnes spent the night with the president and other doctors at the Petersen House and examined his wound with a metal probe. As death approached, he kept his fingers over Lincoln's carotid artery, seeking to detect a pulse. He was the doctor who pronounced Lincoln dead.

William Thomas Carroll — Vault 292

Carroll was the clerk of the U.S. Supreme Court. When Lincoln's son Willie died of a fever in 1862, he was dressed in a soldier's uniform, laid in a coffin, and placed in Carroll's vault. President Lincoln returned to the vault alone several times and lifted the coffin lid to view his son. After Lincoln's assassination, Willie's remains were taken from the vault and carried on the Lincoln funeral train to be buried with his father in Springfield, Illinois.

William W. Corcoran — Lots 1-15 (Corcoran Vault)

Corcoran started his business career as a dry goods merchant in a store on the northwest corner of N Street and Wisconsin Avenue. He was a Southern sympathizer who spent the war in Europe, and his mansion on H Street was seized by the government for use as a military hospital but was never used as such. The Corcoran Gallery of Art was used as an army clothing depot during the war. Harewood Hospital was erected on Corcoran's farm near the Soldiers' Home.

George Eustis — Lots 1-15 (Corcoran Vault)

Eustis was a member of the House of Representatives from Louisiana and was the son-in-law of William W. Corcoran. Eustis was involved in the Trent Affair in November 1861. The Confederate government had selected James Murray Mason of Virginia as its commissioner to Great Britain and John Slidell of Louisiana as commissioner to France. Eustis was the private secretary to Slidell. At the Spanish port of Havana, Cuba, the commissioners booked passage on a British merchant ship, a mail packet named the *Trent.*

The day after leaving port, the ship was stopped by a warship of the United States, the USS *San Jacinto,* commanded by Capt. Charles Wilkes. The commissioners and their secretaries, Eustis and James E. MacFarland, were arrested, removed from the British ship, and placed in confinement in Fort Warren, Boston Harbor. Britain made a formal complaint that a U.S. officer had not only stopped and searched a neutral ship (which was legal but offensive) but also seized passengers claiming diplomatic status—which was quite another matter. Britain sent more warships to her North Atlantic squadron and planned to send troops to Canada, but remarked that perhaps Wilkes had acted on his own. The State Department agreed that he had and apologized. The commissioners and their private secretaries were released, and the United States and Great Britain resolved a major diplomatic crisis.

Eustis, his wife, and their three children moved to France. After he died, Eustis's remains were brought back to the United States and buried in Oak Hill Cemetery.

Joseph Henry — Henry Crescent

Henry was the first secretary of the Smithsonian Institution, established in 1849. He was noted for his work in elec-

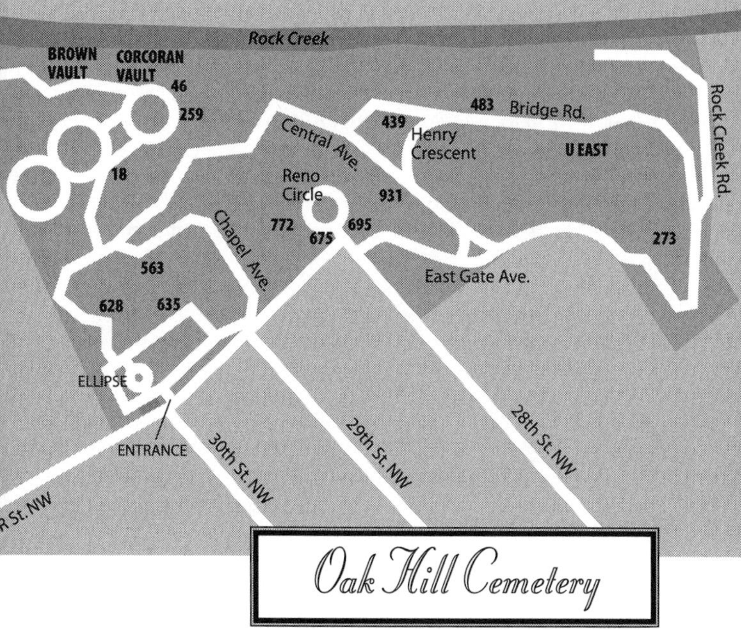

tricity and magnetism. Because of Henry, scientific research was a basic function of the Smithsonian for the 31 years he served as secretary. There was no money to pay scientists and scholars a salary, but they were offered laboratory space and a bed in the tower if they brought their own linens.

Professor Thaddeus S. C. Lowe, a 29-year-old aeronaut, was attracted by Henry's emphasis on scientific research and made several balloon ascents from the grounds near the Smithsonian. Professor Lowe was able to see scattered army camps in neighboring Virginia. Impressed with Lowe's exploits, President Lincoln made him chief of army aeronautics in August 1861, with the rank and pay of a colonel.

Henry also allowed the lecture halls of the Smithsonian to be used by abolitionists Henry Ward Beecher, Horace Greeley, and Wendell Phillips to lecture on the evils of slavery. Henry was criticized by the Washington press, and he said that the Smithsonian was not responsible for the statements made by guest lecturers.

Mary Cogswell Kinney — Lot 931

After President Lincoln was shot and his body taken to the Petersen House, Robert Lincoln, his oldest son, asked that the wife of Senator James Dixon of Connecticut be brought to comfort his mother. The carriage brought Mrs. Dixon to the Petersen House; then it was sent for Mrs. Dixon's sister, Mary Kinney, and her daughter, Constance, who also came to be with Mrs. Lincoln the rest of the night.

William D. Longstreet — Lot 46

William, the 14-month-old son of Maj. Gen. James Longstreet, USA, died in 1854. His father was a West Point graduate promoted for heroism in the Mexican War, a lifelong friend of Ulysses S. Grant, and a future Confederate general. Of James Longstreet's ten children, only five lived to be adults. His daughter, Louise (her married name was Whelchel), died in Liverpool, England, in 1957 and is buried in the Montrose Section, Site 9.

Richard T. Merrick — Lot 635

Richard Merrick was the son of Senator William D. Merrick of Maryland. As an assistant to attorney Joseph H. Bradley, he helped defend John Surratt, an alleged conspirator in the Lincoln assassination. Surratt escaped to Canada when suspects were being arrested. He traveled to Rome, where he joined the Papal Zouaves, but was recognized. He escaped to Egypt but was captured there and was returned to stand trial in 1867. A hung jury set Surratt free. Merrick was described as "the best-dressed man at the bar—not that he is foppish, but that he likes to make a good appearance and isn't above wearing a handsome necktie. Smooth, suave, open-handed, with bright black eyes that meet you frankly—the man makes you see Dick Merrick every time you look his way."

Myrtilla Miner — Lot 439 East

Miss Miner was a young white woman from New York who opened a school for training free black girls in 1851. She was supported by the Society of Friends (Quakers),

Harriet Beecher Stowe, Henry Ward Beecher, and Johns Hopkins. The school was located on New Hampshire Avenue south of Dupont Circle. Many white Washingtonians were afraid that her students would be too well educated and that Washington would become a center for the education of persons of African descent. The present-day University of the District of Columbia can trace its roots to Miss Miner's school.

John B. Montgomery — Lot 772

Montgomery was the commanding officer of the Washington Navy Yard when the remains of John Wilkes Booth were brought in. He also took charge of the suspected conspirators as they were individually arrested and imprisoned on the USS *Saugus.* Montgomery was taken aback and complained to Secretary of the Navy Gideon Welles that Secretary of War Stanton had no authority to give him orders to prevent visitors from coming aboard the ironclads. Montgomery also complained about the removal of Booth's body in an informal and unmilitary manner when a tugboat came alongside the USS *Montauk* at 1:30 a.m. on April 27, and the body was removed.

John George Nicolay — Lot 273 East

Nicolay was one of President Lincoln's private secretaries, John Hay being the other. In later years, with Hay, he wrote a ten-volume biography of Lincoln. Nicolay screened many of the president's visitors, sorted mail, prepared a daily news summary, and wrote letters for Lincoln. He referred to Lincoln with respect and affection as the "Tycoon." In March 1865, he was appointed consul to Paris. Nicolay was on a cruise when Lincoln was assassinated, and he returned to Washington to put the presidential papers in order.

William Pinckney — Ellipse

Pinckney was the rector of the Episcopal Church of the Ascension that stood at the corner of Massachusetts Avenue and 12th Street. He defied the bishop of Maryland's order for prayers for Union victories. Pinckney was also a close friend of William Corcoran and sought to have Corcoran become a communicant of the church. In the 1870s, he became the bishop of Maryland.

Jesse Lee Reno — Lot 686 (Reno Circle)

Reno's name was changed from Renault. He graduated from West Point in 1846, a member of a class that included George B. McClellan, Thomas J. (Stonewall) Jackson, and George Pickett. A captain in the Army's Ordnance Office when the war broke out, he was commissioned a brigadier general of U.S. volunteers. He was commanding a corps in the Army of the Potomac when he was killed on September 14, 1862, while advancing up the slopes of Fox's Gap during the Battle of South Mountain.

Prior to the battle, while General Reno was in Frederick, Maryland, he met Barbara Fritchie. She told him that she waved a U.S. flag at Maj. Gen. Stonewall Jackson as he passed through the city. Miss Fritchie gave General Reno this flag, and it was used to cover his casket at his funeral at Trinity Church in Boston. On April 9, 1867, Reno's remains were removed to Oak Hill.

Edwin McMasters Stanton — Lot 675

As President Lincoln's second secretary of war, Stanton was described as stern, pragmatic, and all business, a man of enormous energy, somber moods, and ferocious temper. He did not believe that the war would last long and closed all of the government recruiting offices in the spring of 1862. He was one of the first members of Lincoln's Cabinet to advocate the use of black troops. His support of the use of blacks was as much a matter of practicality as morality: he believed that diseases such as yellow fever did not affect persons of African descent the way they affected whites.

Secretary Stanton also restricted the freedom of the press, claiming the press gave too much information to the South. All telegraphic messages had to pass through the War Department. On one occasion a dispatch from a general named Rufus Ingalls to Senator Nesmith puzzled everyone at the War Department. Many thought the dispatch was sent in Bohemian (Czech), but an officer who had served on the Pacific Coast recognized it as Chinook, a compound of English, Chinese, and Indian languages used by the whites while trading with the Chinook Indians. The dispatch was a harmless request, but Stanton was always alert to rumors of a plot to kill or kidnap Lincoln.

Stanton believed that Lincoln's assassination was the result of a Confederate plot. He took over after Lincoln was shot, set up headquarters in the back parlor of the Petersen House, and began issuing orders for various government officials, military men, and police to be prepared for all emergencies. Messages concerning Lincoln's condition, as dictated to Assistant Secretary of War Charles A. Dana, went to Maj. Gen. John A. Dix for distribution to the press throughout the country. Stanton was given credit for the famous statement at Lincoln's deathbed: "Now he belongs to the ages," or "Now he belongs to the angels," as he stood with tears running down his cheeks after Lincoln died.

Since Stanton did not want to exploit the assassination as a symbol for the South, he forbade photographs of Lincoln lying in state, closed Ford's Theatre, and had John Wilkes Booth buried in secrecy. He also advocated a military commission to try the conspirators to ensure that they did not escape punishment. Stanton has been accused by many historians of allowing questionable legal methods during the trial. He has also been charged with sending Mary Surratt to her death, even though her guilt was not proven beyond all doubt. It has even been argued that he was part of the conspiracy, but no solid evidence has ever been produced to support this idea. As evidence to the contrary, John Hay, Lincoln's private secretary, wrote to Stanton after the war: "Not everyone knows, as I do, how close you stood to our leader, how he loved you and trusted you, and how vain were all the efforts to shake that trust and confidence, not lightly given and never withdrawn. All this will be known some time, of course, to his honor and yours."

Upon Ulysses S. Grant's election to the presidency, Stanton was offered a seat on the U.S. Supreme Court. He died on December 24, 1869, four days after the Senate confirmed his nomination. Rumor had it that he committed suicide out of remorse over the execution of Mary Surratt.

Joseph Pannell Taylor — Lot 563

Taylor was the youngest brother of President Zachary Taylor. His age kept him from field duty during the war, but he served as commissary general of subsistence. He was the first in that office to hold the rank of brigadier general under an Act of Congress in February 1863. He died in 1864 after a half-century of service. His nephew Richard Taylor became a lieutenant general in the Confederate service, and his niece Sarah Knox Taylor had been the first wife of Jefferson Davis.

Lorenzo Thomas — Lot 259

In August 1861, Thomas became adjutant general. Never in favor with Secretary of War Stanton, he was sent west in 1863 to begin the organization of black regiments in the military district of Mississippi. He carried out this assignment so well that Lincoln praised him highly. At the end of the war, he was promoted to brevet major general; he retired in 1869. After the war, Thomas was involved in the controversy between Stanton and President Andrew Johnson. The president attempted to appoint Thomas as acting secretary of war and tried to remove Stanton, who refused to resign.

Henry Ulke — Lot 483

Henry and his brother Julius were boarders at the Petersen House the night that John Wilkes Booth assassinated President Lincoln. Henry was a talented painter, and Julius was a portrait photographer. They owned a photographic studio on Pennsylvania Avenue and 12th Street. Both brothers spent the night carrying hot water from the kitchen to the back room where Lincoln lay dying. After Lincoln died and all of the people left, Julius brought out his camera to photograph the room and bed where Lincoln had died just minutes earlier.

Many painters have attempted to paint the scene in the small bedroom at the time of Lincoln's death. The number of witnesses has ranged from 11 to 47 people. Henry and Julius certified that when *Frank Leslie's Illustrated Newspaper* published an engraving of the scene at the deathbed, it showed the correct number of people present. That engraving, however, portrayed several people who were not actually present, including Lincoln's oldest son Robert.

Richard Wallach — Vault 278 (Brown Vault)

After Mayor Berret's removal from office for refusing to take the loyalty oath, the Washington Board of Aldermen elected Wallach, the board president, as mayor. He was a lawyer by profession, and his brother owned and edited the *Evening Star.* He was elected by popular vote in June 1862 and served until 1868. Wallach was opposed to President Lincoln signing the act prohibiting slavery in the District. The night Lincoln was shot, Wallach was standing on the sidewalk outside Ford's Theatre. At the suggestion of Clay Ford, one of the Ford brothers, he was summoned back inside to help clear the crowded theater.

Joseph Willard — Lot U East

Joseph joined in business with his brother Henry, who bought the Fuller's City Hotel on Pennsylvania Avenue and 14th Street in 1847 from Benjamin Ogle Tayloe. It soon became the most fashionable hotel in Washington; many politicians and diplomats were guests there. At the beginning of the war, Joseph retired from the hotel business and joined the Union army. He was commissioned a captain, promoted to major, and then served on the staff of Brig. Gen. Irvin McDowell. Willard fell in love with Antonia Ford, who was a Confederate spy supplying information about Union troops in northern Virginia. Miss Ford was arrested in March 1863 and imprisoned in the Old Capitol Prison. She was released seven months later after taking the oath of allegiance to the United States. Willard married her on April 10, 1864, and they had only one child, Joseph E. Willard, who survived to adulthood.

Andrew Wylie — Lot 695

Wylie was one of the judges of the Supreme Court of the District of Columbia. Mary Surratt's attorneys, F. A. Aiken and John W. Clampitt, made application to him for a writ of habeas corpus on behalf of Mrs. Surratt. The writ was served on Maj. Gen. Winfield Scott Hancock, who commanded the Middle Department, or local military sector. Hancock refused to turn over the prisoner because President Andrew Johnson declared that the writ of habeas corpus was suspended in her case. Judge Wylie and the court ruled that it yielded to the suspension by the president. This action terminated all appellate proceedings in her case. The only recourse left was a direct appeal to President Johnson. General Hancock told Mrs. Surratt's daughter, Anna, that the only way to free her mother was to "go to the president, throw yourself upon your knees before him, and beg for the life of your mother." Johnson refused to see Anna Surratt. In 1867, while selecting the jury for the trial of John Surratt, Judge Wylie sat in for Judge George Fisher, who had been taken ill.

Rock Creek Cemetery

Directions—Drive north on North Capitol Street past the Soldiers' and Airmen's Home. Once past the Soldiers' Home, make a left turn on Harewood Road. On the right is Soldiers' Home National Cemetery. Drive past the entrance to Rock Creek Church Road. Make a left turn. The entrance to Rock Creek Cemetery is on the right.

Rock Creek Cemetery is the oldest burial ground in Washington. Burials began in 1719 on its grounds, now 85 acres. Approximately a hundred acres were given by Col. John Bradford to the Chapel of Ease for the establishment of a glebe. Within a year of the donation, the chapel was expanded into St. Paul's Church. A writer in 1816 described Rock Creek as "being in the bosom of the woods." Many local Washingtonians are buried here. Most military funerals were conducted next door at the Soldiers' Home National Cemetery. Among those interred here are members of the military with distinguished careers, civilians who contributed to Civil War society in Washington, and officials of President Lincoln's administration.

Henry Adams — Section E

Adams was the grandson of President John Quincy Adams and great-grandson of President John Adams. He spent seven years in London as private secretary to his father, Charles Francis Adams, who was minister to England during the Civil War. Adams became a distinguished historian and man of letters. His autobiography and his novel *Democracy* provide a searching account of Washington as it emerged from the war.

John Hay was a close friend of Adams, and in the 1880s they both built mansions at 16th and H Streets across from St. John's Church. Adams's home became famous as one of the social centers of the city. The site is currently occupied by the Hay Adams Hotel. When his wife Marion (better known as Clover) committed suicide in 1885, Adams commissioned a monument by Augustus St. Gaudens, simply known today as "Grief," which stands over Marion's grave.

Frank Crawford Armstrong — Section L

Armstrong was a commissioned officer who fought for the Union army at the Battle of First Manassas. After the battle, however, he resigned his commission and joined the Confederate army. Armstrong served on the staff of Brig. Gen. Benjamin McCulloch and was a few feet away from McCulloch when the general was killed at Pea Ridge. Armstrong was promoted to brigadier general in January 1863. He served as a cavalry commander under Confederate generals Sterling Price, Nathan Bedford Forrest, Joseph Wheeler, and Stephen D. Lee.

Montgomery Blair — Section A

Blair was one of the lawyers who represented Dred Scott

in the slave's fight for freedom. During President Lincoln's first administration, he served as postmaster general but resigned the position in 1864. He was a moderate who was not trusted by the Radical Republicans, and in order to gather the support of this faction, Lincoln asked Blair to resign.

His father was Francis Preston Blair, a leader in the founding of the Republican Party. Both father and son had country homes in Maryland at Silver Spring (in what is now Montgomery Blair Park). During Jubal Early's raid in July 1864, Rebel troops despoiled the father's house, stole clothes and liquor, and burned the son's home, but spared crops worth $6,000.

Robert Christie Buchanan — Section A

Buchanan was a nephew by marriage of President John Quincy Adams. At the beginning of the war, he served in the defenses of Washington. He commanded a brigade of Regular Army infantry during the Seven Days' Battles (at Gaines Mill and Malvern Hill), at Second Manassas, and at Antietam. He was breveted major general for his service at Fredericksburg. Relieved from active duty, Buchanan was detailed to assist in raising troops in New Jersey. He was promoted to colonel in the Regular Army in 1864, and was known to his troops as "Old Buck."

William Henry French — Section B

When the secession movement took shape, French was commanding an army garrison in Texas. In March 1861, a brevet major, he was at Fort Taylor in Key West, Florida, ready to defend it. In the Gettysburg campaign, French replaced the wounded Daniel Sickles as commander of the 3rd Corps. He was sent to destroy Gen. Robert E. Lee's pontoon bridges on the Potomac River but chose not to follow too closely, thus allowing Lee to make his escape back to Virginia. He also saw action on the Peninsula, South Mountain, and took part in the futile assaults against the Confederates on Marye's Heights at Fredericksburg. French was commissioned a major general of volunteers in

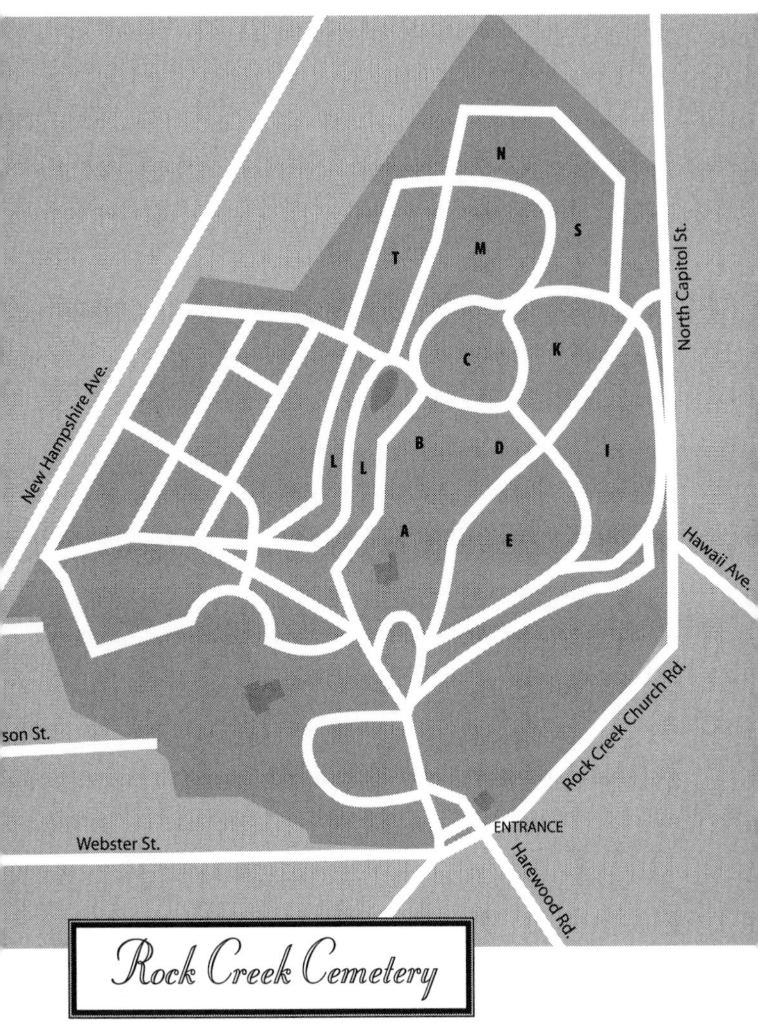

November 1862. When the army was reorganized in 1864, his corps was dissolved, and he never again saw field service.

Hugh McCulloch — Section B

As the president of the National Bank of Indiana, McCulloch traveled to Washington in 1862 to lobby against a national bank bill. He was offered the position of comptroller of the currency by Secretary of the Treasury Salmon P. Chase the following year. In 1865, he was appointed President Lincoln's third secretary of the Treasury, replacing William

Fessenden (who had replaced Chase). He also served as secretary of the Treasury under President Chester Arthur from 1884 to 1885.

Crosby Noyes — Section B

Noyes was the editor-in-chief of the *Evening Star* for almost 50 years. At President Lincoln's first inauguration, Noyes was given the complete text of the original inaugural address. It was taken to the *Star* office, cut into "takes" for handsetting compositors, and published in the *Star* on the day Lincoln delivered it. During the war Noyes, as a reporter and as a member of the Washington City Council, sought to have the federal government assume one half of the debt and expenses of the District of Columbia in the reclamation of the swampy area known as the Potomac Flats.

George Riggs — Section D

Riggs opened a successful commission house in partnership with William W. Corcoran, and together they made a fortune by marketing bonds to finance the Mexican War. They began Corcoran & Riggs in a small shop on Pennsylvania Avenue near 15th Street. In 1845, the business bought the United States Bank on the corner of 15th Street and New York Avenue, and the name was changed to Riggs National Bank. Riggs's summer home on North Capitol Street became the Anderson Cottage on the grounds of the Soldiers' Home, where Lincoln wrote the draft of the Emancipation Proclamation. President Lincoln had an account at the Riggs National Bank.

James Alexander Williamson — Section E

As a fearless volunteer officer, Williamson rose from first lieutenant to brevet major general, even though he had no previous military experience. He fought in Arkansas at Pea Ridge (also called Elkhorn Tavern), and directed the advance of his regiment at Chickasaw Bluffs in Mississippi. For his courage under fire, he was awarded the Medal of Honor, and his regiment was authorized by General Grant to inscribe "First at Chickasaw Bayou" on its regimental flag. Williamson also was a brigade commander at Chattanooga, in the Atlanta campaign, and in Sherman's march to the sea. He was breveted major general of volunteers in 1865.

Scottish Rite Temple

Directions—2800 16th Street NW (16th and S Streets).

This temple is the District of Columbia's Jurisdiction of the Ancient and Accepted Scottish Rite of Freemasonry. The cornerstone was laid in 1939 and dedicated with Masonic ceremonies on May 12, 1940. Steps leading to the entrance are in groups of three, five, seven, and nine. Around the Great Portal are 33 square stones, one for each degree in Scottish Rite Masonry. Within the Great Hall on the stage arch are the 29 jewels of Scottish Rite Masonry.

Freemasonry, which claims origins in antiquity, is a fraternal society that teaches brotherhood, justice, and freedom of religion and expression. It has secret passwords and handshakes. George Washington, Benjamin Franklin, and Paul Revere were Masons.

Albert Pike — Main hallway behind bust

Pike, a large man weighing more than 300 pounds, spent his early career as a lawyer, publisher, and poet. Even though he was originally from Boston, Pike had considerable holdings in Arkansas. As a frontier lawyer, he helped the Creek Indian Nation collect almost $800,000 from the U.S. government. Even though he was opposed to secession, Pike went with the South because he had so much invested in Arkansas. He was made Confederate commissioner to the Indian Territory, and in August 1861, was commissioned a brigadier general. He began training Indians, and his force was part of Maj. Gen. Earl Van Dorn's army in the Battle of Pea Ridge. The Indians initially attacked a federal artillery battery. After overrunning the position, they stopped to celebrate and were repulsed in a federal counterattack. The Federal troops claimed that Pike's Indians had scalped many dead and wounded soldiers. Pike resigned his commission on November 11, 1862.

After the war, Pike moved to Washington, where he studied Freemasonry. When Pike died in 1891, his will stipulated that he be cremated and his ashes sprinkled around roots of trees that stood in front of Washington Temple of the Supreme Council of Freemasonry. The council had other ideas, and he was buried in Oak Hill Cemetery. In 1944, Pike's remains were reinterred in a crypt in the new Scottish Rite Temple.

Soldiers' Home National Cemetery

Directions—Drive north on North Capitol Street past the Soldiers' and Airmen's Home. Once past the Soldiers' Home, make a left turn on Harewood Road. On the right is Soldiers' Home National Cemetery.

The commissioners of the Soldiers' Home offered the U.S. government six acres of land on the premises for use as a cemetery. Adjutant General Lorenzo Thomas accepted the land. The first burials here came from the hospitals and churches caring for the wounded of the Battle of First Manassas. In 1864, space ran out and this shortage necessitated the creation of a new national cemetery across the Potomac River on the grounds of Robert E. Lee's former estate, Arlington.

From 1861 to 1864, more than 5,000 burials were made in the Soldiers' Home National Cemetery. The majority of the interments were of common soldiers, privates, cooks, storekeepers, and ambulance drivers. Approximately 128 Confederate prisoners of war were also buried here. (In 1900 these Confederate dead were exhumed and reinterred in Arlington National Cemetery.) Buried in the cemetery are the remains of 292 unknowns from the Civil War.

In 1867, Congress authorized the secretary of war to appoint national cemetery superintendents and to provide lodges for their housing. The superintendent at Soldiers' Home National Cemetery was Patrick Callaghan, a discharged first lieutenant of the Veteran Reserve Corps.

Originally, burials were restricted to those soldiers

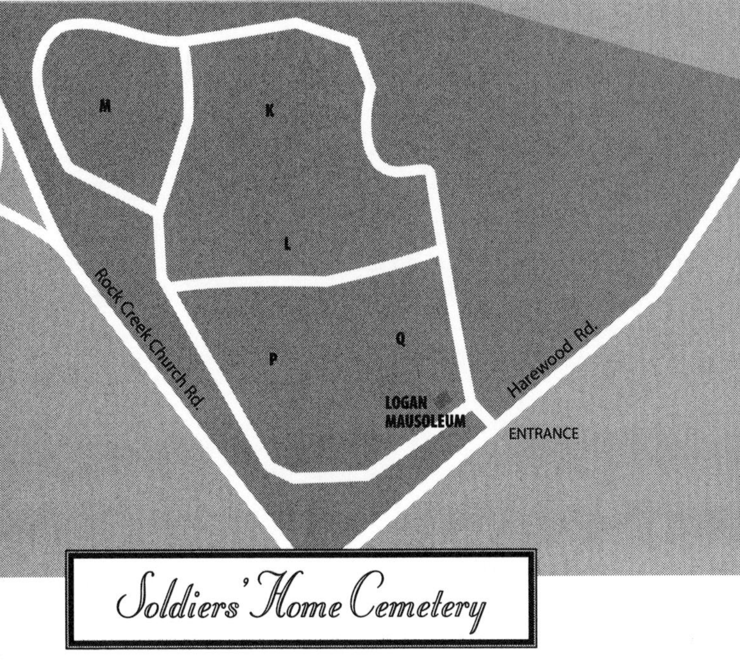

Soldiers' Home Cemetery

killed in battle or who died of wounds or sickness in hospitals during the war. In 1873, an Act of Congress allowed all honorably discharged veterans of the Civil War to be buried in national cemeteries.

The original headstones were made of wood, but in 1873, stone headstones and markers replaced them. In 1883, nine acres were added to the cemetery to give it its present size of fifteen acres.

Benjamin William Brice — Section Q

Brice was a lawyer, judge, and militia officer in Ohio. During the Mexican War, he served as a major in the pay department. During the Civil War, on November 29, 1864, Brice was promoted to colonel and appointed paymaster general. He held that post for the rest of the war and was breveted major general in the Regular Army.

John Alexander Logan — Logan Mausoleum

Logan was a "political general" from Illinois. His brother-in-law enlisted in the Confederacy, and as a state legislator in Illinois, Logan was best known for sponsoring harsh laws barring free blacks from the state. He also defended the Fugitive Slave Act, which required that runaway slaves be returned to their masters. He was elected to the House of Representatives in 1860, and as a congressman, he followed the Union forces on the field at First Manassas. He joined a Michigan regiment and actually fired at the Confederates. Logan soon resigned his congressional seat and raised a regiment of his own, the 31st Illinois. He rose from colonel to brigadier, and was promoted to major general in 1862.

Logan saw action at Belmont, Fort Donelson, and in the Atlanta campaign. When Maj. Gen. James McPherson was killed in July 1864, Logan assumed command of the Army of the Tennessee. General Sherman did not trust Logan's performance as a soldier/politician and replaced him with West Pointer Oliver O. Howard. Logan was, however, given the honor of commanding the Army of the Tennessee in the Grand Review in Washington in May 1865. But, in part because of Sherman's slight, Logan developed a resentment against professional soldiers that lasted the rest of his life.

He was again elected to Congress and served on the committee that voted the articles of impeachment against President Andrew Johnson. He was one of the leaders in the Grand Army of the Republic, a veterans' organization. As commander in chief of that organization, he issued his famous General Order No. 11, on May 5, 1868; it established that the Grand Army of the Republic should begin a practice of putting flowers on the graves of Union soldiers on May 30. The first such observance was in 1869. At Arlington National Cemetery, a wind blew the flowers onto the graves of Confederates. From then on, all graves, both Union and Confederate, were marked with flowers. This practice led to Congressional establishment of May 30 as a day to memorialize the nation's dead. In 1884, Logan ran for vice president on the Republican ticket with James G. Blaine.

Appendices

CIVIL WAR SCULPTURE IN WASHINGTON, D.C.

Henry and Marian Adams—Rock Creek Cemetery

William Worth Belknap—Arlington National Cemetery

James Buchanan—Meridian Hill Park (16th Street and Florida Avenue NW)

Confederate Memorial—Arlington National Cemetery

Rear Adm. Samuel F. Dupont—Dupont Circle (Massachusetts and Connecticut Avenues NW)

Emancipation Monument—Lincoln Park (East Capitol and 11th Streets NE)

John Ericksson—West Potomac Park (Ohio Drive and Independence Avenue SW)

Adm. David G. Farragut—Farragut Square (K Street between 16th and 17th Streets NW)

James Abram Garfield—1st Street and Maryland Avenue SW

Grand Army of the Republic—7th and C Streets NW

Lt. Gen. Ulysses S. Grant—Union Square (east end of Mall)

Maj. Gen. Winfield Scott Hancock—Pennsylvania Avenue and 7th Street NW

Joseph Henry—Smithsonian Institution Building (1000 Jefferson Dr. SW)

Maj. Gen. Philip Kearny—Arlington National Cemetery

Abraham Lincoln—Department of the Interior courtyard (C Street between 18th and 19th Streets NW)

Abraham Lincoln—Lincoln Memorial

Abraham Lincoln—National Cathedral

Abraham Lincoln—Old City Hall (D Street between 4th and 5th Streets NW)

Maj. Gen. John A. Logan—Logan Circle (Vermont Avenue and 13th and P Streets NW)

Maj. Gen. George B. McClellan—Connecticut Avenue and Columbia Road NW

Brig. Gen. James B. McPherson—McPherson Square (15th Street between I and K Streets NW)

Maj. John Rodgers Meigs—Arlington National Cemetery

Navy Yard Urns—Lafayette Park, center (Pennsylvania Avenue between Jackson and Madison Places NW)

Peace Monument—Pennsylvania Avenue and 1st Street NW

Pension Building—G and F Streets, between 4th and 5th Streets NW

Brig. Gen. Alfred Pike—3rd and D Streets NW

Maj. Gen. John Rawlins—Rawlins Park (18th and E Streets NW)

Lt. Gen. Winfield Scott—Scott Circle (Massachusetts and Rhode Island Avenues and 16th Street NW)

Maj. Gen. Philip Sheridan—Sheridan Circle (23rd Street and Massachusetts Avenue NW)

Maj. Gen. William T. Sherman—15th Street, Treasury Place, and Pennsylvania Avenue NW

Maj. Gen. George H. Thomas—Thomas Circle (14th Street and Massachusetts Avenue NW)

WASHINGTON STREET DIRECTORY

This street directory has been adapted from *Boyd's 1860 Directory of Washington and Georgetown.* It represents the street layout of the city as it appeared in 1860. Its purpose is to show the exact location of all numbered buildings in Washington and Georgetown during the Civil War.

There were 1,170 blocks or squares bounded by 21 avenues and more than 100 streets. The Capitol was the division of the alphabetical and numerical streets. Alphabetical streets having North affixed to them were on the north side of the city running in an east-west direction. Alphabetical streets having South affixed to them were on the south side of the city, also running in an east-west direction.

The numerical streets ran north-south and were divided into East and West by Capitol Street. Thus, the city was divided into quadrants North, South, East, and West, each marked with a geographical direction.

With this guide, you can pinpoint the exact location of a Civil War-era building if you know its original address. For example, to use the guide to find the location of a building on H Street (page 192): the guide tells you that H Street ran in an east-west direction in the northern section of the city from 27th Street to Boundary Street. So an address such as 130 H Street North was on the left-hand side of the street near 23rd Street West. 91 H Street was on the right-hand side near 23rd Street. There were no numbered buildings between 130 and 200 H Street North. The directory indicates that the land was open between 23rd Street and 31st Street on the left-hand side of the street.

A North, from N. Capitol to Eastern Branch

Left.	*Rt.*	
2	—	Delaware Av.
40	41	1st E.
—	75	2d E.
—	—	3d E.

Further not numbered.

B, North, from 21st West to Eastern Branch.

Left.	*Rt.*	
272	—	6th W.
274	273	3d W.
296	295	2d W.
Creek, no Bridge.		
—	—	1st W.
—	—	New Jersey Av.
—	—	N. Capitol.
306	305	Delaware Av.
336	327	1st E.

Further not numbered.

C, North, from 22d West to Eastern Branch.

Left.	*Rt.*	
218	—	13 1/2 W.
232	—	13th W.
—	261	12th W.
—	275	11th W.
—	291	10th W.
—	307	9th W.
—	—	Louisiana Av.
—	—	Pennsylvania Av.
306	309	7th W.
—	337	6th W.
372	375	4 1/2 W.
—	409	3d W.
—	433	2d W.
—	—	1st W.
—	—	New Jersey Av.
476	—	N. Capitol.
498	497	Delaware Av.
528	—	1st E.
566	—	2d E.
594	—	3d E.
624	—	4th E.

Further not numb'd.

D, North, from 26th West to Boundary.

Left.	*Rt.*	
70	—	22d W.
—	—	21st W.
—	—	New York Av.
—	—	20th W.
—	—	19th W.
—	—	18th W.
—	—	17th W.
Re-opens at		
220	—	15th W.
218	—	14th W.
266	265	13 1/2 W.
286	285	13th W.
—	—	Penn. Av.
—	311	12th W.
310	327	11th W.
330	329	10th W.
372	361	9th W.
382	367	8th W.
392	375	7th W.
426	—	6th W.
—	—	La. Av.
432	—	5th W.
—	393	4 1/2 W.
—	—	Indiana Av.
434	—	4th W.
440	439	3d W.
474	473	2d W.
498	497	1st W.

E, North, from 26th West to Boundary.

Left.	*Rt.*	
168	—	21st W.
200	—	20th W.
226	—	19th W.
—	—	New York Av.
—	185	18th W.
—	231	17th W.
Re-opens at		
274	275	15th W.
294	—	14th W.
—	305	13 1/2 W.
—	321	13th W.
—	339	12th W.
366	357	11th W.
384	371	10th W.
412	415	9th W.
POD	419	8th W.
436	429	7th W.
478	459	6th W.
492	473	5th W.
496	475	4th W.
498	493	3d W.

F, North, from 26th West to Boundary.

Left.	*Rt.*	
—	1	27th W.
—	17	26th W.
40	39	25th W.
—	—	24th W.
—	—	23d W.
108	—	22d W.
128	127	21st W.
148	—	20th W.
162	—	19th W.
—	175	18th W.
—	207	17th W.
Navy Dept. President's house and Treasury Dept.		
208	207	15th W.
232	231	14th W.
272	279	13th W.
298	301	12th W.
316	315	11th W.
334	331	10th W.
—	369	9th W.
—	383	8th W.
		P.O.
400	401	7th W.
438	445	6th W.
450	—	5th W.
		Judiciary Sq.
—	—	4th W.
460	—	3d W.

G, North, from 26th West to Boundary.

Left.	*Rt.*	
82	—	23d W.
134	—	22d W.
148	147	21st W.
—	169	20th W.
192	193	19th W.
224	215	18th W.
250	245	17th W.
		President Sq.

252	251	15th W.
276	275	14th W.
306	309	13th W.
383	333	12th W.
356	349	11th W.
370	—	10th W.
414	—	9th W.
426	—	8th W.
		Pat't. Off.
442	397	7th W.
478	421	6th W.
482	443	5th W.
540	—	4th W.
556	555	3d W.
584	575	2d W.
—	599	New Jersey Av.
644	645	N. Capitol.
684	—	Delaware Av.

H, North, from 27th West to Boundary.

Left.	*Rt.*	
130	91	23d W.
—	109	22d W.
200	147	31st W.
224	173	20th W.
240	189	19th W.
		Pennsylvania Av.
274	221	18th W.
300	251	17th W.
310	239	16 1/2 W. } Lafayette Square
312	—	16th W. } Lafayette Square
332	—	15 1/2 W. } Lafayette Square
336	333	15th W.
356	365	14th W.
—	—	New York Av.
390	—	13th W.
416	415	12th W.
430	429	11th W.
446	—	10th W.
490	—	9th W.
498	—	8th W.
514	511	7th W.
550	547	6th W.
564	561	5th W.
630	621	4th W.
—	635	Mass. Av.
—	—	3d W.
—	—	2d W.
—	—	New Jersey Av.
—	—	1st W.
—	651	N. Capitol.
—	697	Iron Bridge.
—	713	1st E.

Further not numbered.

I, North, from 27th West to Boundary.

Left.	*Rt.*	
—	99	24th W.
—	115	23d W.
146	139	22d W.
178	169	21st W.
—	—	Pennsylvania Av.
206	203	20th W.
234	209	19th W.
258	247	18th W.
278	281	17th W.
—	—	Connecticut Av.
292	287	16th W.
320	219	15th W.
—	—	Vermont Av.
348	—	14th W.
—	—	Franklin Sq.
374	371	13th W.
400	—	12th W.
—	—	New York Av.
418	407	11th W.
424	427	10th W.
468	467	9th W.
482	—	8th W.
496	493	7th W.
526	531	6th W.
—	—	Mass. Av.
528	555	5th W.
604	605	4th W.
622	—	3d W.
652	—	2d W.
—	—	New Jersey Av.

K, North, from Rock Creek, Georgetown, to Boundary.

Left.	*Rt.*	
2	1	Bridge.
26	25	27th W.
40	49	26th W.
66	65	25th W.
84	83	24th W.
—	—	Circle.
—	—	Pennsylvania Av.
—	91	22d W.
128	121	21st W.
148	—	20th W.
168	167	19th W.
178	177	18th W.
—	189	Connecticut Av.
224	211	17th W.
254	235	16th W.
280	291	15th W.
292	—	Vermont Av.
300	—	14th W.
340	339	13th W.
358	365	12th W.
370	377	11th W.
—	381	10th W.
426	411	9th W.
—	—	Mass. Av.
—	—	N. Market Sp.
—	—	New York Av.
413	—	7th W.
456	451	6th W.
480	461	5th W.
532	531	4th W.
550	547	3d W.

L, North, from Rock Creek, Georgetown, to Boundary.

Left.	*Rt.*	
—	—	26th W.
—	—	Pennsylvania Av.
30	—	25th W.
—	—	24th W.
—	—	23d W.
—	—	22d W.
—	—	21st W.
186	185	20th W.
208	205	19th W.
252	247	18th W.
272	271	Connecticut Av.
—	—	17th W.
340	333	16th W.
366	373	15th W.
388	395	Vermont Av.
400	399	14th W.
442	447	13th W.
466	—	12th W.
—	—	11th W.
470	—	Mass. Av.
490	493	10th W.
532	531	9th W.
544	541	8th W.
556	553	7th W.
592	593	6th W.
—	—	New York Av.
614	—	5th W.
662	661	4th W.
674	675	3d W.
684	685	New Jersey Av.

L, North, from Rock Creek, Georgetown, to Boundary.

Left.	*Rt.*	
2	—	26th W.
—	—	25th W.
76	77	24th W.
—	101	23d W.
—	—	22d W.
—	—	21st W.
174	—	20th W.
204	195	19th W.
—	—	18th W.
—	—	Connecticut Av.
—	—	17th W.

Creek, not open.

354	327	16th W.
344	357	15th W.
—	—	14th W.
416	417	Mass. Av.
—	—	Vermont Av.
446	449	13th W.
476	479	12th W.
488	493	11th W.
508	—	10th W.
542	541	9th W.
564	—	8th W.
584	581	7th W.
614	613	6th W.
624	625	5th W.
686	685	4th W.
—	—	3d W.

N, North, from Rock Creek, Georgetown, to Boundary.

Left.	*Rt.*	
368	—	15th W.
410	—	14th W.
426	—	Vermont Av.
438	439	13th W.
462	405	12th W.
—	—	11th W.
488	485	10th W.
528	525	9th W.
—	—	8th W.
562	561	7th W.
604	605	6th W.
620	—	5th W.
672	—	4th W.
—	—	New Jersey Av.

O, North, from Rock Creek, Georgetown, to Boundary.

Left.	*Rt.*	
560	—	8th W.
—	537	7th W.
—	581	6th W.
—	603	5th W.
—	643	4th W.
—	—	3d W.

P, North, from Rock Creek, Georgetown, to Boundary.

Left.	*Rt.*	
6	—	22d W.
32	—	21st W.
478	—	6th W.
490	491	5th W.
—	—	4th W.

Q, North, from and to Boundary.

Left.	*Rt.*	
476	—	6th W.
494	—	5th W.

R to W North, are partially open and not numbered.

A, South, from New Jersey Av. to Eastern Branch.

Left.	*Rt.*	
—	1	New Jersey Av.
42	47	1st E.
80	81	2d E.
104	109	3d E.
128	—	4th E.
—	143	5th E.

B, South, from 14th W. to Eastern Branch.

Left.	*Rt.*	
—	1	14th W.
—	—	13 1/2 W.
—	123	13th W.
—	—	12th W.
—	135	11th W.
—	145	20th W.
—	191	9th W.
—	—	8th W.
—	215	7th W.
—	257	6th W.
Re-opens at		
208	—	2d W.
242	239	1st W.
—	—	S. Capitol.
Re-opens at		
208	265	New Jersey Av.
—	301	1st E.
350	351	2d E.
—	—	Pennsylvania Av.
381	—	3d E.
384	387	4th E.
—	—	5th W.

C, South, from the Potomac to 19th East.

Left.	*Rt.*	
58	—	14th W.
80	—	13 1/2 W.
106	—	13th W.
142	—	12th W.
150	—	11th W.
170	—	10th W.
—	—	Virginia av.
—	—	Maryland Av.
—	185	6th W.
274	277	4 1/2 W.
316	—	3d W.
332	331	2d W.
—	353	1st W.

Canal (no Bridge) from New Jersey Av. eastward. But partially open, and not numbered.

D, South, from the Potomac to 19th East.

Left.	*Rt.*	
56	55	14th W.
78	77	13 1/2 W.
94	95	13th W.
—	—	12th W.
—	—	Maryland Av.
—	97	11th W.
—	109	10th W.
—	149	9th W.
—	155	8th W.
180	167	7th W.
—	189	6th W.
—	—	Virginia Av.
210	211	4 1/2 W.
248	257	3 W.
208	267	2d W.
—	295	1st W.
Canal (no bridge)		
380	379	S. Capitol.
410	409	New Jersey Av. (not graded)
—	441	2d E.
450	451	3d E.
472	471	4th E.
—	493	5th E.
512	511	6th E.
—	—	7th E.
—	—	8th E.

further not open.

E, South, from the Potomac to 19th East.

Left.	*Rt.*	
54	53	12th W.
62	—	11th W.
—	63	10th W.
—	107	9th W.
—	123	8th W.
122	125	7th W.
148	—	6th W.
192	189	4 1/2 W.
—	241	3d W.
—	275	2d W.
—	—	Virginia Av.
258	—	1st W. Bridge.
Re-opens at		
—	—	2d E.
400	—	3d E.
432	—	4th E.
—	—	5th E.
—	—	S. Carolina Av.
458	457	6th E.
508	505	7th E.
—	—	8th E.
—	—	9th E.
—	551	10th E.
—	—	11th E.
572	571	12th E.
—	607	13th E.

F, South, from the Potomac to S. Capitol.

Left.	*Rt.*	
18	—	11th W.
34	31	10th W.
76	73	9th W.
94	93	8th W.
—	115	7th W.
144	141	6th W.
194	193	4 1/2 W.
238	243	3d W.
272	281	2d W.
304	—	1st W.
—	—	S. Capitol.

G, South, from the Potomac to Eastern Branch.

Left.	*Rt.*	
2	—	11th W.
24	—	10th W.
72	59	9th W.
90	87	8th W.
110	—	7th W.
148	147	6th W.
—	170	4 1/2 W.
202	201	3d W.
—	241	2d W.
Re-opens at		
—	—	3d E.
—	—	4th E.
—	—	5th E.
378	379	6th E.
422	421	7th E.
446	—	8th E.
464	—	9th E.
486	485	10th E.
—	505	11th E.
—	545	12th E.
—	581	13th E.
—	—	Pennsylvania Av.

H, South, from the Potomac to the Canal.

Left.	*Rt.*	
—	31	9th W.
70	61	8th W.
—	—	7th W.
112	—	6th W.
160	—	4 1/2 W.

I, South, from 9th West to 13th East.

Left.	*Rt.*	
—	—	8th W.
—	—	7th W.
—	71	6th W.
—	111	4 1/2 W.
—	—	1st E.
—	—	New Jersey Av.
392	—	2d E.
418	419	3d E.
446	449	4th E.
—	—	Virginia Av.
—	469	5th E.
450	—	6th E.
478	479	7th E.
502	—	8th E.
518	519	9th E.
536	—	10th E.
558	557	11th E.
582	—	12th E.
616	607	13th E.

K, South, from the Potomac to the Eastern Branch.

Left.	*Rt.*	
—	79	6th W.
—	117	4 1/2 W.
—	—	1st E.
—	—	New Jersey Av.
Canal (no bridge)		
340	—	3d E.
370	—	4th E.
400	—	5th E.
—	—	6th E.
442	441	East Market Sp.
—	—	7th E.
—	—	Virginia Av.
—	—	8th E.
466	—	9th E.
484	—	10th E.
506	—	11th E.
532	—	12th E.
—	—	13th E.
—	601	14th E.
—	—	15th E.
670	669	16th E.

L, South, from the Potomac to the Eastern Branch

Left.	*Rt.*	
—	55	6th W.
—	95	4 1/2 W.
—	—	3d W.
—	—	2d W.
Re-opens at		
—	—	New Jersey Av.
Canal (bridge)		
354	355	3d E.
384	383	4th E.
406	401	5th E.
—	—	6th E.
—	—	East Market Sp.
456	455	7th E.
472	471	8th E.
492	491	9th E.
—	—	Virginia Av.
—	—	Georgia Av.

M, South, from 7th West to 11th East.

Left.	*Rt.*	
—	—	7th W.
34	—	6th W.
—	61	Union al.
88	85	4 1/2 W.
—	119	3d W.
—	—	2d W.
Re–opens at		
—	—	South Capitol.
—	—	New Jersey Av.
—	—	2d E.
—	—	3d E.
—	—	4th E.
—	—	5th E.
—	—	6th E.
428	—	7th E.
—	—	8th E.
452	—	9th E.
470	471	10th E.
492	493	11th E.

N, South, from the Potomac to Georgia Av., and from 10th to 12th East—not numbered.

O, South, only one or two blocks open—not numbered.

P, South, only a few houses,—not numbered.

Q to W, South, are not yet opened.

Adams' Express Al., from H North, between 2d and 3d West.

Bates Al., from 462 G to H North, between 6th and 7th West.

Blagden's Al., from M North to N, between 9th and 10th West.

Boundary St., from Rock Creek, round the North side of the City. Partially open.

Brown's Al., rear of K North, South side, between 24th and 25th West.

Cabbage Al., (or Jackson St.) from N. Capitol to 1st East between G and H North.

Carolina Terrace, a row of houses beginning at 351 to 363 I North.

Carroll Pl., from E. Capitol St. to A South, East side of the Capitol.

Carroll St., from 1st to 2d East, between B and C South.

Chestnut, from 14th West, to 15th between P and Q North.

Christian Al., between F South and G and 1/2, and 1st West.

Circle, on Pennsylvania Av. K North and 23d West.

Connecticut Al., from Connecticut Av. to K and L North.

Connecticut Av., from boundary to President Sq.

Cook's Al., rear 351 L North.

Cox's Al., rear E North, between 6th and 7th West.

Crow Hill, between 7th and 4th West, and M and O North.

Delaware Av., from N North to T South.

Left.	*Rt.*	
—	137	I N.
—	167	H N.
not open.		
298	293	E N.
324	329	D N.
—	—	A N.

Douglas Sq., New Jersey Av. corner I North.

E. Capitol St., from 1st East to the Eastern Branch.

Left.	*Rt.*	
2	1	lst E.
48	43	2d E.
76	75	3d E.
104	95	4th E.
126	117	5th E.
140	—	6th E.
—	—	7th E.

Eastern Market space, from K to L South on 5th and 6th East.

Farnham's Row, M North, between 11th and 12th West.

Franklin Pl., between I and K North and 13th and 14th West.

Freeman's Alley, from 7th West, between N and O North.

Georgia Av., from 4 1/2 St. West to 19 East.

Goat Al., between L and M North on 6th West.

Hamilton Pl., on I North, between 11th & 12th West.

Indiana Av., from City Hall, D North, to 1st West.

Left.	*Rt.*	
—	1	D N.
—	—	4th W.
—	39	3d W.
68	—	2d W.
86	67	1st W.

Jackson Hall Al., from 389 C North to 464 Pennsylvania Av. between 3d & 4 1/2 West.

Jackson St., (or Cabbage Al.), from N. Capitol to 1st East between G & H North.

Kendall Green, a lane from M North & 7th East to Mr. Kendall's castle. Numbers from 1 and 2 to 9 and 10. Number 6 is the Deaf and Dumb, and Blind Asylum.

Kendall Green La., Jackson St. from 4 1/2 to 6th West, between D and E North.

Kentucky Av., is to be located on Capitol Hill, between E. Capitol St., & the Potomac.

Lafayette Sq., between 15 1/2 and 16 1/2 West, opposite President's mansion.

Louisiana Av., from the City Hall, D N. to the canal.

Left.	*Rt.*	
2	—	D N.
—	—	5th W.
42	35	6th W.
79	73	7th W.
—	—	Pa. Av.
70	77	9th W.
—	99	10th W.

Madison Al., from 329 1st to 2d West, between E and F North.

Madison St., (or Organ Al.), from 586 M to 595 N North.

Madison Pl., (or 15 1/2 and 16 1/2 West) on both sides of Lafayette Sq. from President's Sq. to H North.

Maine Av., from 6th to 3d West (Island).

Left.	*Rt.*	
—	1	6th W.
—	45	4 1/2 W.
—	75	3d W.

Marble Al., from 391 Pennsylvania Av. to 22 Missouri Av. and 47 4 1/2 West.

Market Space, from Pennsylvania Av. c. 9th to 7th West.

Left.	*Rt.*	
2	—	Pennsylvania Av.
30	—	8th W.
50	—	7th W.

Maryland Av., from N.E. Boundary to the Potomac.

Left. *Rt.*

140	—	11th E.
186	—	10th E.
—	—	9th E.
—	—	8th E.
—	—	7th E.
—	—	6th E.
—	—	5th E.
—	—	4th E.
342	341	3d E.
364	363	2d E.
—	—	1st E.
		Capitol.
—	—	1st W.
—	—	2d W.
—	—	3d W.
474	461	4 1/2 W.
526	529	6th W.
560	561	7th W.
—	565	Virginia Av.
—	585	10th W.
592	599	11th W.
608	—	12th W.
640	631	13th W.
—	651	13 1/2 W.
—	671	14th W.
		Potomac.

Mass. Av., from Boundary to 19th East.

Left.	*Rt.*	
—	—	15th W.
—	—	14th W.
330	327	13th W.
356	355	12th W.
368	357	11th W.
390	369	10th W.
416	409	9th W.
—	—	New York Av.
—	—	N. Market Sp.
416	419	7th W.
456	459	6th W.
476	465	5th W.
534	525	4th W.
542	543	3d W.
568	563	2d W.
—	581	New Jersey Av.
596	585	1st W.
640	—	N. Capitol on

Capitol Hill not numbered.

Missouri Av., from 6th to 3d West, opposite Botanic Garden.

Left.	*Rt.*	
2	—	6th W.
44	—	4 1/2 W.
78	—	3d W.

Mount Pleasant Al., M to N North, between 9th and 10th West.

Naylor's Al., 9th to 10th West between N and O North.

New Hampshire Av., from Boundary to the canal. (But partially open.)

New Jersey Av., from Boundary to Potomac.

Left.	*Rt.*	
506	507	C N.
540	—	B N.
—	—	A N.
		Capitol.
540	—	A S.
556	553	B S.
592	591	C S.
—	623	D S.
—	677	E S.
—	—	Virginia Av.
—	695	I S.
724	721	K S.
740	743	L S.
—	773	M S.
—	827	N S.
		Potomac.

New York Av., from N. E. Boundary to 23d West.

Left.	*Rt.*	
—	—	1st W.
160	—	2d W.
176	—	New Jersey Av.
180	—	3d W.
198	199	4th W.
250	253	5th W.
270	257	6th W.
312	—	7th W.
—	—	N. Market Sp.
—	—	Mass. Av.
316	319	9th W.
360	359	10th W.
—	367	11th W.
370	369	12th W.
406	397	13th W.
440	409	14th W.
470	—	15th W.
		President's Sq.
—	449	17th W.
—	—	18th W.
—	—	19th W.
—	—	20th W.
530	—	21st W.

Nigger Hill, between 9th & 10th West and N & O North.

North Capitol St., from Boundary to the north side of the Capitol.

Left.	*Rt.*	
—	—	I N.
246	—	H N.
268	271	G N.
—	305	F N.
		Not open.
372	—	C N.
400	399	B N.
—	—	A N.

North Carolina Av., from 1st East to Boundary. (But partially opened.)

Northern Market Space, from 9th to 7th West on K North.

Left.	*Rt.*	
2	1	9th W.
18	15	8th W.
32	27	7th W.

Ohio Av., from 15th to 12th West.

Left.	*Rt.*	
2	—	15th W.
30	—	14th W.
62	—	13 1/2 W.
—	—	13th W.

Organ Al., from 586 M to 595 N North, between 6th & 7th West.

Pennsylvania Av., from Rock Creek, Georgetown, to the Eastern Branch.

Left.	*Rt.*	
8	—	25th W.
34	33	24th W.
		Circle.
50	51	22d W.
98	97	21st W.
110	107	20th W.
138	135	19th W.
146	141	18th W.
196	183	17th W.
		War Dept.
		White House.
		State Dept.
		Treasury Dept.
198	201	15th W.
—	233	14th W.
232	235	13th W.
270	265	12th W.
—	267	11th W.
292	285	10th W.
340	317	9th W.
		Centre Market.
344	319	7th W.
378	359	6th W.
444	413	4 1/2 W.
492	463	3d W.
536	2d W.	} Botanic Garden
570	1st W.	
Capitol.		
—	571	1st E.
620	619	2d E.
—	656	3d E.
—	683	4th E.

Pierce St., from 211 New Jersey Av. to N. Capitol St., between M and N North.

Plater's Al., between I and K North, and 4th and 5th West.

President's Sq., between 15th & 17th West, on Pennsylvania Av.

Rhode Island Av., from Boundary to Connecticut Av. (But partially open.)

Ridge St., from 149 4th to 208 5th West, between M and N North.

Simms Al., O North, between 9th and 10th West.

Snow's Al., from 94 I North between 24th and 25th West.

South Capitol St., from the South side of the Capitol to Bartholow's wharf, Potomac. (But two or three blocks open.)

South Carolina Av., from 3d East to Mass. Av. (But partially open.)

Temperance Hall Al., from 362 D North, between 9th & 10th West.

Tennessee Av., will be located on Capitol Hill, between the Boundary and E. Capitol St.

Tin Cup Al., from 171 2d to 3d West, between B and C North.

Union Al., from 61 M to O South, between 4 1/2 and 6th West.

Union Al., from 596 6th to 4 1/2 West, between D and E South.

Union Row, from 401 to 413 F North, between 6th and 7th West.

Upper Water St., from foot of 21st to 23d West.

Van St., from 390 4 1/2 to 771 3d West, between M and N South.

Vermont Av., from Boundary to Lafayette Sq.

Left.	*Rt.*	
—	243	L N.
—	265	K N.
254	267	I N.
284	285	H N.

Virginia Av., from 27th West to Eastern Branch.

Left.	*Rt.*	
—	—	26 W.
Re-opens at		
170	—	22d W.
Re-opens at		
—	231	12th W.
—	243	11th W.
274	261	10th W.
304	—	9th W.
—	—	Mass. Av.
306	285	7th W.
334	315	6th W.
352	331	4 1/2 W.
390	385	3d W.
418	405	2d W.
—	435	1st W.
—	—	N. Capitol.
—	—	New Jersey Av.
—	459	2d E.
502	503	3d E.
526	523	4th E.
—	527	5th E.
—	—	6th E.
582	583	7th E.
594	603	8th E.
—	621	9th E.
618	—	Georgia Av.

Washington St., from 378 5th to 4th West, between G. and H North.

Water St., begins at the Potomac, cor. 21st West, and ends at the Observatory.

Western Market Space, on K North, between 19th & 20th West.

Willow Tree Al., from 289 B South, between New Jersey Av. and 1st East.

Wiltberger St., from S North, between 6th and 7th West.

1–2 East, open at F, and from N to O South.

1st East, from Boundary to the Eastern Branch.

Left.	*Rt.*	
164	—	K N.
194	—	I N.
214	—	H N.
		Not open.
226	329	D N.
360	361	C N.
394	393	B N.
—	—	A N.
418		E. Capitol.
		Carroll Pl.
—	—	A S.
—	—	Pennsylvania Av.
456	—	B S.
—	—	C S.

2d East, from Boundary to the Eastern Branch.

Left.	*Rt.*	
380	377	A N.
410	409	E. Capitol.
—	427	A S.
446	445	Pennsylvania Av.
—	459	Carroll St.
—	473	C S.
750		Virginia Av.

3d East, from Boundary to the Eastern Branch.

Left.	*Rt.*	
362	363	C N.
386	385	Maryland Av.
—	—	B N.
416	—	A N.
436	—	E. Capitol.
458	457	A S.
482	481	B S.
490	—	Pennsylvania Av.
506	—	C S.
548	—	N. Carolina Av.
566	—	E S.
—	—	S. Carolina Av.
—	—	G S.
—	639	Virginia Av.
—	663	I S.
—	683	K S.
—	697	L S.
—	723	M S.
764	765	N S.
778	787	Georgia Av.

4th East, from Boundary to the Eastern Branch.

Left.	*Rt.*	
416	—	A N.
—	—	E. Capitol.
—	—	A S.
—	—	B S.
—	—	Pennsylvania Av.
—	517	C S.
544	545	D S.
570	571	E S.
—	—	S. Carolina Av.
—	—	G S.
—	—	Virginia Av.
658	659	I S.
678	679	K S.
700	705	L S.
718	—	M S.
—	—	N S.

5th East, from Boundary to M South.

Left.	*Rt.*	
452	—	B S.
—	—	Pennsylvania Av.
—	—	D S.
—	—	S. Carolina Av.
518	519	E S.
554	555	G S.
—	—	I S.
602	—	Virginia Av.
—	—	K S.
638	637	L S.
648	649	M S.

6th East, from Boundary to L South.

Left.	*Rt.*	
470	471	Pennsylvania Av.
502	501	D S.
—	519	S. Carolina Av.
—	521	E S.
—	515	G S.
578	575	Virginia Av.
—	—	K S.

7th East, from Boundary to Navy Yard.

Left.	*Rt.*	
—	—	Pennsylvania Av.
528	523	E S.
564	555	G S.
612	603	I S.
616	615	Virginia Av.
638	639	L S.
664	657	M S.

8th East, from Boundary to Navy Yard.

Left.	*Rt.*	
484	—	Pennsylvania Av.
—	511	E S.
550	551	G S.
596	597	I S.
622	615	K S.
624	617	Virginia Av.
632	627	L S.
650	—	Georgia Av.
		Navy Yard.

9th East, from Boundary to Eastern Branch.

Left.	*Rt.*	
—	393	B S.
412	—	C S.
—	—	S. Carolina Av.
474	—	D S.
—	—	
		Pennsylvania Av.
—	—	E S.
540	539	G S.
576	—	I S.
—	—	K S.
—	—	Virginia Av.
—	595	Georgia Av.
600	—	M S.
—	—	Georgia Av.

10th East, from Boundary to Eastern Branch.

Left.	*Rt.*	
—	—	Pennsylvania Av.
540	539	G S.
—	585	I S.
593	?99	K S.
608	—	Virginia Av.
628	—	M S.
642	—	N S.

11th East, from Boundary to L South.

Left.	*Rt.*	
442	—	C S.
—	—	S. Carolina Av.
474	—	D S.

— — Pennsylvania Av.
— — E S.
476 469 G S.
510 511 I S.
532 531 K S.
— — Georgia Av.
— — Virginia Av.
— — I S.
546 — M S.
590 595 N S.
636 — O S.

12th East, from Boundary to Eastern Branch.

13th East, from Boundary to Eastern Branch.

14th East, from Boundary to Eastern Branch.

15th to 30th East, not open.

1/2 West, from F South to Eastern Branch.

1st West, from Boundary to W South.
Left. Rt.
— 319 E N.
— — D N.
426 — C N.
— 457 B N.
— 491 Pennsylvania Av.
— — Maryland Av.
514 511 B S.
534 — C S.
— 515 D S.
— 559 Virginia Av.

2d West, from New Jersey Av. to W South.
Left. Rt.
58 61 Mass. Av.
76 79 G N.
104 — F N.
110 — E N.
140 — D N.
— — Indiana Av.
166 159 C N.
— 199 B N.
— — Pennsylvania Av.
Re–opens at
200 — Maryland Av.
— — B S.
224 — C S.
268 267 D S.
812 — Virginia Av.
— 347 F S.
— — G S.

3 West, from Boundary to U South.
Left. Rt.
168 167 New York Av.
198 199 L N.
— 225 K N.
— 267 I N.
— — H N.
286 283 Mass. Av.
316 315 G N.
342 — F N.
— 363 E N.
394 — D N.
388 387 Indiana Av.
396 399 C N.
— — B N.
420 — Pennsylvania Av.
Botanic Garden.

— 433 Missouri Av.
Canal (bridge)
472 471 Maryland Av.
— 521 C S.
— 541 D S.
570 571 Virginia Av.
576 577 E S.
594 597 F S.
628 — G S.
— — H S.
— — I S.
— 695 K S.
— 715 L S.
— 747 M S.
— 801 N S.

4th West, from Boundary to D North.
Left. Rt.
114 — N N.
162 169 M N.
176 175 New York Av.
204 201 L N.
228 229 K N.
264 259 I N.
288 279 Mass. Av.
290 283 H N.
334 G N.
358 F N. } Judiciary Square
382 E N. }
414 D N.

4 1/2 West, from City Hall to T South.
Left. Rt.
1 D N.
16 19 C N.
42 31 Pennsylvania Av.
54 45 Missouri Av.
Canal (bridge)
62 67 Maine Av.
78 69 Maryland Av.
122 105 C S.
146 131 D S.
156 — Virginia Av.
186 171 E S.
216 185 F S.
242 211 G S.
208 239 H S.
— — I S.
— 291 K S.
— 309 L S.
362 337 M S.
390 Van St.
— 377 N S.
— 401 O S.
— — P S.

5th West, from Boundary to D North
Left. Rt.
124 — P N.
148 147 O N.
190 193 N N.
240 239 M N.
— — New York Av.
284 — L N.
314 315 K N.
— — Mass. Av.
342 341 I N.
364 351 H N.
303 G N.
417 F N. } Judiciary Square
429 E N. }
447 D N.

6th West, from Boundary to the Potomac.
Left. Rt.
54 — R N.

110 — Q N.
— — P N.
158 161 O N.
194 197 N N.
246 245 M N.
— 295 L N.
— 301 New York Av.
318 321 K N.
340 — Mass. Av.
340 347 I N.
368 369 H N.
408 413 G N.
428 433 F N.
454 447 E N.
470 479 D N.
— — Louisiana Av.
— 495 C N.
— — Pennsylvania Av.
508 — Missouri Av.
Canal (no bridge)
— — Maine Av.
— — B S.
— — Maryland Av.
— 549 C S.
— — Virginia Av.
560 563 D S.
596 Union Al.
608 605 E S.
630 — F S.
664 661 G S.
— 685 H S.
710 709 I S.
730 — K S.
754 — L S.
780 — M S.
828 817 N S.
844 — O S.

6 1/2 West, from D to E South.

7th West, from the Boundary to the Potomac.
Left. Rt.
2 1 Boundary.
— 19 T N.
— 53 S N.
— 79 R N.
— — Q N.
— — P N.
178 179 O N.
2?6 213 N N.
264 269 M N.
304 317 L N.
336 — New York Av.
338 — Mass. Av.
342 345 N. Market Sp.
374 381 I N.
400 411 H N.
444 }
440 } G.N.* } Patent Office
464 }
456 } P.O.F.N.* }
482 491 E N.
526 515 D N.
542 531 Market Sp.
546 mkt. Pennsylvania Av.
566 B N.
Bridge.
568 567 B S.
582 595 Maryland Av.
— — Virginia Av.
— 597 C S.
586 615 D S.
626 657 E S.
638 683 F S.
656 699 G S.
— 729 H S.
— 751 I S.

8th West, from Boundary to I South.

Left.	*Rt.*	
—	147	Q N.
—	179	P N.
—	207	O N.
246	245	N N.
290	289	M N.
350	325	L N.
374	339	N. Market Sp.
—	—	Mass. Av.
—	—	New York Av.
390	369	I N.
396	397	H N.
432	437	G N.
		Patent Office.
P.O.	439	F N.
—	455	E N.
440	475	D N.
450	499	Market Sp.
Re-opened.		
—	—	B S.
—	—	Maryland Av.
—	—	C S.
—	—	Virginia Av.
510	511	D S.
548	549	E S.
566	557	F S.
578	—	G S.

9th West, from Boundary to H South.

Left.	*Rt.*	
140	—	Q N.
184	—	P N.
218	217	O N.
252	253	N N.
300	301	M N.
338	341	L N.
360	357	Mass. Av.
—	—	K N.
362	365	New York Av.
396	391	I N.
416	413	H N.
444	433	G N.
446	451	F N.
460	475	E N.
494	505	D N.
514	519	Pennsylvania Av.
—	521	C N.
mkt.	523	Louisiana Av.
—	553	B N.
Re-opens.		
—	—	B S.
—	—	Virginia Av.
—	—	C S.
—	—	Maryland Av.
—	555	D S.
582	581	E S.
—	—	F S.
600	—	G S.
620	—	H S.

10th West, from Boundary to G South.

Left.	*Rt.*	
—	231	Q N.
—	—	P N.
290	—	O N.
310	315	N N.
340	345	M N.
376	361	L N.
376	367	Mass. Av.
382	373	K N.
394	391	New York Av.
398	393	I N.
410	403	H N.
—	439	G N.
438	449	F N.
458	471	E N.
482	—	D N.
482	491	Pennsylvania Av.
494	505	C N.
510	521	Louisiana Av.
—	—	B N.
		Bridge.
—	—	B S.
524	523	Virginia Av.
—	541	C S.
—	551	Maryland Av.
—	—	D S.
586	585	E S.
—	605	F S.
—	617	F S.

11th West, from Boundary to the Potomac.

Left.	*Rt.*	
270	—	P N.
310	—	O N.
336	—	N N.
354	351	M N.
—	—	Mass. Av.
382	371	L N.
402	383	K N.
404	403	I N.
430	411	H N.
458	447	G N.
468	461	F N.
490	491	E N.
—	—	D N.
520	507	Pennsylvania Av.
—	521	C N.
—	537	B N.
Re-opens.		
—	—	B S.
—	529	Virginia Av.
—	543	C S.
—	—	Maryland Av.
570	571	D S.
612	605	E S.
636	617	F S.

12th West, from Boundary to F South.

Left.	*Rt.*	
—	259	P N.
284	281	O N.
322	323	N N.
358	351	M N.
380	373	Mass. Av.
382	381	L N.
398	393	K N.
418	413	I N.
420	423	New York Av.
438	439	H N.
464	473	G N.
478	489	F N.
498	513	E N.
518	521	Pennsylvania Av.
524	523	D N.
550	549	C N.
558	559	B N.
		Bridge
—	—	B S.
570	559	Virginia Av.
636	—	E S.

13th West, from Boundary to Maryland Av.

Left.	*Rt.*	
—	289	O N.
—	321	N N.
—	—	M N.
338	349	Mass. Av.
—	369	L N.
—	—	K N.
370	371	I N.
386	383	New Jersey Av.
386	395	H N.
420	433	G N.
430	449	F N.
462	471	E N.
472	471	Pennsylvania Av.
480	485	D N.
498	507	C N.
—	—	B N.
Re-opens.		
526	525	B S.
546	561	C S.
568	587	D S.
580	—	Maryland Av.

13 1/2 West, from D North and to Maryland Av.

Left.	*Rt.*	
—	—	D N.
10	11	C N.
32	31	Ohio Av.
—	—	B N.
Re-opens.		
60	61	B S.
86	85	C S.
112	111	D S.
—	133	Maryland Av.

14th West, from Boundary to the Potomac.

Left.	*Rt.*	
170	—	S N.
194	—	R N.
—	—	Q N.
—	—	P N.
—	—	O N.
—	205	Rhode Island Av.
—	—	N N.
—	—	M N.
—	—	Vermont Av.
404	391	L N.
—	—	K N.
406	431	I N.
434	—	H N.
—	—	New York Av.
454	443	G N.
464	463	F N.
480	465	Pennsylvania Av.
482	477	D N.
498	479	C N.
520	493	Ohio Av.
—	—	B N.
		Bridge.
534	539	B S.
574	575	C S.
586	—	D S.
616	—	Maryland Av.

15th West, from Boundary to B North

Left.	*Rt.*	
328	327	M N.
372	365	L N.
390	367	K N.
404	405	I N.
416	413	H N.
440	433	New York Av.
446	—	G N.
468	—	F N.
486	—	Pennsylvania Av.
493	—	E N.
503	—	D N.

15 1/2 West, Madison Pl., from President Sq. to H North.

16th West, from Boundary to Lafayette Sq.

Left.	*Rt.*	
366	361	L N.
394	397	K N.
414	—	I N.
432	—	H N.

16 1/2 West, from Madison (or Madison Pl.) from President Sq. to H North.

17th West, from Boundary to B North.

Left.	*Rt.*	
470	483	I N.
—	507	H N.
—	525	Pennsylvania Av.
—	529	G N.
		War Dept.
		Navy Dept.
		Winder's bldg.
—	541	F N.
—	—	New York Av.
—	569	E N.
—	—	D N.
—	605	C N.
—	—	B N.

18th West, from Boundary to the Canal.

Left.	*Rt.*	
302	305	L N.
326	339	K N.
342	347	I N.
366	371	H N.
—	373	Pennsylvania Av.
—	393	G N.
—	407	F N.
—	—	New York Av.
446	—	E N.

19th West, from Boundary to the Canal.

Left.	*Rt.*	
326	333	K N.
—	351	I N.
—	363	Pennsylvania Av.
360	375	H N.
868	387	G N.
—	—	F N.
406	—	E N.
—	—	New York Av.
412	409	D N.

20th West, from Boundary to the Canal.

Left.	*Rt.*	
—	85	R N.
—	—	Q N.
—	—	P N.
—	—	O N.
194	195	N N.
244	243	M N.
364	301	L N.
326	333	K N.
—	351	I N.
304	351	Pennsylvania Av.
394	375	H N.
416	397	G N.
426	399	F N.
450	327	E N.
—	431	D N.

21st West, from Boundary to the Canal.

Left.	*Rt.*	
2	—	Boundary
34	—	R N.
—	71	Q N.
—	135	P N.
—	159	Q N.
—	—	N N.
222	281	M N.
—	275	L N.
—	—	K N.
326	—	I N.
—	—	Pennsylvania Av.
350	349	H N.
380	—	G N.
388	379	F N.

22d West, from Boundary to the Canal.

Left.	*Rt.*	
—	19	O N.
—	—	N N.
—	—	M N.
128	—	L N.
156	—	K N.
158	151	Pennsylvania Av.
180	179	I N.
212	109	H N.
—	241	G N.

23d West, from Boundary to the Canal.

Left.	*Rt.*	
88	—	M N.
128	—	L N.
Circle.		
100	159	I N.
192	193	H N.
224	223	G N.
—	—	F N.
258	—	E N.

24th West, from Rock Creek to Observatory.

Left.	*Rt.*	
84	87	M N.
132	—	L N.
144	—	Pennsylvania Av.
—	147	K N.
—	183	I N.

25th West, from Rock Creek to the Canal. But partially open, and only two or three houses numbered.

26th West, from Rock Creek to the Canal.

Left.	*Rt.*	
—	45	Pennsylvania Av.
72	—	K N.
114	—	I N.
—	—	H N.
—	—	G N.
179	—	F N.
—	199	E N.

27th West, from Rock Creek to the Canal. Only two or three houses numbered.

GEORGETOWN DIRECTORY

Back St., west side of High St. above Eighth. Not opened.

Bank Al., from Bridge St., between Market and Frederick Streets, to Prospect.

Beall St., from Rock Creek to High St.

Left.	*Rt.*	
—	18	North
39	—	Monroe
63	64	Montgomery
69	—	Greene
85	86	Washington
119	134	Congress
179	190	High

Bridge St., from Rock Creek to the corporation limit.

Left.	*Rt.*	
—	10	Rock
—	24	Montgomery
37	50	Greene
47	66	Washington
67	—	Jefferson
89	112	Congress
127	144	High
167	188	Potomac
179	—	Market
—	—	Bank Al.
221	218	Frederick
245	—	Fayette

Cecil Al., from Cherry Al. to Water St.

Cherry Al., from High St. to Market Sp.

Congress St., from 30 Water to Road St.

Left.	*Rt.*	
—	—	Water
48	45	Bridge
84	75	Gay
104	—	Dunbarton
122	—	Beall
138	—	West
158	—	Stoddart

Dunbarton St., from Rock Creek to 112 High St.

Left.	*Rt.*	
—	2	Creek
21	22	Monroe
63	64	Montgomery
63	68	Greene
—	88	Washington
121	114	Congress
165	150	High

East St., a row of houses on the road to Lyons' Mill.

Fayette St., from 245 Bridge to 340 High St.

Left.	*Rt.*	
31	30	First
53	66	Second
87	76	Third
91	90	Fourth
—	—	Sixth
—	—	Seventh
183	180	Eighth

Frederick St., from 160 Water to High St.

Left.	*Rt.*	
31	32	First
49	—	Second
67	68	Third
93	94	Fourth
—	112	Fifth
—	140	Sixth
—	166	Seventh

Gay St., from Rock Creek to 92 High St.

Left.	*Rt.*	
—	2	Creek
27	82	Montgomery
39	46	Greene
61	60	Washington
101	102	Congress
139	140	High

Greene St., from Water St. to the Cemetery.

Left.	*Rt.*	
1	2	Water
58	60	Bridge
59	70	Olive
75	—	Gay
91	88	Dunbarton
107	108	Beall
—	126	West
—	128	Stoddart

High St., from Water St. to the Corporation limit.

Left.	*Rt.*	
1	2	Water
45	48	Bridge
65		Prospect
	92	Gay
81		First
	112	Dunbarton
111		Second
	132	Beall
137		Third
	152	West
161		Fourth
181		Fifth
207		Sixth
—		Seventh
	840	op. Fayette

Jefferson St., from 30 Water to 67 Bridge

Left.	*Rt.*	
1	2	Water
43	42	Canal
67	68	Bridge

Lingan St., from Prospect to Third St.

Left.	*Rt.*	
7	—	Prospect
33	—	First
—	—	Second
	66	Third

Madison St., west side of High St. above Eighth. Not opened.

Market Sp., from 167 Bridge to the Canal.

Left.	*Rt.*	
2	1	Bridge
26	25	Canal

Market St., from 130 Water to High St.

Left.	*Rt.*	
—	2	Water
—	24	Bridge
31	30	Prospect
—	48	First
—	—	Second
65	64	Third
83	88	Fourth
—	106	Fifth
—	—	Sixth
	140	High

Mill St., a road leading from 30 West St. to Lyons' Mill.

Monroe St., from 22 Dunbarton to 39 Beall.

Montgomery St., from Rock Creek to the Cemetery.

Left.	*Rt.*	
9	18	Bridge
25	34	Olive
35	—	Gay
49	—	Dunbarton
67	70	Beall
79	92	West
91	—	Stoddart
		Cemetery.

North St., crosses West St. at No. 21.

Olive St., from 25 Montgomery to 121 Washington St.

Left.	*Rt.*	
15	—	Montgomery
43	—	Greene
—	—	Washington

Potomac St., from 118 Water to 2d St.

Left.	*Rt.*	
—	—	Bridge
17	22	Prospect
35	—	First

Prospect St., from 65 High to 5 Lingan St.

Left.	*Rt.*	
1	2	High
51	52	Potomac
71	72	Market
Bank Al.		
—	98	Frederick
—	110	Fayette
129	130	Lingan

Road St., from Montgomery to High St.

Left.	*Rt.*	
39		Washington
59		Congress

South St., from Congress to High St., between Water St. and the Canal.

Stoddart St., from 91 Montgomery to 158 Congress St.

Left.	*Rt.*	
81	—	Greene
—	106	Washington
—	170	Congress

Valley St., from 166 West to Road St.

Warehouse Al., from 157 Bridge, between High St. and Market Sp.

Warren St., from 136 First to Third St.

Left.	*Rt.*	
—	74	Third

Washington St., from 2 Water St. to the Cemetery.

Left.	*Rt.*	
51	—	Water
103	—	Bridge
123	—	Olive
135	118	Gay
139	124	Dunbarton
—	140	Beall
—	154	West
190	172	Stoddart
		Cemetery

Water St., from foot of Washington to above Frederick St.

Left.	*Rt.*	
35	30	Jefferson
55	50	Congress
81	—	High
99	—	Cecil Al.
—	118	Potomac
—	130	Market
—	160	Frederick

West St., from Rock Creek Road to 152 High St.

Left.	*Rt.*	
21	18	North
37	30	Mill Road
61	56	Montgomery
81	68	Greene
97	98	Washington
133	128	Congress
	166	Valley
181	182	High

1st St., from 81 High to Warren St.

Left.	*Rt.*	
1	2	High
33	36	Potomac
41	48	Market
69	80	Frederick
91	—	Fayette
109	—	Lingan
—	136	Warren

2d St., from 111 High St. to the College.

Left.	*Rt.*	
1	2	High
31	32	Potomac
43	56	Market
63	—	Frederick
85	94	Fayette
101	110	Lingan
121	126	Warren
		College

3d St., from 137 High to the end.

Left.	*Rt.*	
1	2	High
35	36	Market
—	56	Frederick
—	—	Fayette
87	—	Lingan
109	—	Warren
—	122	End

4th St., from 161 High to 90 Fayette St.

Left.	*Rt.*	
1	2	High
21	34	Market
57	64	Frederick
79	—	Fayette

5th St., from 161 High to 112 Frederick St.

Left.	*Rt.*	
—	2	High
—	12	Market
—	40	Frederick

6th St., from Market to Fayette St.

Left.	*Rt.*	
—	2	Market
—	46	Frederick
—	—	Fayette

7th St., from High to Fayette St., & further.

Left.	*Rt.*	
1	—	High
33	—	Frederick
63	64	Fayette

8th St., from High to Fayette St.

Left.	*Rt.*	
1	—	High
	12	Frederick
	24	Fayette

APPENDIX III

CIVIL WAR FORTS IN WASHINGTON, D.C.

After Virginia left the Union and joined the Confederacy, the federal government saw that the capital was in a vulnerable position and subject to capture. Maj. Gen. George McClellan, commander of the Army of the Potomac, chose Maj. Gen. John Barnard of the Corps of Engineers to direct the building of a string of 68 enclosed forts and batteries. By the war's end, 20 miles of rifle pits and more than 30 miles of military roads encircled the city. Most of the forts had earthwork walls supported by logs. For most of these forts, only tree- or grass-covered hills remain. During the war, the forts had clear fields of fire in front of them. Trees were cut down and their branches left to obstruct infantry movements.

Battery Cameron
Location: 1900 block of Foxhall Road. High ground on west side of Foxhall Road NW.

Battery Jameson
Location: Bladensburg Road to Fort Lincoln Cemetery entrance. Right onto grounds past mausoleum and Lincoln oak to battery.

Battery Kemble
Location: Chain Bridge Road near Loughboro Road. On left.

Battery Martin Scott
Location: 5600 block of Potomac Street NW. Battery on river side of street.

Battery Parrott
Location: 2300 block of Foxhall Road. West side of Foxhall Road NW on grounds of Belgian ambassador's house.

Battery Terrill
Location: Opposite 5301-5303 29th Street (Jenifer Street).

Fort Davis
Location: South on Alabama Avenue SE to intersection with Pennsylvania Avenue. To the right in park area.

Fort DeRussy
Location: Military Road NW to Oregon Avenue. Turn left. Walk up unpaved bridle path.

Fort DuPont
Location: Alabama Avenue SE to Fort DuPont Park.

Fort Reno
Location: 40th Street past Woodrow Wilson High School to Chesapeake Street NW. Turn toward reservoir.

Fort Ricketts
Location: Corner park across from Reynolds Place at Bruce Place and Fort Place SE, near Anacostia Museum.

Fort Slemmer
Location: Taylor Street to Harewood Road, left to first major street at edge of Catholic University. Note sign for O'Boyle and Marist Hall, left for one half block. To the left of the street on knoll north of Marist Hall.

Fort Stanton
Location: Fort Place to Erie Street to Morris Road (all the same street). Remnants behind Our Lady of Perpetual Help School and Church.

Fort Slocum
Location: Bordered by Kansas Avenue, Blair Road, Milmarson Place, and Nicholson Street NW. In Fort Slocum Park.

Fort Totten
Location: Blair Road south to Madison Street, zigzag left which becomes Fort Totten Drive after crossing Riggs Road. Entrance on left.

Argument of John A. Bingham. Special Judge Advocate. Washington, D.C.: Government Printing Office, 1865.

Atwood, Albert W. *Gallaudet College: Its First 100 Years.* Lancaster, Pennsylvania: Intelligencer Printing Company, 1964.

Bassler, Roy, ed. *The Collected Works of Abraham Lincoln.* New Brunswick, New Jersey: Rutgers University Press, 1953.

Battles and Leaders of the Civil War. New York: Thomas Yoseloff, Inc. 1936.

Beale, Marie. *Decatur House and Its Inhabitants.* Washington, D.C.: National Trust for Historic Preservation, 1954.

Biographical Dictionary of the United States Congress 1774-1989. Washington, D.C.: Government Printing Office, 1989.

Bishop, Jim. *The Day Lincoln Was Shot.* New York: Harper & Row Publishers, 1955.

Borchert, James. *Alley Life in Washington: Family, Community, and Folklife in the City, 1850-1970.* Urbana: University of Illinois Press, 1980.

Brown, Glenn. *History of the United States Capitol.* Washington, D.C.: Government Printing Office, 1901-1904.

Bryan, Wilhelmus B. *A History of the National Capital from Its Foundation through the Period of the Adoption of the Organic Act.* New York: The McMillan Company, 1914 & 1916.

Busey, Samuel C. *Pictures of the City of Washington in the Past.* Washington, D.C.: William Ballantyne & Sons, 1898.

Cable, Mary. *The Avenue of the Presidents.* New York: Houghton Mifflin Co., 1969.

Coggeshall, E.W. *The Assassination of Lincoln.* Chicago: Walter M. Hill, 1920.

Centennial Papers, Saint Elizabeths Hospital. Baltimore: Waverly Press, Inc., 1956.

Cole, Donald B. ed. *Witness to the Young Republic, A Yankee's Journal 1828-1870, Benjamin Brown French.* Hanover: University Press of New England, 1989.

Confederate Veteran Magazine. Nashville: 1893.

Cooling, Benjamin F. *Jubal Early's Raid on Washington 1864.* Baltimore: The Nautical & Aviation Publishing Company of America, 1989.

Cooling, Benjamin F. *Mr. Lincoln's Forts.* Shippensburg, Pennsylvania: Beidel Printing House, Inc., 1988.

Cooling, Benjamin F. *Symbol, Sword and Shield, Defending Washington During the Civil War.* Hamden, Connecticut: Archon Books, 1975.

Crew, Harvey W., ed. *Centennial History of Washington, D.C.* Dayton, Ohio: United Brethren Publishing House, 1892.

Downtown Urban Renewal Area, Landmarks Washington, D.C. Washington, D.C.: National Capital Planning Commission, 1970.

Durkin, Joseph T., S.J., *Georgetown University: The Middle Years, 1840-1900.* Washington, D.C.: Georgetown University Press, 1963.

Eberlein, Harold D. *Historic Houses of Georgetown and Washington City.* Richmond: The Dietz Press, 1958.

Ecker, Grace D. *A Portrait of Old Georgetown.* Richmond: The Dietz Press, 1951.

Eisenschiml, Otto. *In the Shadow of Lincoln's Death.* New York: Wilfred Funk, Inc., 1940.

Eisenschiml, Otto. *Why Was Lincoln Murdered?* Boston: Little, Brown and Company, 1937.

Eskew, Garnett L. *Willards of Washington.* New York: Coward-McCann, Inc., 1954.

Federal Writers' Project. *Washington, City and Capital.* Washington, D.C.: Government Printing Office, 1937.

Gallaudet, Edward M. *History of the College for the Deaf 1857-1907.* Washington, D.C.: Gallaudet College Press, 1983.

Glicksberg, Charles L. ed. *Walt Whitman and the Civil War.* Philadelphia: University of Pennsylvania Press, 1933.

Goode, James M. *Capital Losses: A Cultural History of Washington's Destroyed Buildings.* Washington, D.C.: Smithsonian Institute Press, 1979.

Goode, James M. *The Outdoor Sculpture of Washington, D.C.: A Comprehensive Historical Guide.* Washington, D.C.: Smithsonian Institute Press, 1974.

Green, Constance M. *Washington: Village and Capital.* Princeton: Princeton University Press, 1962.

Gutheim, Frederick. *The Potomac.* New York: Rinehart and Company, 1949.

Gutheim, Frederick. *Worthy of the Nation.* Washington, D.C.: Smithsonian Institute Press, 1977.

Hanchett, William. *The Lincoln Murder*

Conspiracies. Urbana: University of Illinois Press, 1986.

Hargrave, Thomas B., Jr. *Private Differences-General Good, A History of the YMCA of Metropolitan Washington.* Washington, D.C.: YMCA, 1985.

Hazelton, George C., Jr. *The National Capitol, Its Architecture, Art, and History.* New York: J. F. Taylor and Company, 1902.

Hines, Christian. *Early Recollections of Washington City.* Washington, D.C.: Chronicle Book and Job Printing, 1866.

Hutchinson, Louise D. *The Anacostia Story: 1608-1930.* Washington, D.C.: Smithsonian Institute Press, 1977.

Jackson, Richard P. *The Chronicles of Georgetown, D.C. from 1751 to 1878.* Washington, D.C.: R. O. Polkinhorn, 1878.

Junior League of the City of Washington. *The City of Washington, An Illustrated History.* Thomas Froneck, ed. New York: Alfred Knopf, 1977.

Kayser, Elmer L. *Bricks Without Straw: The Evolution of George Washington University.* New York: Appleton-Century Crofts, 1970.

Kimmel, Stanley. *Mr. Lincoln's Washington.* New York: Coward-McCann, Inc., 1957.

King, LeRoy O., Jr. *100 Years of Capital Traction: The Story of Streetcars in the Nation's Capital.* Dallas: Taylor Publishing Company, 1972.

Kirk, Elise K. *Music at the White House.* Urbana: University of Illinois Press, 1986.

Kunhardt, Dorothy M. *Twenty Days.* New York: Castle Books, 1965.

Latimer, Louise P. *Your Washington and Mine.* New York: Charles Scribners Sons, 1930.

Leech, Margaret. *Reveille in Washington, 1860-1865.* New York: Harper and Brothers, 1941.

Logan, Mrs. John A. *Thirty Years in Washington.* Hartford, Connecticut: A. D. Worthington & Company, 1901.

Mackall, Sally S. *Early Days of Washington.* Washington: The Neale Company, 1889.

Maddex, Diane. *Historic Buildings of Washington, D.C.* Pittsburg: Ober Park Associates, Inc., 1973.

McCue, George. *Octagon.* Washington, D.C.: American Institute of Architects Foundation, 1976.

Mitchell, Mary. *Divided Town.* Barre, Massachusetts: Barre Publishers, 1968.

Mitchell, Mary. *A Walk in Georgetown.* Barre, Massachusetts: Barre Publishers, 1966.

Murdock, Myrtle C. *Constantino Brumidi.* Washington, D.C.: Monumental Press, Inc., 1950.

Myer, Donald B. *Bridges and the City of Washington.* Washington, D.C.: Commission of Fine Arts, 1974.

Newcomb, S. *Reminiscences of an Astronomer.* New York: Houghton Mifflin and Company, 1903.

Nicolay, Helen. *Our Capital on the Potomac.* New York: The Century Company, 1924.

Places and Persons on Capitol Hill. Washington, D.C.: The Capitol Hill Southeast Citizens Association, 1960.

Poore, Ben P. *The Conspiracy Trial for the Murder of the President.* New York: Arno Press, 1972.

Poore, Ben P. *Reminiscences of Sixty Years in the National Metropolis.* Philadelphia: Hubbard Brothers, 1886.

Proctor, John C. *Washington Past and Present: A History.* New York: Lewis Historical Publishing Co., Inc., 1930 & 1932.

Reck, W. Emerson. *Lincoln, His Last 24 Hours.* Jefferson, North Carolina: McFarland & Company, 1987.

Ridgely, Helen. *Historic Graves of Maryland and the District of Columbia.* Westminster, Maryland: Family Line Publications, 1992.

Sandburg, Carl. *Abraham Lincoln: the War Years.* New York: Harcourt Brace & Company, 1939.

Schuon, Karl. *Home of the Commandants.* Washington, D.C.: Leatherneck Association, 1966.

Schwartz, Nancy B. comp. *District of Columbia Catalog 1974.* Charlottesville: University Press of Virginia, 1976.

Seale, William. *The President's House.* Washington, D.C.: White House Historical Association, 1986.

Sherwood, Susan B. *Foggy Bottom 1888-1975: A Study in the Uses of an Urban Neighborhood.* Washington, D.C.: The George Washington University, 1978.

Shutes, Milton H. *Lincoln and the Doctors.* New York: The Pioneer Press, 1933.

Smith, Kathryn S., ed. *Washington at Home.* Northridge, California: Windsor Publications, Inc., 1988.

Staudenraus, P. J. ed. *Mr. Lincoln's Washington, The Civil War Dispatches of Noah Brooks.* New York: Thomas Yoseloff, 1967.

Tayloe, Benjamin 0. *Our Neighbors on Lafayette Square.* Washington, D.C.: Private Printing, 1872.

Thomas, Benjamin P. *Abraham Lincoln, A Biography.* New York: Alfred Knopf, 1952.

Torbert, Alice. *Doorways and Dormers of Old Georgetown.* Washington, D.C.: Alice Coyle Torbert, 1930.

Truett, Randall B., ed. *Washington, D.C.* New York: Hastings House, 1942.

U.S. Army Corps of Engineers. *A Historical Summary of the Work of the Corps of Engineers in Washington, D.C. and Vicinity, 1852-1952.* Sacket Duryee, ed. Washington, D.C.: 1952.

U.S. Commission of Fine Arts. *Georgetown Architecture.* Washington, D.C.: USCFA and HABS, 1970.

U.S. Commission of Fine Arts. *Georgetown Architecture—Northwest.* Washington, D.C.: USCFA and HABS, 1970.

U.S. Commission of Fine Arts. *Georgetown Architecture—The Waterfront.* Washington, D.C.: USCFA and HABS, 1968.

U.S. Commission of Fine Arts. *Georgetown Commercial Architecture—M Street.* Washington, D.C.: USCFA and HABS, 1967.

U.S. Commission of Fine Arts. *Georgetown Commercial Architecture- -Wisconsin Avenue.* Washington, D.C.: USCFA and HABS, 1967.

U.S. Commission of Fine Arts. *Georgetown Residential Architecture—Northeast.* Washington, D.C.: USCFA and HABS, 1970.

Georgetown Historic Waterfront, Washington, D.C. Washington, D.C.: USCFA and Office of Archeology and Historic Preservation, National Park Service, 1968.

Massachusetts Avenue Architecture. Vols. I & II. Washington, D.C.: Government Printing Office, 1973 & 1975.

Wallace, Richard. *The Willard Hotel, An Illustrated History.* Washington, D.C.: Dicmar Publishing, 1986.

War of the Rebellion: Official Records of the Union and Confederate Armies. Washington, D.C.: Government Printing Office, 1892.

Washington and Georgetown City Directories. 1860, 1862, 1863, 1864, 1865.

Washington Post. *A History of the City of Washington, Its Men, and Its Institutions.* Allan Slauson, ed. Washington, D.C.: Washington Post Company, 1903.

Weichmann, Louis J. *A True History of the Assassination of Abraham Lincoln and of the Conspiracy of 1865.* New York: Alfred Knopf, 1975.

NEWSPAPERS

National Intelligencer 1861-1865

Evening Star 1861-1865

Daily Morning Chronicle 1862-1865

Index to Buildings and Sites

Arlington National Cemetery, 122-43
Arsenal Memorial, 145-46
Battleground National Cemetery, 143-44
Blair Lee House, 85
Bodisco House, 67-68
Capitol, 105-08
Chesapeake & Ohio Canal, 76-77
Church of the Epiphany, 101
Congressional Cemetery, 144-63
Constantino Brumidi House, 108
Convent of the Visitation, 65
Cox's Row, 66
Customs House, 76
Cutts Madison House, 88
Decatur House, 86
Dodge Warehouse, 77
Dumbarton House, 69
Dumbarton Oaks, 68-69
Ebenezer United Methodist Church, 108
Ellipse, 104
Evermay, 69
Ford's Theatre, 93-96
Forrest Hall, 62
Forrest Marbury House, 62
Fort Carroll, 113
Fort Leslie McNair, 115-17
Fort Stevens, 118-19
Gallaudet University, 117-18
Georgetown University, 64
Glenwood Cemetery, 163-66
Grafton Tyler House, 75
Halcyon House, 62-63
Jacqueline Kennedy House, 75
John Haw House, 73
Kennedy House, 67
Lafayette Park, 86-87
Lincoln Memorial, 80
Lock Keepers House, 80-81
Louis Mackall House, 70
Lydia English's Georgetown Female Seminary, 74
Maj. Henry Rathbone House, 85
Marine Corps Barracks, 108-109
Mathew Brady's Photography Studio, 100-01
Methodist Episcopal Church, 73
Mount Olivet Cemetery, 166-70
National Portrait Gallery, 99-100
National Theatre, 92
Naval Observatory, 79-80
New York Avenue Presbyterian Church, 91
Oak Hill Cemetery, 69, 170-80
Octagon House, 82
Old City Hall, 98-99
Petersen House, 96-97
Prospect House, 63
Renwick Gallery, 84-85
Riley Shinn House, 73-74
Robert Dodge Mansion, 70
Rock Creek Cemetery, 180-85
St. Elizabeths Hospital, 110-13
St. John's Episcopal Church, 68, 87
St. John's Parish House, 87-88
St. Patrick's Church, 101
Samuel Hein House, 67
Scott Grant House, 68
Scottish Rite Temple, 185-86
Smithsonian Building, 103-04
Soldiers' Home National Cemetery, 186-88
Surratt Boardinghouse, 97-98
Tudor Place, 71-72
Treasury Building, 88-89
Trinity Church, 64-65
United States Soldiers' Home, 119-20
Washington Circle, 79
Washington Monument, 102
Washington Navy Yard, 113-15
Wheatley Row, 76
White House, 89-91
Willard Hotel, 92
Winder Building, 83-84

Index to Street Addresses of Buildings and Sites

Northwest

1st and East Capitol Streets, 105-08
4th and D Streets, 98-99
8th Street between G and I Streets, 108-09
511 10th Street, 93-96
516 10th Street, 96-97
10th and G Streets, SE Corner, 101
600 17th Street, 83-84
17th Street and Constitution Avenue, SW Corner, 80-81
23rd and E Streets, 79-80
1524 28th Street, 69-70
1534 28th Street, 70
1623 28th Street, 69
1633 29th Street, 70
30th Street, 69, 76-77
1300 30th Street, 75
1311 30th Street, 74
1517 30th Street, 70-71
1215 31st Street, 76
1644 31st Street, 71-72
35th and P Streets, 65
36th and O Streets, 64-65
37th and O Streets, 64
F Street between 7th and 9th Streets, 99-100
1317 G Street, 101
604 H Street, 97-98
1520 H Street, 88
1525 H Street, 87-88
3350 M Street, 62
2808 N Street, 73
2812 N Street, 73-74
3017 N Street, 75
3033 N Street, 75
3038 N Street, 76
3043 N Street, 76
3249 N Street, 67
3307 N Street, 67
3311 N Street, 66
3327-3339 N Street, 66
3340 N Street, 65-66
N Street and Wisconsin Avenue, NW Corner, 67
3240 O Street, 68
3322 O Street, 67-68
2805 P Street, 72-73
2819 P Street, 72
3116 P Street, 72
2715 Q Street, 69
3101 R Street, 68-69
3238 R Street, 68
Constitution Avenue, E Street, 17th to 15th Streets, 104
3127 Dumbarton Street, 73
712 Jackson Place, 85-86
748 Jackson Place, 86

1000 Jefferson Drive, 103-04
Mall between 15th and 17th Streets, 102
Mall at 23rd Street, 80
1799 New York Avenue, 82
New York Avenue and H Street, 91
633 Pennsylvania Avenue, 100-01
1321 Pennsylvania Avenue, 92
1401 Pennsylvania Avenue, 92
1650 Pennsylvania Avenue, 85
Pennsylvania Avenue and 15th Street, 88-89
Pennsylvania Avenue and 16th Street, 89-91
Pennsylvania Avenue and 17th Street, NE Corner, 84-85
Pennsylvania Avenue between Madison and Jackson Places, 86-87
Pennsylvania and New Hampshire Avenues, K and 32rd Streets, 79
3400 Prospect Street, 62-63
3425 Prospect Street, 63-64
3508 Prospect Street, 63
Rock Creek Church Road and Upshur Street, 119
1256 Wisconsin Avenue, 62
Wisconsin Avenue and Water Street, 77

Southwest

4th and P Streets, 115-17

Northeast

13th and Quackenbos Streets, 118
Florida Avenue and 7th Street, 117-18

Southeast

4th and D Streets, 108
326 A Street, 108
M and 9th Streets, 114-15
2700 Martin Luther King Jr. Avenue, 110-13
Martin Luther King Jr. Avenue and South Capitol Street, 113

Index to Names Associated with Gravesites and Houses

Adams, Henry, 181
Adams, John Quincy, 69
Addison, Henry Clay, 66, 70, 171
Ainsworth, Fred Clayton, 127
Alexander, Joseph Bell, 145
Allen, Dr. Charles E., 145
Almy, John Jay, 145
Anderson, Robert, 119
Armstrong, Frank Crawford, 181
Augur, Christopher Columbus, 127-28
Augusta, Alexander T., 128
Ayres, Romeyn Beck, 128
Bache, Alexander Dallas, 146
Baker, Lafayette, 66
Baker, Newton, 75
Barnes, Dr. Joseph, 171
Beall, Ninian, 69
Belknap, William Worth, 128
Benham, Henry W., 146
Benjamin, Judah P., 86
Berdan, Hiram, 128-29
Berret, James G., 146-47
Blair, Francis Preston, 85
Blair, Montgomery, 85, 181-82
Bodisco, Alexander, 67
Bohrer, George A., 147
Booth, John Wilkes, 92-97, 114-16
Brady, Mathew B., 100-01, 147-48
Brewer, Henry, 72
Brice, Benjamin William, 187
Browning, William A., 148
Brumidi, Constantino, 108, 163-64
Buchanan, Robert Christie, 182
Buckingham, John Edward, 148-49
Calhoun, James, 68
Calhoun, John C., 69
Carroll, Samuel Sprigg, 113
Carroll, William Thomas, 171
Cattell, Henry Pratt, 149
Charmes, John, 111
Clarvoe, John Alexander W., 149
Clem, John Lincoln, 129
Cooke, Henry, 68, 71
Corcoran, William Wilson, 67, 84, 171-72
Cox, John, 66
Croggon, James, 149
Crook, George, 129
Crumbaugh, John, 65
Cummins, Edmund, 69-70
Cutts, Richard, 88
Dahlgren, John, 113-14
Dahlgren, Ulric, 113-14
Davis, Charles W., 149
Davis, Jefferson, 83
Daw, Reuben, 72
Decatur, Mrs. Stephen, 73
Decatur, Stephen, 86
Dent, Josiah, 69
Dick, Robert, 75
Dix, Dorothea Lynde, 109-11
Dodge, Alexander Hamilton, 72
Dodge, Charles, 69
Dodge, Francis, 70, 76
Dodge, Robert, 69, 70
Doherty, Edward, 129
Doubleday, Abner, 129-30
Dunlop, James, 75
Emory, William H., 149-50
English, Lydia, 73-74
Eustis, George, 172
Ezekial, Sir Moses, 130
Forbes, Charles, 150
Ford, Dr. Charles Mason, 150
Forrest, French, 150
Forrest, Bladen, 62, 66
Forrest, Uriah, 62
French, Benjamin Brown, 150-51
French, William Henry, 182-83
Gales, Joseph, 151
Gardner, Alexander, 164
Gibbon, John, 130
Gilliss, James M., 79
Gordon, William A., 76
Grant, Ulysses S., 68
Greenleaf, James, 115
Gurley, Phineas, 91
Gurowski, Count Adam, 151-52
Hadfield, George, 98
Hall, Charles, 101
Hall, James Crowhill, 152
Halleck, Henry, 68
Hammond, William Alexander, 130-31
Hanscom, Simon P., 152
Hansell, Emerick W., 153
Harney, William Selby, 131
Hartley, E. D., 66
Harriman, Pamela, 76
Harris, Clara, 86
Haw, John Stoddert, 73
Hazen, William Babcock, 131

Hein, Samuel, 67
Henningsen, Charles P., 153
Henry, Joseph, 103, 172-73
Herold, David (Davy), 153-55
Herr, Abraham, 67-68, 70
Heywood, Charles, 131-32
Hoban, James, 166
Holmes, Oliver Wendell, 132
Holt, Joseph, 84
Hopkins, Juliet Opie, 132
Howe, Julia Ward, 92
Hoxie, Vinnie Reem, 136
Humphries, Andrew A., 155
Hunter, William, 66
Ingalls, Rufus, 132
Jefferson, Thomas, 69
Kearny, Philip, 132-33
Keilholtz, William Henry, 155
Kendall, Amos, 117, 164
Kennedy, Jacqueline, 75
Kennedy, John F., 67
Kennon, Britannia Peter, 71-72, 75
Kidwell, John, 63
King, Horatio, 155-56
Kinney, Mary Cogswell, 174
Larner, Noble D., 156
Latrobe, Benjamin Henry, 86, 87
Laub, Charles H., 66
Lee, Samuel Phillips, 85
Letterman, Jonathan, 133
Lincoln, Robert Todd, 133
Linthicum, Edward, 69
Logan, John Alexander, 187-88
Longstreet, William D., 174
MacArthur, Arthur, 133-34
Mackall, Louis, 70
Madison, Dolley, 69, 88
Madison, James, 69
Marbury, John, 62
Maury, Matthew Fontain, 79
McCallum, Daniel Craig, 63
McClellan, George, 88
McKim, Dr. Samuel A. H., 156
Marbury, John, 62
Mason, George, 63-64
Meigs, John Rodgers, 134
Meigs, Montgomery Cunningham, 64, 84, 134
Merrick, William Matthew, 166
Merrick, Richard, T., 174
Merritt, John G., 156
Miles, Nelson Appleton, 135
Mills, Clark, 164-66
Mills, Robert, 157
Miner, Myrtilla, 174-75
Monroe, James, 69
Montgomery, John B., 175
Moore, William George, 157-58
Morris, George Upham, 63
Mosby, John, 77
Munroe, Frank, 158
Munroe, Seaton, 158
Nayes, Crosby, 184
Nicholay, John George, 90, 175
Nichols, Dr. Charles Henry, 111-12, 158
Nokes, James, 158-59
Ord, Edward Otho Cresap, 135
Petersen, William 96
Pike, Albert, 185-86
Pinckney, William, 175-76
Plant, Joseph T.K., 159
Pleasonton, Alfred, 159
Porter, David Dixon, 135
Powell, John Wesley, 136
Pumphry, James W., 159
Rathbone, Henry, 86
Rawlins, John Aaron, 136
Redin, William, 75
Reno, Jesse Lee, 176
Renwick, James, 84
Ricketts, James Brewerton, 136-37
Ridgley, William, 66
Riggs, George, 75, 119, 184
Riley, Joshua, 76
Rind, William, 73
Rodgers, John, 137
Rosecrans, William Starke, 137
Rousseau, Lovell Harrison, 137-38
Rucker, Daniel, 138
St. Clair, James Henry, 160
Sampson, William Thomas, 138
Sands, Frank T., 160
Scala, Francis Maria, 160
Schoepf, Albin F., 160
Schofield, John McAllister, 138-39
Scott, Mrs. Alfred Vernon, 68
Scott, Winfield, 65, 119
Seaton, William Winston, 160-61
Shelton, Joseph G. 161
Sheridan, Philip Henry, 139
Shinn, Riley, 74
Shoemaker, George, 72
Sickles, Daniel Edgar, 139-40
Slemmer, Charles, 66
Smith, William Russell, 166
Sprigg, Ann G., 161
Stahel, Julius, 140
Stanton, Edwin McMasters, 176-78
Steele, Franklin, 63
Steele, Mary Chase, 63
Sternberg, George, 140
Stevens, Isaac, 118
Stoddert, Benjamin, 62
Sturgis, Samuel Davis, 140-41
Surratt, Mary Elizabeth, 97-98, 167-68
Taltavull, Peter, 161
Tanner, James, 141
Tayloe, John, 82
Taylor, Joseph Pannell, 178
Taylor, Vincent, 67, 70
Taylor, Walter, 70
Temple, William Grenville, 162
Templeman, George, 63
Tilinghast, Nicholas P., 67-68, 70
Thomas, Lorenzo, 178
Thornton, William, 82
Totton, Joseph G., 162
Tyler, Grafton, 75
Ulke, Henry, 178-79
Vaux, Calvert 72
Wainwright, Richard, 162
Wallach, Richard, 179
West, Joseph Rodman, 141-42
Wheatley, Francis, 76
Wheeler, Joseph, 142
Whitall, Sarah, 69
White, Charles, 82
Whiton, William, 63
Wilkes, Charles, 89, 142
Willard, Joseph, 92, 179-80
Willard, Henry, 92
Williamson, James Alexander, 184-85
Winder, William, 83
Wirz, Henry, 108, 168-70
Wood, William P., 162
Worthington, Henry Gaither, 162-63
Wright, Horatio Gouverneur, 142
Wright, Marcus Joseph, 143

Acknowledgments

I could not have put together a book like this without the help of many people. I would especially like to thank the staff at the Special Collections Room at the Gelman Library at George Washington University and Roxanna Dean of the Washingtoniana Room at the Martin Luther King Jr. Library for helping me to understand how to effectively access the material in their collections. John Hanley, Executive Director of Congressional Cemetery; John Metzler, Jr., Superintendent, and Tom Sherlock, Historian, at Arlington National Cemetery provided records, stories, and anecdotes on the persons interred in their cemeteries. Sarah Turner, archivist for the United States House of Representatives, and Dr. Michael Crawford, Senior Historian at the Naval History Center at the Washington Navy Yard, patiently answered my questions and willingly opened their files for my perusal. Kerri Childress, Public Affairs Officer at the United States Soldiers' and Airmen's Home, provided information on Abraham Lincoln's involvement with the home. Steven E. Mirsky, Esquire, helped me untangle the bureaucratic legalese of 19th-century Washington. Patty Murray and Annette Leak typed part of the manuscript.

My heartfelt thanks goes to my publishers Doug Elliott and Carolyn Clark for having faith in this project. Their guidance and direction made the book a reality. Thanks to my editor Mary Ann Harrell who put my thoughts into a logical order.

Most of all, I would like to thank my loving wife Fran, who always accompanies me on my perambulations throughout Washington. She carries books, cameras, paper, pens, pencils, tape recorders, and candy bars without complaining. For her love and support, I am eternally grateful.